Introduction

As literacy consultants with our hearts still in the classroom, Carrie Ekey and I visit schools around the world, learning alongside students and teachers as we explore how to teach writing. For the last three years we've visited classrooms, asked questions, read as many books as we could, and collected hundreds of pictures and ideas on a worldwide scavenger hunt. We deluged teachers and coaches with pleas for specific examples of how they incorporated the ideas presented in professional books in the very real world of their classrooms. We have learned so much as we read, viewed, listened, talked, and wrote.

This book is a synthesis of our findings: photographs, book lists, descriptions of the best and newest resources about writing, and classroom stories. You'll recognize some of these insights, since you've probably read some of the same books and articles. As you read about the classroom teaching we describe, you'll also probably recognize strategies, minilessons, and units that you are implementing yourself. We hope you'll feel validated by all that *works well* in your classroom, then decide *what's next* in your own journey as a teacher of writing. Just as we want all our students to feel valued, wherever they are on a continuum of becoming writers, we hope you'll feel affirmed for the good work you're doing, inspired to read further and incorporate new ideas so that you can teach writing even more effectively, intentionally, responsively, and joyfully.

Who We Are

Bonnie

After teaching in elementary schools in Boulder, Colorado, and Seattle, Washington, I returned to graduate school to get my doctorate in education and began to teach at the university level. Instead of guiding thirty students each year, I could guide thirty teachers, each of whom had twenty to thirty students. The teachers I worked with in the Seattle area shared what they were doing, and I was often able to visit their classrooms, learning alongside them. I began presenting at state and national conferences, often in conjunction with these outstanding classroom teachers. Eventually, I began writing professional books in order to share what I was learning and the amazing work these teachers were doing. Many of the teachers I met through my college classes contributed ideas and even co-authored some of these professional books.

With the publication of my books came invitations to speak at conferences for international schools in various parts of the world, followed by invitations to work at some of these schools. Since I spent third, fourth, and fifth grade at an international school in Istanbul, Turkey, and have a deeply ingrained love of travel, I jumped at these amazing opportunities. At this point I've worked with over fifty international schools and spoken at conferences in Central and South America, Eastern and Western Europe, Africa, Asia, and the Middle East. I hope to share with you some of what I've learned about successful classroom environments from teachers and students in classrooms around the world.

Much of my initial work in schools involves "putting the pieces together"— linking a school's philosophy, standards, curriculum, instruction, assessment, and reporting. That's a lot to tackle at once, so after discussions about what pieces of the puzzle each school has in place, the administrators, teachers, and I usually create a four-year plan for implementing change, new ideas, and best practices in literacy. Since my time with each school is usually limited to a few days or a week, my friend and colleague Carrie Ekey provides follow-up support to these schools based on their specific needs as they expand their expertise in literacy instruction and assessment.

Carrie

I officially retired from the Denver metro area's Jefferson County School District in 2002. I've been an elementary classroom teacher, a lead district staff developer, and a curriculum specialist. I was also a core coordinator and instructor at a master's program for teachers at Regis University in Denver. Since Bonnie Campbell Hill first convinced me to begin consulting overseas, I've visited over twenty-five international schools. After Bonnie's initial visit to a school, I help the staff reach a common understanding of a balanced literacy program, as well as help develop literacy curriculum. Often I help administrators create a vision, goals, and a long-range plan. I then introduce literacy instructional strategies to teachers through workshops and demonstration lessons and develop common understanding and practices around literacy instruction and assessment in grade-level team meetings. I sometimes work on improving classroom libraries and often hold literacy workshops for parents.

In addition to my ongoing work with international schools, I served as a consultant-in-residence for one year at the International School of Beijing and for two years at Hong Kong International School. I've worked harder in the last eight years than ever before and hardly feel "retired"!

Most recently, I've developed initial units of study in literacy for schools that don't have the staff to do this themselves. I've also begun to train literacy coaches for international schools with the support of NESA (the Near East South Asian group of schools). I recently completed the first iteration of this two-year training program with twenty-five teachers from fourteen international schools in twelve countries. This fall, I began training a second cadre of twenty-one additional international school teachers who will meet in various countries four times over the next two years. Many of these teacher leaders and coaches have contributed ideas and photographs for this book.

Enhancing
Writing Instruction

RUBRICS AND RESOURCES FOR SELF-EVALUATION AND GOAL SETTING

FOR LITERACY COACHES, PRINCIPALS, AND TEACHER STUDY GROUPS, K–6

Bonnie Campbell Hill & Carrie Ekey

HEINEMANN
Portsmouth, NH

Heinemann
361 Hanover Street
Portsmouth, NH 03801–3912
www.heinemann.com

Offices and agents throughout the world

Library of Congress Cataloging-in-Publication Data
Hill, Bonnie Campbell
    The next-step guide to enhancing writing instruction : rubrics and resources for self-evaluation and goal setting / Bonnie Campbell Hill and Carrie Ekey.
        p. cm.
    Includes bibliographical references.
    ISBN-13: 978-0-325-03045-6
    ISBN-10: 0-325-03045-6
    1. English language—Composition and exercises—Study and teaching.
2. Language arts.   I. Ekey, Carrie.   II. Title.
LB1576.H351 2010
428.0071—dc22   2010008486

Editor: Kate Montgomery
Production: Lynne Costa
Cover design: Jenny Jensen Greenleaf
Cover photograph: Megan Sloan
Interior design and typesetting: Gina Poirier
Manufacturing: Steve Bernier

Printed in the United States of America on acid-free paper
14   13   12   11   10   VP   1   2   3   4   5

Contents

What We Do

In our ongoing tag-team work with schools, Carrie and I continue to build on each other's work, share ideas, and swap travel tips. Between us, we've racked up a slew of frequent-flyer miles. The twenty- or even thirty-six-hour flights are physically exhausting, and we don't stop running from the minute we hit the ground until we fly out. Since our jobs are fairly unusual and the examples we will share come from teachers and classrooms around the world, we'd like to begin with a short explanation of our roles and the context for our work.

Most of our careers have been spent working in classrooms in the United States, and we continue our connections with many of these teachers, especially those close to our homes in Denver and Seattle. These teachers have contributed many of the examples and photographs in this book and on my website. However, a great deal of our time recently has been spent working with international schools. These K–12 schools are most often created for the expatriate communities living in these countries, and most have an American curriculum and classrooms much like ones down the street from our houses. These international schools are essentially a miniature school district with a director (superintendent) and a high school, a middle school, and an elementary school. The teachers are primarily from the United States, Canada, Great Britain, Australia, and New Zealand, although some are from other countries as well. The schools in Africa and South and Central America have a higher percentage of teachers from the local country.

The students in these schools come from all over the world. Some are members of embassy families and some have parents who work for huge international companies or non-governmental agencies (NGOs). Postings are usually for two to five years, although some families stay longer. The number of local students varies greatly from school to school, although it's usually less than 20 percent. We have also had the privilege of occasionally working with local schools, such as two amazing bilingual (Arabic/English) schools in Bahrain and Saudi Arabia. Each school has its own challenges related to student and staff turnover (sometimes as high as 50 percent!), access to resources, the added responsibility of teaching the local language to students, access to professional learning experiences like conferences, and politics.

However, the most astonishing aspect of our work is that the major educational challenges are the same, whether it's a classroom in North Dakota, London, or Tanzania. Good teachers around the world all want to know how to improve their instruction to better meet their students' needs. The dedicated teachers we work with, whether they're from Denver, Colorado, or Doha, Qatar, all want to keep up with current research and best practices.

This book was a daunting undertaking. Carrie and I were often emailing each other from around the globe as I worked with a school in Paris and she was busy doing classroom demonstrations in Indonesia. Thank heavens for email and Skype phone calls! In the two years it took us to write this book, we've been interrupted by a tornado and blizzard (Colorado); a typhoon (Hong Kong); an earthquake (Indonesia); surgery (both Carrie and her husband, Glenn); the death of Carrie's mother; and innumerable power outages, computer glitches, and flight disasters. Despite the challenges of weather, technology, and daily life, we persevered because of our deep desire to help teachers and our belief in the value of this project. Our floors, dining room tables, and nightstands have overflowed with stacks of professional books. We enlisted the help of two knowledgeable colleagues, Sandy Garcia Figueroa (a principal in Arizona) and Laura Benson (a literacy consultant in Colorado), to help us read and annotate hundreds of professional books and DVDs. We've tried to create a "metabook" in which we synthesize everything we've ever read about writing instruction and list the most helpful resources about each topic. We've also gone into classrooms and emailed the wonderful teachers we know in order to gather stories and photographs showing what these cutting-edge ideas look like in practice. Our stack of permission forms for the hundreds of photographs we collected is three feet high! So although our names are on the cover of this book, it's truly been a worldwide collaborative project and journey.

As we wrote, we discovered that it was simply too confusing for readers if we wrote in two voices, so Carrie graciously allowed me (Bonnie) to write in the first person. I've occasionally woven in Carrie's stories in her own words, but much of the text is a combination of our experiences and knowledge.

About the Staff Development Rubrics

To support teachers and schools, Carrie and I created a rubric so that teachers can assess their strengths and areas for growth in teaching writing and word study. The rubric can be found at the end of this introduction. When we first shared the writing instruction rubric, most teachers were very accurate, if anything underestimating their abilities. Others who were clearly novices marked themselves as "leaders." We realized that the rubric couldn't stand alone. Some teachers "didn't know what they didn't know." We needed to share key ideas gleaned from the best books and DVDs on each aspect of teaching writing and make them come to life through photographs and examples from classrooms around the world. That's what you'll find in the chapters of this book.

If you are a literacy coach, assistant principal, or principal, you will read this book through a different lens. Therefore, we've also created a version of the rubric specifically for literacy coaches and principals. As you try to help teachers in your building expand and deepen their knowledge of best practices, you may want to use the "school" version of the writing instruction rubric to ascertain *what works* for your staff and *what's next* so that you can provide time, resources, and professional development opportunities based on those goals.

Warning!

Because Carrie and I created these staff development rubrics as tools for teachers to evaluate their own teaching and set their own goals, we want to emphasize that they should *not* be used by administrators for evaluation. The rubrics can help principals, coaches, and teachers identify best practices, but as soon as they take on the aura of evaluation, they lose all their potential for change. Teachers won't be honest about their strengths and areas for growth unless they are part of a supportive and risk-taking environment in which everyone is viewed as a learner.

The Teacher Rubric in Action

I asked Melissa White, who teaches second grade at the American Embassy School in New Delhi, India, about how her writing instruction has changed over the past few years. She wrote:

> Twelve years ago when I started my teaching career as a third-grade teacher, I used a writer's workshop model to teach students how to write. My lessons were based primarily on 6+1 traits of writing or formulaic writing with little emphasis on writing strategies. Students occasionally self-selected writing topics and were invited to confer about their writing piece during the editing and revising stages of the writing process. Word study consisted of weekly spelling lists with words taken from guided reading stories. Students had the freedom to choose words from their reading or writing to add to their weekly spelling list. Writing for most of my students was uninteresting and not enjoyable. They put in their daily writing time and came away with a few published pieces that lacked creativity and voice. Once they published a piece of writing, students could opt to share their work with peers. According to the writing instruction rubric by Bonnie Campbell Hill and Carrie Ekey, I was a writing teacher in the Apprentice stage in all categories.
>
> I knew I had to figure out how to make each lesson more meaningful, help my students grow as writers, improve my understanding of writing pedagogy, and, most important, instill a love of writing in each of my students. I began talking to my colleagues about how they taught writing. I also took the time to observe writing instruction in a number of classrooms. At the same time, I was working on a master's degree in

elementary education, which provided me the opportunity to familiarize myself with current best practices. I was introduced to Lucy Calkins' *The Art of Teaching Writing* (1994) and *Units of Study for Primary Writing* (2003). All of these experiences showed me that my idea of writer's workshop lacked a number of the necessary components to build strong writers. I began to implement daily minilessons that taught specific writing strategies and modeled these strategies in my own writing. Students chose interesting topics and engaged in daily independent writing. Their writing became more focused and they published more frequently, while sharing their work with peers throughout the writing process.

My current school developed a schoolwide philosophy about writing, began using the writing continuum (from *Developmental Continuums*, 2001) by Bonnie Campbell Hill to communicate student writing development and brought in consultants to model and guide curriculum building and writing instruction. My professional development growth continued through the Summer Writing Institute with Lucy Calkins at Columbia Teachers College, where I learned that an effective individual writing conference would help me to understand the needs of my students, lift their writing through the reinforcement of effective writing strategies, and get my students excited about their work. In addition, I strengthened my new knowledge through attendance at regional educational conferences, served as grade-level leader on my school's literacy committee, and joined the International Literacy Coaching Cohort led by Carrie Ekey. During the past few years, our school literacy committee has undertaken a number of projects including collecting anchor papers to evaluate student work with detailed lists of descriptors to guide that evaluation and developing grade-level yearly curriculum maps of units of study in writing.

These professional experiences have allowed me to increase my capacity to write and to teach writing and have enhanced the educational experience for my students. Currently, I see myself moving from the Practitioner stage on the rubric into the Leader stage. The greatest reward has come from seeing the love of writing my students now exude. My students get excited about writing and make the most of their writing time. They spring into action by quickly finding their writing folders and locating a comfortable place to work. The writing instruction rubric allows me to reflect on where I have been as a teacher and the progress I have made. The rubric also helps me focus on what I need to still work on.

The next area of growth that I see for myself using the rubric is in the area of word study. I have grown in this area as I moved away from using whole-class spelling lists and began incorporating strategies from *Phonics*

Lessons (2006) by Gay Su Pinnell and Irene Fountas. I have also incorpo-rated lists of words and strategies from a program by Rebecca Sitton. Our whole elementary staff, myself included, has discovered that we had not been differentiating instruction to meet the needs of individual students. I began studying *Word Crafting* (2003) by Cindy Marten and *Words Their Way* (2008) by Donald Bear and his colleagues with my school literacy commit-tee as we began working on a schoolwide word study philosophy and plan for instruction. So I would put myself at the very beginning of the Practitioner stage. I'm just beginning to use a pre- and post-test develop-mental spelling inventory as well as observations during writing workshop, which help me monitor my students' word study knowledge in order to design specific word sorts and other activities to meet their needs. I'm also supporting my students in automaticity by having them use sight words in authentic writing situations. I would like to deepen my understanding of best practices for word study so that I can provide stronger individualized instruction and best utilize classroom instructional time.

Melissa told me that the writing rubric had really helped her affirm what was working well and see where she could improve. It's a delight to learn alongside teachers like Melissa who are so reflective, dedicated, and such lifelong learners.

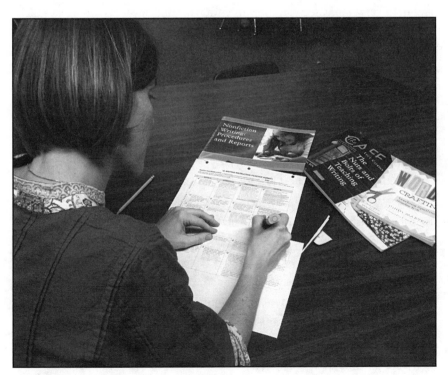

Melissa White Using a Rubric for Self-Evaluation

Administrator Susan Young (Principal) and Kathy Zabinski (Literacy Coach) Filling Out the School Version of the Rubric

The School Rubrics in Action

Both Carrie and I have visited the American Embassy School in New Delhi, India, and have been very impressed with how intentionally and effectively they have tackled the challenge of improving instruction and student learning in the area of writing. We wrote to Kathy Zabinski, the current literacy specialist, and asked her to describe their journey.

I joined AES as a fourth-grade teacher four years ago (school year 2006–2007). I was part of a team of five fourth-grade teachers and we met weekly to plan our curriculum collaboratively. I represented my grade-level team on the elementary school literacy committee and reported back to the team regarding literacy initiatives being worked on at the committee level. Our school was in the second year of working with a literacy specialist, Stacey DuPont, who was helping us develop a balanced literacy framework for our school. As a school, we had adopted a set of "Essential Literacy Agreements" that included word study, shared writing, and writing workshop, including minilessons, conferring, and independent writing as elements of a balanced writing program. We had also worked with Bonnie and Carrie to build proficiency in using the reading and writing continuums to inform our instruction.

With thirty classrooms in the elementary school (soon to become thirty-six), there was a range of experience with a workshop model. However, most teachers were developing literacy plans based on our essential agreements, incorporating writing workshop with a predictable schedule three or four days a week, and offering students regular and authentic opportunities to share published work that had been taken through the writing process. During those first two years of work, the literacy committee helped move our school from the Apprentice stage on the writing rubric to the Practitioner stage as we began to understand and articulate the components of a balanced writing program based on beliefs and agreements adopted by our entire school.

Initially, Bonnie worked with our school on providing the big picture and introduced her reading and writing continuums and assessment tools. Our professional development next focused on developing expertise with the components of our balanced literacy framework and learning to use the reading and writing continuums with our students. Carrie supported this work in small- and large-group professional development sessions on three separate visits to our school from 2006 to 2008. We also used faculty meetings to talk about instruction and to examine student writing by using the continuum alongside anchor papers. Additionally, some teachers joined professional book clubs to deepen their practice. Some teachers studied *The Art of Teaching Writing* (1994) by Lucy Calkins and *Writing Essentials* (2005) by Regie Routman, while the kindergarten teachers focused on *Talking, Drawing, Writing* (2007) by Martha Horn and Mary Ellen Giacobbe. During grade-level collaborative planning, teachers often shared what they were learning from their readings and discussions in their book clubs. While we were moving more fully into the Practitioner stage as a school for our writing instruction and writing workshops, our units of study throughout the school were often based on genres and/or 6+1 traits, and conferences were primarily focused on editing and conventions (Apprentice stage). Our word study programs differed widely across the school.

For our next steps in professional development, we focused on creating units of study for writing. One teacher at each grade level spent a year piloting the *Units of Study* (2003, 2006) by Lucy Calkins. We shared highlights with our grade-level teams, which were then reported back to the literacy committee. As we piloted the units, it soon became clear that we needed to revise our writing curriculum. The following summer, those of us who had piloted the units attended the weeklong writing institute with the Reading and Writing Project at Teachers College and returned to school ready to lead our teams as teachers developed and implemented units of study in writing. Supported by the literacy committee, we developed a schoolwide, articulated sequence of units of study in writing, along with structured minilessons. While we were working on the units of study across the grades, I returned to Teachers College with Stacey to attend a special session for literacy coaches as I prepared to step into her position as literacy specialist. The coaching workshop really helped us to refine our understanding of the structure of a minilesson and techniques for conferring with students about writing. I started this school year with demonstration lessons designed to highlight the elements of a focused minilesson and effective methods of conferring.

This intense two-year focus on writing instruction has moved our school much closer to the Leader descriptors on the rubric. This year, we've tackled the challenging issue of how to incorporate word study into a writing workshop model. Last year, our first-grade team worked collectively to develop beliefs and agreements for their grade-level word study program. Building on their work, the literacy committee has begun work on schoolwide belief statements and essential agreements for word study. Our school was fortunate to have the time, resources, and support to engage in effective professional development. The combination of grade-level collaboration and implementation of whole-school initiatives by the literacy committee effectively moved our school along the continuum of development in writing instruction.

About This Book Series

Carrie and I originally began this literacy-focused project intending to include writing, reading, assessment, and reporting. However, as we worked with teachers and schools, we realized that the conditions for learning were vital to the success of any literacy initiative. We learned the hard way that our presentations on writing workshop rarely took root in schools in which teachers had not read professionally or considered why and how to teach responsively. Literacy initiatives sometimes fell short when the majority of students were pulled out of the classroom for English language support. And sometimes the swirl of politics and personalities within a school created an atmosphere of resistance and animosity toward any ideas we presented. It became clear that a healthy, respectful classroom and school environment were fundamental to change and that we needed this necessary foundation before we could help schools build meaningful and long-lasting literacy initiatives. For these reasons, in the first book in our series, *The Next-Step Guide to Enriching Classroom Environments* (2010), we focused on setting the groundwork so that literacy initiates could be successful.

In this second book, we zoom in specifically on ways to create classrooms in which young writers can flourish so that you can explore new ideas and resources alongside your own practices. Do you like to write? Do you love to teach writing? I enthusiastically jumped into my first year of teaching with my own love of writing and of children but with no clue how to teach my eager second graders how to write. I'd taken a class on children's literature, but there was nothing in my coursework about teaching writing. I spent the last weekend before school began jotting down possible "story starters." I also bought thirty-two stenographer's notebooks and carefully glued in alphabet tabs along one edge to make "word books." After handing out the notebooks and explaining their use that first Monday, I soon had six students dutifully lined up with their word books flipped open to the appropriate letter so I could spell the words they needed. The first two students watched as I wrote the correct spelling for their words. The next two kids in line were thumb wrestling. By the time the last two kids reached me, they couldn't remember what word they needed and had long since forgotten my story starter and what they were writing. I remember thinking, "There's something wrong with this picture."

Luckily, Donald Graves came to speak in Boulder a few weeks later and the way I taught writing changed forever. I realized that I didn't need to spend my weekends coming up with creative prompts; my students needed to discover their own writing topics. As I listened to Don speak, I felt a huge sense of relief as he talked about the writing *process* and the value of students getting their ideas down independently without focusing on spelling every word correctly. Teaching writing suddenly seemed doable and natural. Thirty years later, most teachers have a strong grasp of the writing process and a writing workshop approach, yet writing instruction still varies widely from school to school and teacher to teacher.

Key Components

In this book, we explore five aspects of teaching writing:

- ▶ Writing workshop.
- ▶ Units of study.
- ▶ Writing instruction.
- ▶ Writing conferences.
- ▶ Word study.

These five components form the five categories on the writing rubric, and each is discussed in a separate chapter.

Chapter 1: Writing Workshop

If a parent asked you how you teach writing, what would you say? What are the components of your writing program? How knowledgeable are you about writing workshop? Chapter 1 begins with an overview of teaching writing, then explores each of six key components of writing workshop—time, predictable schedule, choice, risk-taking environment, modeling, and response—and the components of a gradual release instructional model—modeled, shared, interactive, guided, and independent writing.

Once you've figured out a structure for writing workshop, the next question is *what* to teach. As you model your own writing, students share their pieces, and you explore the work of published writers, you'll want to explore specific aspects of the writing process. How do you help your students choose topics? What are some good books about teaching revision? How often should your students publish their work?

The final section of this chapter offers ideas about the five interwoven components of writing process: prewriting, drafting, revising, editing, and publishing.

Chapter 2: Units of Study

How do you decide which genres and forms of writing to teach? Do you have a schoolwide plan or calendar? Chapter 2 provides ideas and resources for designing individual, grade-level, and schoolwide plans for units of study for writing. It offers specific ideas and resources for teaching eight genre-based units: poetry, fiction, nonfiction, persuasive writing, memoir and personal narrative, essays, writing to a prompt, in addition to writing in other genres.

Chapter 3: Writing Instruction

How do you develop minilessons? How can you help reluctant writers? Chapter 3 delves into nine specific aspects of teaching writing: minilessons, using a writer's notebook, demonstrating with mentor texts, supporting struggling or reluctant writers, addressing gender issues, supporting English language learners, incorporating technology, considering the politics of writing instruction, and communicating with families.

Chapter 4: Writing Conferences

In addition to whole-class and small-group instruction, you probably also hold individual writing conferences. How many students do you confer with each day? How do you decide the one teaching point that will best help each writer? The heart of writing workshop is the one-to-one interaction that occurs during individual writing conferences. This chapter presents tips, quotes, and insights from writing experts and classroom teachers about writing partnerships as well as individual and peer conferences.

Chapter 5: Word Study

Do you have a clear philosophy statement and vision for how you teach word study? Is there schoolwide agreement about best practices? Has your school had conversations about how you teach controversial topics like phonics, spelling, and handwriting? Are there fun ways to incorporate minilessons about punctuation where you can see results appear in students' writing? Word study is more than just teaching spelling. In this chapter, I'll present ideas about how to weave word study into a writing workshop approach, with ideas and practical suggestions for teaching phonological awareness, phonics, spelling, vocabulary, and other conventions of language (including handwriting, punctuation, and grammar).

Book Lists, Annotations, and Professional Book Log

If you are like me, you probably agonize over which professional books to purchase with a limited budget. I want to know as much as I can about a book in order to ascertain if it will address a particular need I have for my learning and "next steps." I want to know the grade-level range, the topics covered, and if this book has new and practical ideas I would find helpful. Most publishing companies now provide book annotations on their websites; however, most of those annotations still do not have enough information for me to make my final decision about whether to buy a book. At workshops and conferences, Carrie and I often "book-talk" the best professional books we read and are often asked by teachers, coaches, and principals for advice about helpful books on specific topics. For this reason, Carrie and I (with help from Sandy Figueroa and Laura Benson) have written over three hundred annotations that we feel will help you decide which professional books and DVDs to add to your personal library about writing instruction and word study. We have included annotations and bibliographic information on my website (www.bonniecampbellhill.com) as a free resource to educators who have bought this book. The annotations are linked to every descriptor at the Leader stage of the writing instruction rubric.

I encourage you to look up the annotation for *A Place for Wonder* (2009), Georgia Heard and Jen McDonough's new book, to try out the website. It will only take you a few minutes and I believe it will hook you into using the database. I promise to add new resources as they are published, which will help you to keep up to date with all the latest professional resources, even after you read this book.

I also know that a "picture is worth a thousand words." When Carrie and I present, teachers often ask for copies of the pictures of classrooms that we insert in our PowerPoint presentations. They tell us that actually *seeing* photographs of writing instruction in real classrooms makes the ideas more tangible and inspiring. For these reasons, I have also posted additional photos of writing instruction and word study on my website. I believe that just looking at these glimpses from exemplary classrooms will inspire you as you rethink your writing program. I would encourage you to go to my website, click on the link to this book, then explore these photos. We hope that in addition to this book, my website and database will provide additional inspiration and ongoing support for your professional learning about teaching writing. I want to give a special thank-you to Carrie's husband, Glenn, for his help taking and organizing many of the photographs in this book and on the website. I also want to thank my very tech-savvy sons, Keith and Bruce, who designed the website and database as a way to share our annotations and photographs with readers.

As you read this book, you may want to glance at the book lists in each section and highlight or put a check (✓) by the books you've already read and use an asterisk (*) to denote the books you'd like to read next. If you find an area you'd like to explore further, you may want to read the annotations on the website in order to determine which books would be most helpful to read on your own or with a colleague. The Professional Reading Log (Appendix A) can help you prioritize your "to read" list of professional books. As a literacy coach or principal, you may want to note individual or grade-level teachers who may find specific books helpful, or indicate books you want to read to deepen your knowledge about teaching writing and word study. You might also want to offer professional book studies focused on some of these titles.

What Works? What's Next?

As you read this book, you can examine the writing rubric to determine your (or your school's) areas of strength (*what works?*) and the concepts you might want to explore further (*what's next?*). The corresponding rows of both the teacher and the school versions of the rubrics are broken out at the end of each chapter, along with a "ponder box" of self-evaluation questions, to make it easy for you to pause and reflect on your or your school's teaching and learning.

Highlight the specific descriptors in the rubric that reflect your practices and knowledge, pat yourself on the back, and celebrate all that you already have in place. Then, use a different-colored highlighter to indicate areas for improvement. Or you might want to use one color this year for aspects you already have incorporated and use a different color next year as you implement new ideas and dig deeper into a topic as a way to visually track your professional growth. After making those changes, observe your students and evaluate the effect the changes have had on their writing.

Some of you may decide to read one or two professional books on your own during the school year or during your vacation. If you have colleagues with similar interests, you may want to read a book with another teacher, in grade-level teams, or maybe study a professional book with a cross-grade-level group of colleagues. If you're a real techie, you may want to keep a blog about the books you read. If you are a principal or literacy coach, you might choose a few books to read, as well as facilitate grade-level or small-group professional book studies about how to create classrooms that nourish and support young writers.

One more warning: As you read about all these fabulous books and ideas about teaching writing, it's very easy to become overwhelmed. Remember that no one teacher implements all these ideas, and no one could possibly read all these books. Whenever you start feeling inadequate, take a deep breath and remember that change takes time. It's important to start small. The only way to continue the literacy journey is to take one step at a time. All the ideas and books I share are exciting, but pick just one or two intriguing ideas to try and one or two books to read. Once those are under your belt, you can come back and pick a new goal. Remember that your ultimate purpose is to create classrooms that are both rigorous and joyful in which writers will flourish.

And one final tip: Learning is so much more fun when you work alongside a friend. Work with a colleague or your literacy coach (if you're lucky enough to have one). Celebrate when you try something new; when new ideas work, share your learning with other colleagues. If you are a principal or coach, affirm teachers who take risks and incorporate new ideas, and encourage and structure opportunities for collaboration and sharing.

Patrick Lee and Sally Disher Examine Student Writing and Share Ideas

Writing Instruction (Teacher Rubric)

Teacher and Grade Level: _____   **Date:** _____

Check the boxes that apply, perhaps using a highlighter to mark some or all of the specific descriptors. Use the back for comments.

	NOVICE	APPRENTICE	PRACTITIONER	LEADER
Writing Workshop and Writing Process	☐ I teach writing primarily through whole-group assignments, after which students work independently; I provide writing time once or twice a week; otherwise writing is integrated throughout the day and focuses mostly on other content areas; I determine writing topics and/or provide story starters or writing prompts; I am the primary audience for student writing; as students write, I usually work at my desk; student writing is completed as a draft that is copied neatly into a final draft with little or no revision; I display little student writing in my classroom or hallway	☐ I am beginning to incorporate writing workshop with some instruction and mini-lessons; I teach writing two or three times a week for thirty minutes a day; I direct the writing and occasionally allow students to choose topics or give students free rein during writing workshop; during writing workshop, I monitor student writing or work at my desk; during writing workshop, students occasionally share their writing with peers (author's chair); student writing is taken through the writing process and published a few times during the year, often for a writing contest, class book, bulletin board display, or celebration; I display some student writing in the classroom and hallway	☐ I have implemented writing workshop with minilessons, independent writing, and some sharing; I also teach writing through some modeled, shared, and interactive writing; I teach writing with a predictable schedule three or four days a week for thirty to forty minutes a day; students write independently, often on topics they have chosen themselves; students write in a variety of genres and text types; students regularly share their writing with peers (author's chair) and begin to share in writing partnerships; student writing is taken through the writing process and published and shared often during the year; I display a variety of student writing in my classroom and hallway	☐ I have implemented writing workshop with clear components (minilessons, independent writing, sharing, and some guided writing when necessary); I also teach writing through modeled, shared, and interactive writing; I teach writing with a predictable schedule for forty-five to sixty minutes a day, as well as across the curriculum; students write independently on topics they choose themselves, often within a unit of study; at times they choose their own genres or text types; students share their writing with writing partners, in writing groups, with peers (author's chair), and with authentic audiences outside the classroom; I foster a risk-taking environment in which students are comfortable giving and receiving feedback from me and their peers; student writing is taken through the writing process and published and shared frequently and consistently, often in connection with units of study; I display student writing in my classroom and hallway that reflects range, variety, and the steps in the writing process
Units of Study	☐ My individual lessons may or may not be connected with one another or to a specific genre or unit; I may provide some genre study; my writing instruction often focuses on grammar, spelling, and penmanship	☐ I provide a sequence of skills and writing activities that may or may not be part of a genre study; my minilessons are based primarily on the 6+1 traits or on a pre-determined structure (formulaic writing)	☐ I am beginning to develop some units of study with a sequence of minilessons (e.g., Calkins, Allyn, Ray); my other writing minilessons are based on the 6+1 traits or writing in specific genres	☐ I have developed a clearly articulated curriculum calendar and set of well-developed units of study (e.g., Calkins, Allyn, Ray) with a sequence of focused, connected minilessons; my grade level has developed a calendar with specific units of study within a schoolwide plan to provide consistency

	NOVICE	APPRENTICE	PRACTITIONER	LEADER
Writing Instruction	☐ My instruction focuses on conventions rather than on writing strategies and the writing process; I often assign rather than teach writing	☐ I provide some instruction about writing strategies and the writing process; my students keep writing journals	☐ I explore the writing process and writer's craft, as well as teach revision and editing strategies through minilessons; I am beginning to modify my instruction for ELLs and learners with special needs; I am beginning to use mentor texts to teach writer's craft; my students keep writing folders; I provide some explanation of writing instruction and writing workshop to parents at Open House and in newsletters	☐ I provide intentional, focused minilessons (five to ten minutes) about the writing process, writer's craft, and revision and editing strategies based on my planned curriculum, as well as on assessed student needs; I use engagement strategies like "turn and talk"; I modify my instruction for ELLs and learners with special needs; I often use mentor texts and teach students to read like writers; my students keep writing folders (K–5) and/or writer's notebooks (3–5); I provide clear, ongoing communication with parents about how I teach writing and what they can do to support writers at home
Conferences	☐ I often sit at my desk grading papers, completing administrative paperwork, or checking email while students write; I correct completed student papers and mark errors	☐ I occasionally confer with individual students; my student conferences focus primarily on editing and conventions	☐ I regularly hold individual conferences in which I often teach a new strategy; I usually direct the conversation during conferences; my conferences focus on revision and editing; my conferences are also beginning to focus on process and writer's craft; I am beginning to implement some writing partnerships (K–5) and peer conferences (3–5)	☐ I hold focused individual writing conferences using Lucy Calkins' research, decide, teach format; I use the information I gather and record to guide my individual and whole-class instruction; my conferences focus on process, writer's craft, initiative, specific writing strategies, and student self-reflection; I implement effective writing partnerships (K–5) and peer conferences (3–5)
Word Study	☐ I rely on a published program and teacher's manual or a designated spelling list for spelling instruction; I give weekly spelling tests with little instruction; I rely on worksheets and memorization to teach vocabulary, grammar, and punctuation	☐ I use a published program and teacher's manual flexibly to determine which spelling skills and strategies to teach; I group students for spelling instruction and give weekly spelling tests; I rely on memorization and student activities to teach vocabulary, grammar, and punctuation; I introduce our word wall all at once and students occasionally refer to it	☐ I use a variety of resources to teach spelling skills and strategies; I am beginning to replace weekly spelling tests with individualized and small-group spelling instruction and assessment; I use minilessons, exemplars, word sorts, and activities to teach vocabulary, grammar, and punctuation; I am beginning to use our word wall effectively to teach spelling and vocabulary; students are beginning to use the word wall during independent work time; the students and I develop and add to our word wall throughout the year; I provide information about how I teach word study, spelling, and vocabulary to parents at Open House and in newsletters	☐ I use a variety of resources as part of a schoolwide approach to intentionally teach spelling skills and strategies based on students' needs and to facilitate student inquiry; I teach spelling as a part of word study, and group students or individualize instruction based on students' needs; I integrate vocabulary and grammar instruction throughout the day based on students' needs; I explicitly teach vocabulary and word study as part of a systematic schoolwide approach and facilitate student inquiry; I continually monitor the effect of word study on students' independent writing; I use our word wall effectively to teach spelling and vocabulary; my students and I continually develop, add to, and delete words from our word wall; I provide clear, ongoing communication with parents about how I teach word study, spelling, and vocabulary, and how families can provide support at home

© 2010 by Bonnie Campbell Hill and Carrie Ekey from *The Next-Step Guide to Enhancing Writing Instruction*. Portsmouth, NH: Heinemann.

Writing Instruction (School Rubric)

School Position: _____ **Date:** _____

Check the boxes that apply, perhaps using a highlighter to mark some or all of the specific descriptors. Use the back for comments.

	NOVICE	APPRENTICE	PRACTITIONER	LEADER
Writing Workshop and Writing Process	☐ Most teachers teach writing primarily through whole-group assignments, after which students work independently; teachers provide writing time once or twice a week at most; otherwise writing is integrated throughout the day and focuses mostly on other content areas; teachers determine writing topics and/or provide story starters or writing prompts; in most classrooms, teachers are the primary audience for student writing; most teachers work at their desks when students are writing; in most classrooms, student writing is completed as a draft that is transcribed neatly into a final copy with little or no revision; little student writing is displayed in classrooms or hallways	☐ Some teachers are beginning to incorporate writing workshop with some instruction and minilessons; in most classrooms, writing is taught two or three times a week for thirty minutes a day; most teachers direct the writing and occasionally allow students to choose topics or give students free rein during writing workshop; during writing workshop, most teachers monitor student writing or work at their desks during writing workshop; in some classrooms, students share their writing with peers (author's chair); in most classrooms, student writing is taken through the writing process and published a few times during the year, often for a writing contest, class book, bulletin board display, or celebration; teachers display some student writing in classrooms and hallways	☐ Most teachers have implemented writing workshop with minilessons, independent writing, and some sharing; in all classrooms, writing is also taught through some modeled, shared, and interactive writing; writing is taught with a predictable schedule three or four days a week for thirty to forty minutes a day; in most classrooms, students write independently, often on topics they have chosen themselves; in most classrooms, students write in a variety of genres or text types; in most classrooms, students regularly share their writing with peers (author's chair) and begin to share in writing partnerships; in most classrooms, student writing is taken through the writing process and published and shared often during the year; teachers display a variety of student writing in classrooms and hallways throughout the school	☐ All teachers have implemented writing workshop with clear components (minilessons, independent writing, sharing, and some guided writing when necessary); in all classrooms, writing is also taught through modeled, shared, and interactive writing; writing is taught daily with a predictable schedule for forty-five to sixty minutes a day, as well as across the curriculum; in all classrooms, students write independently on topics they choose themselves, often within a unit of study; at times they choose their own genres or text types; in all classrooms, students share their writing with writing partners, in writing groups, with peers (author's chair), and with authentic audiences outside the classroom; each teacher fosters a risk-taking environment in which students are comfortable giving and receiving peer and teacher feedback; in all classrooms, student writing is taken through the writing process and published and shared frequently and consistently, often in connection with units of study; student writing is displayed in classrooms and hallways throughout the school that reflects range, variety, and the steps in the writing process
Units of Study	☐ In most classrooms, individual lessons may or may not be connected to one another or to a specific genre or unit; most teachers provide some genre study; in most classrooms, writing instruction often focuses on grammar, spelling, and penmanship	☐ Most teachers provide a sequence of skills and writing activities that may or may not be part of a genre study; in most classrooms, minilessons are based primarily on the 6+1 traits or on a predetermined structure (formulaic writing)	☐ Teachers at some grade levels are beginning to develop units of study with a sequence of minilessons (e.g., Calkins, Allyn, Ray); other lessons are based on the 6+1 traits or writing in specific genres	☐ Teachers have developed a schoolwide, clearly articulated curriculum calendar and set of well-developed units of study (e.g., Calkins, Allyn, Ray) with a sequence of focused, connected minilessons; teachers have developed a calendar with specific units of study within a schoolwide plan to provide consistency within and between grade levels

	NOVICE	APPRENTICE	PRACTITIONER	LEADER
Writing Instruction	☐ In most classrooms, instruction focuses on conventions rather than on writing strategies and the writing process; in most classrooms, writing is assigned rather than taught	☐ In most classrooms, teachers provide some instruction about writing strategies and the writing process; a few teachers are beginning to modify instruction for ELLs and learners with special needs; in most classrooms, students keep writing journals	☐ Most teachers explore the writing process and writer's craft, as well as teach revision and editing strategies through minilessons; some teachers modify instruction for ELLs and learners with special needs; some teachers are beginning to use mentor texts to teach writer's craft; in most classrooms, students keep writing folders; in most classrooms, teachers provide some explanation of writing instruction and writing workshop to parents at Open House and in newsletters	☐ Teachers in all classrooms provide intentional, focused minilessons (five to ten minutes) about the writing process, writer's craft, and revision and editing strategies based on the planned curriculum as well as assessed student needs; teachers in all classrooms use engagement strategies like "turn and talk"; all teachers modify their instruction for ELLs and learners with special needs; all teachers use mentor texts and teach students to read like writers; in all classrooms, students keep writing folders (K–5) and/or writer's notebooks (3–5); all teachers provide clear, ongoing communication with parents about how writing is taught schoolwide and how families can support writers at home
Conferences	☐ In many classrooms, teachers often sit at their desk grading papers, completing administrative paperwork, or checking email while students write; in most classrooms, teachers correct completed student papers and mark errors	☐ Teachers in some classrooms occasionally confer with individual students; in most classrooms, student conferences focus primarily on editing and conventions	☐ In all classrooms, teachers regularly hold individual conferences in which they often teach new strategies; conferences are mostly teacher directed; in most classrooms, student conferences focus on revision and editing; in some classrooms, student conferences are also beginning to focus on process and writer's craft; in some classrooms, teachers are beginning to implement writing partnerships (K–5) and peer conferences (3–5)	☐ In all classrooms, teachers hold focused individual writing conferences using Lucy Calkins' research, decide, teach format; they use the information they gather and record to guide instruction for individual writers and the whole class; in all classrooms, student conferences focus on process, writer's craft, initiative, specific writing strategies, and student self-reflection; in most classrooms, teachers implement effective writing partnerships (K–5) and peer conferences (3–5)
Word Study	☐ In most classrooms, teachers rely on a published program and teacher's manual or a designated spelling list for spelling instruction; in most classrooms, teachers give weekly spelling tests with little instruction; in most classrooms, teachers rely on worksheets and memorization to teach vocabulary, grammar, and punctuation	☐ In most classrooms, teachers use a published program and teacher's manual flexibly to determine which spelling skills and strategies to teach; in most classrooms, teachers group students for spelling instruction and give weekly spelling tests; in most classrooms, teachers rely on memorization and activities to teach vocabulary, grammar, and punctuation; most teachers introduce the entire word wall all at once and students occasionally refer to it	☐ In all classrooms, teachers use a variety of resources to teach spelling skills and strategies; teachers begin to develop a schoolwide philosophy and plan for spelling instruction; teachers are beginning to replace weekly spelling tests with individualized and group spelling instruction and assessment; teachers use minilessons, exemplars, word sorts, and student activities to teach vocabulary, grammar, and punctuation; teachers in most classrooms use their word walls effectively to teach spelling and vocabulary; in most classrooms, students are beginning to use the word walls when they are working independently; in most classrooms, teachers develop and add to their word wall throughout the year; all teachers provide information to parents about how word study and spelling are taught	☐ In all classrooms, teachers systematically use a variety of resources to intentionally teach word study, which includes spelling, vocabulary, and grammar based on student needs as part of a schoolwide approach; spelling skills and strategies are taught individually or in small groups; all teachers integrate vocabulary and grammar instruction throughout the day; all teachers explicitly teach word study including vocabulary as an inquiry approach; all teachers continually monitor the effect of word study on students' independent writing; all teachers use their word walls effectively to teach spelling and vocabulary; teachers and students continually develop, add to, and delete words from their word walls; grade level teams collaborate to provide parent communication about word study instruction and home support

Writing Workshop and Writing Process

Teaching writing can be incredibly exciting and rewarding. Some of you may be experienced writing workshop teachers who want to hone specific areas of your instruction. Some of you may want to create more in-depth units of study with your grade-level colleagues. Some of you may be fortunate enough to be part of a schoolwide focus on teaching writing. Whatever your goal—whether you're just getting started or ready to dig into some aspect of writing at a deeper level—you'll want a mentor or two. If you could invite anyone to your school to talk about teaching writing, who would you pick? Regie Routman, Lucy Calkins, Ralph Fletcher, and Katie Wood Ray would be at the top of my list. These remarkable educators have written seminal books about the teaching of writing that I consider mandatory reading for every elementary teacher. The book lists on page 7 (and the annotations on my website) include works by these four literacy "gurus" and other experts.

Essential Books and Resources About Teaching Writing

When I taught graduate courses in writing as part of a teacher education curriculum, I used *The Art of Teaching Writing* (1994), by Lucy Calkins, as a text. The second edition is over fifteen years old, but as I recently skimmed my copy, which has yellow highlighting and sticky notes on almost every page, I marveled at how well Lucy writes (I quote from this book all the time). Year after year, teachers tell me how much they enjoy reading this book and how much it impacts their teaching. If you're new to writing workshop or your school is implementing writing workshop for the first time, this is the first book you'll want to read. It delves deeply into the rationale and structure of writing workshop; looks closely at writing at each grade level; and includes all the specifics about writing process, minilessons, and writing conferences that you need to get started.

In many schools I visit, writing instruction looks very different in each classroom. Even if there are overall writing standards, teachers "do their own thing"; there are no common schedules, structures, or expectations. In some classrooms, writing occurs every day at the same time; in other rooms, writing occurs in spurts or takes a backseat to other content areas. Schools that decide to explore the teaching of writing together as a staff might begin by studying Regie Routman's *Writing Essentials* (2005). Regie writes with passion about what matters most in teaching writing and provides the philosophical underpinnings that I've come to believe are necessary before writing instruction can change. Her subtitle—*Raising Expectations and Results While Simplifying Teaching*—captures the essence of her popularity. She challenges us to provide more time and choice for students in the face of the growing demands of curriculum and assessment. I've heard Regie speak numerous times, and I believe the reason her sessions at conferences are standing room only is that she does four things with great eloquence:

❶ She affirms what we know in our hearts about good teaching.

❷ She challenges our complacency by claiming, "You can do better," and shows us stunning examples from the largely high-poverty schools in which she works.

❸ She reminds us to cling to our beliefs and to speak out for what's good for students.

❹ She encourages us to work smarter and have a life outside school so that we'll have the energy we need to teach.

After reading both *The Art of Teaching Writing* and *Writing Essentials,* elementary school teachers at the American School in London met in grade-level teams to develop a philosophy of teaching writing and created a common statement (see Figure 1.1) that forms the framework for their writing curriculum.

The American School of London's Philosophy Statement on Writing Instruction

❶ Our mission is to create a community of lifelong writers who enjoy experimenting with writing in different genres and for different purposes. We place importance on students writing for authentic purposes.

❷ We value diversity in approaches to teaching writing, but we encourage teachers to try a workshop approach. Even so, teachers are encouraged to achieve the goals set out in this document in a variety of ways.

❸ We see the teaching of writing as explicit and occurring daily but also as integrated throughout the curriculum and across content areas.

❹ Our teaching of writing is based on a differentiated approach and therefore caters to writers of all abilities and interest levels. We pride ourselves on providing instruction that is individualized for each student. We offer this through differentiated instruction and expectations as well as through feedback during individual conferences.

❺ We believe it is essential that students learn and apply the skills of conventions and mechanics to their writing in order to communicate most effectively. Mechanics and conventions are taught both during discrete lessons and as part of a daily writing workshop.

❻ We believe the assessment of writing is important and it takes place on an ongoing basis. It is both formative and summative. Rubrics and checklists are used. Students are involved in setting their own goals for the development of their writing.

Figure 1.1

The American School in London was fortunate to have Regie Routman visit, but not all schools are that lucky. Her weeklong residencies in schools have been so transformative that she recently developed three demonstration programs, each providing thirteen weeks of professional development centered on DVD clips of Regie in action. Each staff development session lasts 90 to 120 minutes and outlines the activities as if Regie were right there at your school. One program focuses on the reading/writing connection (*Regie Routman in Residence: Transforming Our Teaching Through Reading/Writing Connections*, 2008), another on teaching writing (*RRIR: Transforming our Teaching Through Writing for Audience and Purpose*, 2008), and a third on reading (*RRIR: Transforming Our Teaching Through Reading to Understand*, 2009). Regie spends the first two sessions setting the scene by discussing the importance of professional development and focusing on the optimal learning (or gradual release) model of teaching and learning. In schools that use Regie's resources, teachers read, write, watch teachers in action, and discuss ideas with colleagues. (The gradual release model is explained in detail in Regie's books and in our book *The Next-Step Guide to Enriching Classroom Environments* [2010]).

The primary division of the Singapore American School, one of the largest international schools in the world (there are thirteen classrooms at each grade level), adopted Regie's reading/writing connections program. A leadership team made up of Louise Donaghey (the literacy coach), Debbie Woodfield (a first-grade teacher), Peggy Moineau (a second-grade teacher), and David Hoss (the primary school principal) met before each session to plan the agenda and preview the videos. Louise developed a PowerPoint presentation for every session so teachers didn't have to flip backward and forward through books and articles. Each teacher kept a professional development notebook. After viewing the introductory video clips, teachers posted their beliefs about teaching writing and reading around the room. Every teacher put a sticker on the three statements she or he found most significant as together they created a philosophy statement about teaching reading and writing at their school. The leadership team facilitated professional conversations all year. Even though their prekindergarten through second-grade staff had been focusing on literacy for the previous three years, teachers overwhelmingly found this resource to be validating, informative, relevant, helpful, and professionally meaningful. David, the primary school principal, says:

> [Regie's program] really tightened up the common agreements within our grade levels for what we do within classrooms. The videos were particularly effective in modeling appropriate practices and strategies for teaching reading and writing. The teachers enjoyed them and each session validated things they were already doing, reinforced the need to do more appropriate modeling, or revealed some new strategies they could use. One teacher told me her students left her classroom better writers this year because she started sharing her personal life stories. Her sharing propelled the students to craft more personal stories, which provided a real context for their writing. Another overall positive result was that it enabled us to have professional dialogue across the grade levels. Louise and I mixed up the groups of teachers at each session and ensured there was a good mix of grade-level teachers, resource teachers, ESOL teachers, counselors, librarians, and so on. People really enjoyed the camaraderie and became informed about how all of our literacy practices support one another.

The literacy coach, Louise Donaghey, adds:

> Regie's resource has been the most significant professional development opportunity we have had in our primary division. Sixty teachers are implementing the ideas over a two-year period. I think it's an excellent program for any school, at any stage of development. It has helped our teachers gain common experiences, use common language, and better align our philosophies and instruction. Perhaps most valuable is the time spent engaged in discussions with colleagues, whether based on an article or a teaching experience. Teachers value and appreciate these opportunities to share with colleagues.

The most significant change is that teachers are spending more time on "shared experiences" with the students. They are truly considering the gradual handover of responsibility to students when they plan their lessons; as a result students are more confident and better equipped for success in their reading and writing as they progress from "you do it" through "you help me do it" to "I do it." It's rewarding to hear Regie's language in planning meetings and during discussions. As a division, we're beginning to understand the need to "teach with a sense of urgency" and apply the optimal learning model in all areas of the curriculum. Regie has taken the hard work out of planning and implementing successful literacy-based professional development—*just add teachers and snacks!*

Sandy Figueroa also used Regie's reading/writing resource last year. She says: "This resource provided a framework for our instruction. It has been by far the most cost-effective, easy, and powerful way to provide professional development for my staff. As a result, our high-poverty, predominately ELL school made significant gains in only one year. We became a professional learning community able to collaborate, reflect on learning, assess our progress, and discuss professional readings and video clips of effective reading/writing instruction being conducted in schools and classrooms around the country. Watching Regie Routman as she models instruction and talks with teachers and their students was far more powerful for my teachers than simply asking them to read her books."

Whether you study *The Art of Teaching Writing*, *Writing Essentials*, or one of the Regie Routman programs on your own, with a colleague, with your grade-level team, or as a staff, these professional resources will enable you to reflect on your teaching and collect a wealth of ideas about how to improve writing instruction. As you read these and other books about teaching writing, common elements of a workshop approach will start to emerge. You may want to develop a philosophy statement about how writing is taught in your classroom and include it in a parent letter to hand out at curriculum night. Some teachers develop philosophy statements about teaching writing with their colleagues in order to demonstrate consistency within a grade level. Others, like the American School in London, have created a schoolwide philosophy statement that becomes part of their curriculum documents and is included on their school website. Carrie and I developed a list of thirteen statements that we feel are essential components to writing workshop (see Figure 1.2).

Several other books also provide general information about writing workshop. If you're a brand-new teacher and *The Art of Teaching Writing* seems too daunting, you can get started by reading Ralph Fletcher and JoAnn Portalupi's shorter book, *Writing Workshop* (2001). If you're a teacher in grades 2–8 who has already established writing workshop in your classroom and want more detailed information about curriculum, instruction, assessment, and evaluation, you will savor *The Writing Workshop* (2001), by Katie Wood Ray. Katie does a fabulous job of articulating the meaning of writing process and writing workshop and showing the interconnectedness of the two concepts. She describes the importance of helping each of your students develop a writing identity. If you feel comfortable with writing workshop in second through sixth grade but have specific questions or aspects that you'd like to improve, you'll appreciate *When Writing Workshop Isn't Working* (2005), by Mark Overmeyer, which is structured around the ten most frequent questions teachers ask. All of these experts stress how important it is for teachers to see themselves as a writer and to experience writing from the inside.

Writing Workshop Essentials

❶ All children are writers.

❷ Students need predictable, uninterrupted blocks of time in which to write every day.

❸ Students need a climate of trust in which to write and share their writing.

❹ Students need high expectations and a clear structure within a well-managed classroom.

❺ Students need real purposes and audiences for their writing.

❻ Students need choices about what they write in order to be successful.

❼ Students learn best in the context of their own writing, especially through individual writing conferences.

❽ Students need opportunities to give and receive responses about writing. They deserve time to talk about their own writing and receive response from teachers, their peers, and the wider community. They also need opportunities to listen to their classmates talk about their writing and then provide feedback to their peers.

❾ Students need explicit instruction that includes the teacher modeling his or her own writing.

❿ Students learn insights from focused periods of study, such as a genre study or a process study.

⓫ Students need explicit instruction about a variety of genres.

⓬ Students need support in understanding and using all parts of the writing process.

⓭ Students need sharing and publishing rituals that provide real audiences for their writing

Figure 1.2

Book List 📖

General Resources for Writing Workshop

- [ ] *The Art of Teaching Writing* by Lucy Calkins (1994) (Grades K–5)
- [ ] *Writing Essentials* (with DVD) by Regie Routman (2005) (Grades K–8)
- [ ] *Regie Routman in Residence: Transforming Our Teaching Through Writing for Audience and Purpose* (2008) (Grades K–6)
- [ ] *Regie Routman in Residence: Transforming Our Teaching Through Reading/Writing Connections* (2008) (Grades K–6)
- [ ] *Writing Workshop* by Ralph Fletcher and JoAnn Portalupi (2001) (Grades K–8)
- [ ] *The Writing Workshop* by Katie Wood Ray (2001) (Grades 2–8)
- [ ] *When Writing Workshop Isn't Working* by Mark Overmeyer (2005) (Grades 2–5)
- [ ] *When Students Write* by Ralph Fletcher and JoAnn Portalupi (DVD) (2006) (Grades K–5)
- [ ] *What Really Matters in Writing* by Patricia and James Cunningham (2010) (Grades K–8)

Resources for Writing Workshop in Prekindergarten and Kindergarten

- [ ] *Already Ready* by Katie Wood Ray (2008)
- [ ] *The Castle in the Classroom* by Ranu Bhattacharyya (2010)
- [ ] *Talking, Drawing, Writing* by Martha Horn and Mary Ellen Giacobbe (2007)
- [ ] *Joyful Learning in Kindergarten* by Bobbi Fisher (1998)
- [ ] *Growing Up Writing* by Connie Campbell Dierkling and Sherra Ann Jones (2003)
- [ ] *The Art of Teaching Writing* (Chapters 6 and 7) by Lucy Calkins (1994)
- [ ] *Conversations* (Chapters 6, 7, 8, and 9) by Regie Routman (2000)
- [ ] *Literacy and the Youngest Learner* (Chapters 8 and 11) by Susan Bennett-Armistead, Nell Duke, and Annie Moses (2005)
- [ ] *About the Authors* by Katie Wood Ray (2004) (Grades 1–2)
- [ ] *The Teaching Behind About the Authors* by Katie Wood Ray with Lisa Cleaveland (DVD) (2005) (Grades 1–2)
- [ ] *Literate Days* by Gretchen Owocki (with DVD) (2007) (Grades PreK–2)

Book List *(continued)*

Resources for Helping You Implement Writing Workshop in the Primary Grades

☐ *. . . And with a Light Touch* by Carol Avery (2002) (Grade 1)

☐ *On Their Way* by Jane Fraser and Donna Skolnick (1994) (Grade 2)

☐ *Significant Studies for Second Grade: Reading and Writing Investigations for Children* by Karen Ruzzo and Mary Anne Sacco (2004) (Grade 2)

☐ *A Quick Guide to Teaching Second-Grade Writers with Units of Study* by Lucy Calkins (2009) (Grade 2)

☐ *Into Writing* by Megan Sloan (2009) (Grades K–3)

☐ *Engaging Young Writers* by Matt Glover (2009) (Grades PreK–1)

☐ *Raising Writers* by Ruth Shagoury (2009) (Grades PreK–1)

☐ *Inside Reading and Writing Workshop* (DVD) by Joanne Hindley (2006) (Grades K–3)

☐ *In the Beginning* by JoAnn Portalupi and Ralph Fletcher (DVD) (2006) (Grades K–3)

☐ *Of Primary Importance* by Ann Marie Corgill (2008) (Grades K–3)

☐ *Everything You Need to Know to Teach First Grade* (Chapter 11) by Pat Barrett Dragan (2003) (Grade 1)

☐ *Scaffolding Young Writers* by Linda Dorn and Carla Soffos (2001) (Grades 1–2)

☐ *Organizing for Literacy* (DVD) by Linda Dorn (1999, 2006) (Grades K–3)

☐ *Apprenticeship in Literacy* by Linda Dorn, Cathy French, and Tammy Jones (1998) (Grades K–3)

☐ *Developing Independent Learners* (DVD) by Linda Dorn and Carla Soffos (2006) (Grades K–3)

☐ *Teaching Writing in a Title I School* by Nancy Akhavan (2009) (Grades K–3)

☐ *No More "I'm Done!"* by Jennifer Jacobson (2010) (Grades K–2)

Resources for Writing Workshops in the Intermediate Grades

☐ *In the Company of Children* by Joanne Hindley (1996) (Grades 3–5)

☐ *Celebrating the Fourth* by Joan Servis (1999) (Grade 4)

☐ *The No-Nonsense Guide to Teaching Writing* by Judy Davis and Sharon Hill (2003) (Grades 3–8)

☐ *Writing Through the Tween Years* by Bruce Morgan with Deb Odom (2004) Grades 3–6)

Providing Writing Workshop Essentials

How many children were in your family when you were growing up? Did you build forts or climb trees? What games or sports did you like to play? Did you have a pet? Do you have a pet now? What do you like to do on weekends? When Regie Routman works in classrooms, she always begins by telling stories about her family and her own life. Sharing family events and stories in brief minilessons (ten or fifteen minutes) is a way to build relationships with students. We need to demonstrate that students can write about ordinary things that happen and that their lives have significance.

But then what? The hard part about teaching writing is that there are so many factors to consider. There are so many genres you're supposed to teach, as well as minilessons to develop and exemplars to find for each one. You want to introduce all those writing traits, and your students are all writing different pieces. They're all at various stages of the writing process and at different developmental stages; some are just learning English. How do you juggle all these challenges?

The key ingredients that help students become successful writers (based on the conditions of learning initially outlined by Brian Cambourne [1993]) are:

▶ Uninterrupted chunks of time for writing.

▶ A predictable schedule for writing.

▶ Choice about what they write.

▶ A supportive, risk-taking classroom environment.

▶ Models of good writing.

▶ High expectations.

▶ Response from readers.

Time

One key to improving writing is giving students the opportunity to write every day. Students need a predictable schedule and large chunks of uninterrupted time in which to write. So do adult writers. When I worked on this book, I quit traveling because I found it too hard to plunge into writing and then have to stop for a week or two. I stayed home for nine months and wrote every single day. Waking in the middle of the night or standing in line at the grocery store, I thought of things I needed to revise. Because I had a predictable routine, I could chip away at my task, chapter by chapter. Students also need predictability in order to think like writers. Megan Sloan's second and third graders know that every morning at nine o'clock they will gather on the rug for a minilesson and then begin writing. Her students produce more pieces and longer pieces than students in classrooms where writing is sporadic.

In any kind of intense work, we need a continuous chunk of time in which to do something or produce something. Ralph Fletcher and JoAnn Portalupi call this the "flow zone," a time in which we become so immersed in what we are doing that we often lose track of time. They ask, "How do you make it so your students open their notebooks, pick up markers or pencils, and really want to write? There's no magic answer, and it's a fact that certain kids will stubbornly resist the invitation to write. But it starts by giving them regular time, real choice, and your genuine interest in what they put down on paper" (2001, 23). By the middle of first grade, in addition to time for minilessons and sharing, students need to spend *at least* thirty to forty-five minutes every day writing independently. I love Katie Wood Ray's wish that writing workshop could be as dependable as lunchtime (2001, 52)!

Predictable Structure

I've already mentioned how important it was for me to set aside some time for writing this book. What I also needed was a daily predictable schedule for my writing. Each day, I checked my "to do" list, reread what I had written the day before, and created a plan for myself for the day. As I drafted and revised, I referred to research, my journals, emails from colleagues, and my professional books. I also often needed answers to questions or a response to a new section, so I would email Carrie, hoping she was at her computer and could answer quickly. Once in a while I would email her a new draft and ask her to read through the whole chapter, looking just for a logical flow.

It's important to set up a similar type of predictable structure for your writing workshop. Students' materials—paper, writing utensils, writing folders, writer's notebooks, and children's books and other mentor texts—need to be available and ready to use. Students need a routine: a minilesson, followed by independent writing, followed by a response from you (during conferences) and from their peers (during share sessions and in writing partnerships).

In *Writing Workshop* (2001, 22), Ralph Fletcher and JoAnn Portalupi note that too often teachers leap right into improving student writing or revision; instead they suggest starting the year with three short-term goals:

- ▶ Getting students to love writing.
- ▶ Establishing a risk-taking environment.
- ▶ Setting up a system for writing folders (grades K–2), writer's notebooks (grades 3–5), and materials and forms.

For teachers starting writing workshop for the first time, Ralph and JoAnn offer specific recommendations about how to launch writing workshop on those first few days and entice students to fall in love with writing. You'll know you've succeeded when your students groan if they have to miss writing workshop or beg to stay in at recess to finish writing!

Choice

It's hard to strike a balance between maintaining consistency within and between grade levels and honoring choice and remaining flexible. Most teachers find common units of study at each grade level helpful. On the other hand, we still want the freedom to follow the kids' interests when they're captivated by the Olympics or incensed about an injustice. Thomas Newkirk writes, "Standard curricula (and the more recent state frameworks) typically focus on coverage to the extent that one wonders how sustained, self-chosen writing can survive at all amid the various objectives" (2002, 183). As you develop units of study, I hope you can also build in room for serendipity. Students can also choose meaningful topics within the genres we ask them to explore. They can decide what and how to revise, and how they want to publish their work. They can explore topics and genres on their own in their writer's notebook and during independent writing. Choice is what gives teachers and writers ownership. It's a juggling act, but without choice and flexibility, we lose the magic.

Risk-Taking Environment

In *The 9 Rights of Every Writer*, Vicki Spandel states, "Writers need a classroom culture that supports writing, a culture in which everyone, including the teacher, is part of a writing community. They need a supportive environment in which they feel safe. . . . In a supportive, nurturing environment, the *act of writing* always meets with approval and deep appreciation, even when the writing itself needs revision" (2005, 41). Writers need to know that they can take risks and share their writing without being shot down or ridiculed. If you've ever shared your writing with a group of people you don't know well, you are very aware of how your heart races, how anxious you are about whether people will appreciate your writing, and how relieved you feel when people are complimentary. Unfortunately, some of you may carry permanent scars because a peer made a scathing comment or a professor went wild with a red pen. I was a prolific poet in high school, but a college poetry professor was so derogatory that it took me almost ten years before I felt confident enough to share my poetry again.

Lucy Calkins says that "the quality of writing in our classrooms grows more from the tone, values, and relationships of our classroom communities than from anything else" (1994, 142). Tommy Duncan works hard from the first day of school to build a welcoming and strong classroom community for his fifth-grade writers. He says, "The most important element of my classroom is a sense of belonging, acceptance, community, and a place where it is safe to take risks and make mistakes. This is particularly true when it comes to writing. From the first minilesson on writing or writer's notebooks, it's important to emphasize the importance of individuality and the acceptance of others' differences." We need to create a supportive environment in which all writers can take risks, try out new forms, explore new genres, and experiment with language.

Models of Good Writing

Your students need models of good writing. As you read good writing aloud, your students get a peek inside the real world of writing and begin to notice writer's craft and how authors write about what they know well or want to explore. You can also bring in samples of your own writing—cards, notes to yourself, a parent newsletter, your writing notebook—and describe your purpose and how you write. In order for writing to flourish, you also need to celebrate your students' effort and growth and will want to create a bulletin board where your writers can display their work.

When I read *Choice Words*, by Peter Johnston (2004), I was struck by his comment that if we use the terms "good" readers and "good" writers, some children immediately wilt because they don't ever envision themselves being "good." It makes more sense to just say we are all writers (without a qualifier) and expect all students to write, so that everyone is included in the "writers club."

High Expectations

In my experience, I've found that in most schools, expectations are too low; we need to set high expectations for our students. All students travel along the same developmental journey as writers. Regie Routman writes, "All students, advantaged or disadvantaged, go through similar stages of literacy development. Therefore, they need the same excellent instruction, not different instruction. Disadvantaged students just need more of it: more demonstrations, more shared experiences, and more guided practice in order to become successful independent learners" (2005, 56). She advises us to "teach with a sense of urgency" since it's so important that those students progress quickly in order to be successful.

Response from Readers

Response carries two meanings in connection with writing workshop. In order for writing to flourish, students need authentic purposes and audiences for their writing. All authors, whether students or adults, then need *response* from readers. As we venture into new writing territory, we need encouragement and support. Katherine Bomer explores how we can focus on each writer's strengths and learn "how to notice and name positive aspects in every student's writing" (2010, 4). We also need mentors and teachers who can help us hone our craft. As teachers, our duty is then to teach *responsively*, which means we need to be so tuned to our students and know so much about writing that we can help each writer based on what he or she needs.

Putting the Pieces Together

So what does this look like in a day-to-day writing workshop? Three components emerge as "nonnegotiables":

▶ Minilessons

▶ Independent writing with teacher conferences

▶ Sharing

I asked two dozen teachers how they incorporated these three components in their busy classrooms. The schedule for most teachers was similar to this:

Writing Workshop
(60–75 minutes a day, four to five days a week)

- ▶ 10–15 minutes minilesson
- ▶ 30–45 minutes writing/conferring
- ▶ 10 minutes sharing/debriefing

Like most teachers, Melissa Clark always begins writing workshop with a short, focused minilesson based on the needs of her students, their current unit of study, and her school's writing curriculum. Immediately following her minilesson, her first graders begin writing independently. When you walk into her classroom, you can hear the buzz of productive conversation as students think, talk, jot, sketch, write, and read their own writing, often incorporating the skills and strategies from her minilessons. Students often work on a piece of writing over several days, polishing and revising their work based on their growing understanding of the genre and feedback from Melissa and their peers.

As students work independently, Melissa provides differentiated instruction by conferring with individuals or small groups about their writing. (Writing conferences are explored further in Chapter 4.) In each of these conferences, she honors what children are able to do on their own and moves each child forward with one new teaching point.

Melissa sometimes also makes brief teaching points informally while students are working independently or during sharing sessions. For instance, one day she noticed that several students were not punctuating their sentences until after they finished their drafts. Melissa asked for everyone's attention. "You all know that when your mom asks you to clean your room, it's so much easier if you have kept it pretty tidy beforehand. Then you just have to pick up a few things. Writing is the same way. You have grown so much as writers that you understand how important punctuation is. You know that it helps the reader to know when your idea is complete. But I've noticed that many of you are not adding any punctuation until you finish writing your whole piece and then you go back and reread and decide where to add it. It's just like cleaning your room at home. If you put that punctuation in when you are writing the sentence, then it doesn't take nearly as long to check for correct punctuation after you have finished your piece. Right now look down at your paper and reread the last two lines and see where you should have punctuation. If you didn't add it before, do it now. For the rest of our workshop today, I want you to stop and add that punctuation when you finish each sentence." Melissa was able to insert tips about punctuation and revision at two different points—during her minilesson and again more

Melissa Clark's Writing Workshop Schedule

informally during this mid-workshop lesson—all during one sixty-minute period. Part of responsive teaching involves watching students carefully so that you know the best time to slip in tips that will be most helpful for your group of writers.

During the last ten minutes or so of a workshop, the students share their writing with their classmates. In Melissa's class, long-term partners usually share their writing and respond to each other's work. Often there is a whole-class share as well, when she asks a few students to talk about the new strategies or techniques they have applied in their writing or worked on with her during a conference. The last time I visited Melissa's classroom, I overheard one first grader say, "Dominic and I worked really hard on asking each other questions today. This helped us both figure out where we needed to add more details."

Megan Sloan also often ends writing workshop with a whole-class share. As her second- and third-grade students sit in the author's chair and share their work, Megan interjects small teaching points based on what she has noticed during writing workshop. She sometimes asks students who've done things she wants to highlight to share a portion of their writing.

Starting the first week of school, Megan gives specific feedback. Students learn that they should address their comments directly to the author and that specific comments are more helpful than "I liked your story." Eventually, Megan demonstrates how to ask questions that help an author and how to make tactful suggestions. As with everything else, lots of modeling and practice are required. Megan also takes one or two anecdotal notes about writing that is shared, records comments from other students, and jots down possible minilesson ideas. Once in a while, Megan asks every child to share one powerful sentence, phrase, or word in a "read around" so that every child's writing voice is heard.

Having an audience is so motivating for writers. Once students realize they can evoke response from readers (tears, sighs of empathy, chuckles, a round of applause), they'll be motivated to keep writing, to improve their writing, and to elicit more responses. "As writers, what we all need more than anything else in the world is listeners, listeners who will respond with silent empathy, with sighs of recognition, with laughter and tears and questions of their own. Writers need to be heard" (Calkins 1994, 14–15).

I sometimes shortchanged sharing when I'd let the composing part of writing workshop or my minilesson run on too long. Leah Mermelstein's book *Don't Forget to Share* (2007) is a great reminder about the power of sharing among a community of writers. She elevates this one very *small* part of the writing workshop (sharing) to a very *big* deal. Leah admits that she used to struggle with whole-class sharing: "I would usually have a few kids read their writing aloud and talk about what they had tried. I spent most of my time reminding the other kids that it was their job to listen. There were very few bits and pieces of any of my students in these earlier shares, and in my heart of hearts I knew the children were not benefiting from them" (6). Leah describes several types of more focused sharing (content, craft, process, progress, partner, and small group), along with a definition and classroom example of each, transcripts of sample conversations, and teaching tips. Leah adds, "Teach your students their roles in a share conversation, and make sure you understand your own role as well. When you do, you'll help your students not only as writers but also as thinkers, speakers, and listeners in the world" (31). If your writing workshop is running smoothly, you may want to read this thought-provoking book and zero in on how to make the sharing portion more intentional and productive as students support each other as writers and linger over ideas.

Many teachers don't have fifty or sixty minutes a day to devote to writing workshop. How do they cope? Carol Dulac has only forty minutes, so some days she launches writing workshop with a minilesson; other days her third graders get right to work.

Doriane Marvel allows more time for minilessons (fifteen to twenty minutes), followed by twenty minutes for writing and conferring. During a minilesson, her primary students might participate in a shared writing activity, or she might read and discuss a mentor text or discuss a new writing strategy. On Fridays, the students have twenty minutes to share their writing. Students sometimes explain how they have used the strategy presented in the minilesson; Doriane then highlights examples she's noticed in other students' writing. On other days, she uses the final twenty minutes of the workshop for word study or to develop and use rubrics pertaining to particular genres. Doriane finds that more students apply the new learning when she makes explicit connections between her minilessons, anchor texts, and the students' own writing.

Jodi Bonnette can't block out an hour every day, so she has writing workshop three consecutive days each week (a five- to ten-minute minilesson, thirty to forty minutes for writing/conferring, ten minutes for sharing). She finds that three consecutive writing days are better than a little here and there. (On the other two days, she incorporates a brief period of independent writing or word study.)

Whatever your situation, students need *time* to write within a *predictable* structure they can count on. They need *choice* in what they are writing and in the crafting strategies they employ in their writing. They need to work in a *risk-taking environment* in which they know they are safe and can dabble in new genres and techniques. Each day you need to present *models of good writing*—your own, mentor texts, and that of other students. Even though your students know they are safe to take risks in

Book List 📖

Resources for Helping You Launch Writing Workshop

- [ ] *Launching the Writing Workshop* (from *Units of Study for Primary Writing*) by Lucy Calkins and Leah Mermelstein (2003) (Grades K–2)
- [ ] *The Nuts and Bolts of Teaching Writing* (from *Units of Study for Primary Writing*) by Lucy Calkins (2003) (Grades K–2)
- [ ] *Launching the Writing Workshop* (from *Units of Study for Teaching Writing, Grades 3–5*) by Lucy Calkins and Marjorie Martinelli (2006)
- [ ] *Don't Forget to Share* by Leah Mermelstein (2007) (Grades K–5)

their writing, they also must understand that you have *high expectations* of them as writers according to their individual strengths and needs. Finally, students consistently need to receive a *response* to their writing, either from you or from their peers. That is a lot to happen in less than an hour every day, but with these components in place, writers blossom every year in thousands of classrooms around the world.

Articulating a Gradual Release Framework for Teaching Writing

In *The Next-Step Guide to Enriching Classroom Environments* (2010), I wrote about the gradual release model of instruction that underpins writing workshop. The process begins as you model your thinking using your own writing. You gradually turn more and more of the responsibility over to students as they grow as writers and become more proficient. Soon you just hold the reins as you guide students through new genres and help them revise. Eventually, you hope that your students will gallop away as independent writers. Five components of writing instruction support students in this journey toward independence:

▶ Modeled writing

▶ Shared writing

▶ Interactive writing

▶ Guided writing

▶ Independent writing

Before we explore each of these components separately, check out the interconnections between reading and writing workshop depicted in Figure 1.3.

Modeled Writing

> During minilessons or at other times throughout the day, the teacher composes a piece for the whole class or a small group or shares other mentor texts, all the while thinking aloud and modeling thought processes.

After hearing Donald Graves speak in 1980, I implemented writing workshop. My students chose topics and began to write with more energy and enthusiasm. Looking back, however, I realize that what I *wasn't* doing was talking about myself as a writer and sharing my struggles and breakthroughs alongside my students. When I work in classrooms now, instead of deluging students with questions about their lives and proposing possible topic after topic, I start by telling stories about my childhood—when my brother broke his arm jumping down a sand hill or how my gruff grandfather used to bark at me to "pull on the reins" when he took me horseback riding through the cotton fields in Arkansas. Jotting words and phrases on a sticky note or chart paper, I'm demonstrating both *how* to start a piece and the fact that small moments are worth capturing. I then have students turn and talk to their neighbors about their possible topics. This is particularly helpful for students new to English, who are often reluctant to raise questions or speak up in front of the whole group. It's easy to check for understanding and pick up teaching points as I move around and listen in on these paired conversations.

Regie Routman also does a great deal of her teaching by sharing her own writing and observes, "When my teaching breaks down, it's almost always because my demonstration has not been sufficient" (2005, 71). Modeling provides a bridge between new learning and the skills your students already have mastered. When you write aloud, students not only see the writing itself but also witness your inner dialogue as you talk through your struggles and decisions as a fellow author.

Megan Sloan writes, "I always say you need to do three things when you teach writing: model, model, and model some more" (2008, 42). At the beginning of the year, she models her topic choices, shares stories about the people and places in her life,

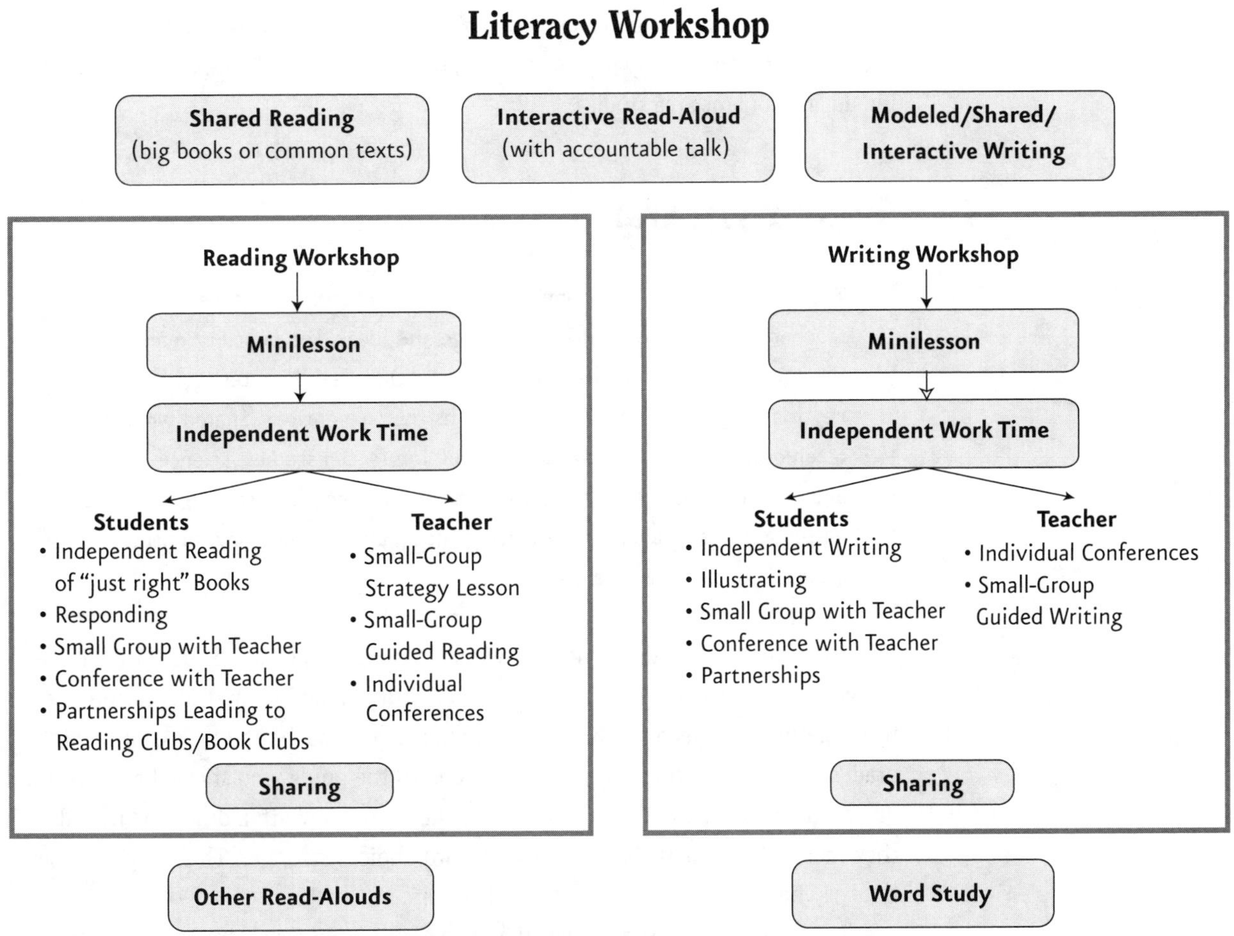

Literacy Workshop

Figure 1.3 Literacy Instruction Within a Workshop Model

Modeled Writing in Megan Sloan's Classroom

then thinks out loud as she decides on her topic and begins to write. Megan demonstrates not only the *how* and *what* of writing but also how much fun this process can be and how satisfying it is to create a draft that captures an image or event. (For example, when she's finished revising her story about shopping with her niece, she mentions how eager she is to share the vignette with her niece the following weekend.) Katie Wood Ray states, "In the best writing workshops I have ever seen, the students can tell you all about their teacher as writer, and that teacher can tell you all about his or her students as writers too. *They know each other in that way* and this changes everything; this changes the whole tone of the classroom" (2001, 47).

Although it's important to share your own writing and think aloud about your own strategies as a writer with the class, you probably won't do so every day. Remember, too, that you can also share your own writing during content area studies.

Shared Writing

> The teacher and children compose messages and stories together as the teacher scaffolds the children's language and ideas. The pencil or marker remains in the hand of the teacher. The teacher demonstrates, guides, and negotiates the craft of writing as well as the conventions. Shared writing often occurs during content area instruction (social studies, science, math) and is used to clarify or record the concepts students are learning. In kindergarten and first grade, shared writing occurs almost every day; in other grades it is used less often, as needed.

Shared writing can be done with the whole class, with a small group, or during an individual conference. You still hold the pen, but you and your students compose a text together. For instance, Kerry Harder (a literacy coach) and a class of third graders composed a thank-you letter to send to the guide who showed them around during their field trip to a museum. First they came up with a draft; the next day, they revised to make the sentences and word choices stronger. This support is particularly helpful for English language learners.

Lev Vygotsky (1978) describes the *zone of proximal development* as the range of learning that lies between what students can do already and what they can do with help. In shared writing, you're "in their zone" as you encourage and acknowledge students' contributions and talk about the craft of writing. Regie Routman writes: "It is through shared writing and scaffolded conversations before, during, and after writing that I do much of my teaching. Shared writing experiences make it possible to write challenging text that no single child could write independently; they raise expectations for what's possible" (2005, 71).

Interactive Writing

> The teacher and students share the pen as they compose collaboratively. Younger children write the letters and words they are able to tackle on their own; the teacher contributes to the text as well. The teacher and older students may take turns writing chunks of text. Interactive writing usually occurs in primary classrooms or with English language learners. Whole-group interactive writing is usually not part of writing workshop; it's much more effective with small groups or during word study or content area learning.

During shared writing, the teacher does the transcription; during interactive writing, the teacher and student (or students) share the pen. Both Cheryl Perkins and Megan Sloan usually use interactive writing with small groups or individuals, composing just a few sentences with them. Megan writes, "Interactive writing is a great strategy because it involves discussion about ideas as well as conventions of print such as spelling, spacing, and directionality. It actively involves students in a non-threatening and focused way" (2009, 141).

When interactive writing was first introduced, teachers had one child come up to the chart paper, take the marker, and fill in the missing sound, word, or phrase. But you can make interactive writing participatory for *all* children at the same time, by having each student write on an individual whiteboard or use their fingers to write on their knee or the carpet. When you come to a letter, word, or phrase that needs to be added to the text, ask all children to try it out on their whiteboard as one child comes to the chart paper to write the missing piece. By glancing around, you'll see which students have internalized a strategy and who needs more support.

Barb McCallister, a first-grade teacher in Colorado, writes interactively with her students for five minutes at the end of every day. She wants them to reflect on their learning, and she knows the power of modeling for and interacting with them. She chooses a different "reflector of learning," who identifies one important highlight of the day. For instance, a child might comment, "We learned that if you have a reading partner, you can practice reading together and you get stronger as readers. And you get to talk about the story." Barb then rephrases these statements to match the wording that will allow practice of developmentally appropriate skills and strategies: "So we might say, *We have learned how to read together with a partner to help us get stronger. We get to talk about the story.*"

Interactive Writing in Cheryl Perkins' Classroom

She asks everyone how to spell *we* and writes that word on the paper. Then she says *have*; a child points out this word on the class word wall, and Barb copies it down. Next she writes the word *learned*, saying out loud why she is placing each letter where she does. Coming to the word *how*, she asks the students to try it out on their whiteboards. Many children spell it quickly; others look on a neighbor's board and copy the word. Then she asks a student to tell her what to write on the chart paper, emphasizing the *h* sound followed by the *ow* sound. She writes *to* quickly; since it is a high-frequency word everyone should know how to spell it. As she begins writing *read*, a child says, "Look on the schedule where it says *reading* and take off the *ing*." Writing the word *together*, Barb stretches the word out into three parts, working on each part by itself, then saying the whole word. Beginning to write *with*, she decides to include it on the word wall; she sounds out each part as she writes it on the chart paper and then writes it on a card for the word wall. While she puts the card on the wall, each child practices writing *with* three times on his or her whiteboard.

Barb continues in the same manner with the rest of the first sentence and then the second sentence, emphasizing various phonetic elements the children still need to learn and pointing out high-frequency words they should be able to spell independently. Throughout the year, she is able to focus on ideas, word choice, sentence structure, and voice, as well as conventions.

At the end of each month, the children participate in a shared reading of the month's reflections and choose their favorite, which then becomes part of a year-long reflection journal, with one entry per month. At the end of the year, Barb gives each child a copy of the year's journal to take home and read over the summer. Barb began this routine her second year of teaching and believes it provides great support for phonics, reading, and writing. It's also a wonderful way for students to reflect on what they are learning.

Interactive Writing (2000), by Andrea McCarrier, Gay Su Pinnell, and Irene Fountas, is an in-depth, detailed resource about interactive writing in primary classrooms. Barb's interactive writing lesson proves these authors' claim that interactive writing "allow[s] children to reach far beyond their present skills so that they [can] participate in the construction of a text, using words and conventions that they could not have controlled while working alone" (8–9). During both shared and interactive writing, you're holding onto the handlebars as you run alongside your writers. Expert teachers know when to correct a wobble and when to let go; these on-the-run decisions will vary from child to child and from task to task.

Guided Writing

The teacher provides instruction and guidance as small groups of students or an individual student in a writing conference focus on aspects of writing process, strategies, craft, and conventions. Groups are temporary, based on students' needs. Guided writing is an integral, daily part of writing workshop.

In guided writing, the students hold the writing implements and are the decision makers. Guided writing groups usually meet during writing workshop when the teacher is there to check in informally, nudge, and offer support. Unlike with guided reading, teachers usually don't form groups based on ability levels. Instead, they gather groups together for specific strategy lessons based on students' needs.

Here's an example of a guided writing lesson in Anne Klein's fifth-grade writing workshop. She's modeled how to "explode a moment"—an idea from Barry Lane's book *After The End* (1993)—in a series of minilessons, but four students are still struggling with this concept. Rather than confer with each of them individually, Anne pulls them together and as a group they craft language to "explode" the moment the fire alarm went off on a snowy day. They talk about the strategies they have used and which ones they might try in their own writing. The four students then apply this new crafting strategy with Anne close by to point out additional tips to the group or to coach individuals. This guided practice pays off as they share their successful elaboration with one another.

The composition of your flexible guided writing groups will be based on your ongoing formative assessment. For instance, after you teach a minilesson about using dialogue, you can circulate as you confer with students and take anecdotal notes. If you notice a number of students struggling with how to punctuate dialogue, you can pull them together to look more closely at some examples.

First-grade teacher Cheryl Perkins carries around a clipboard containing a grid, one box for each student, on which she records anecdotal notes and jots down her compliment and teaching point after each conference. This whole-class portrait lets her see whether there are children with similar needs she may want to group together for a small-group writing lesson.

Guided writing also occurs informally when students help one another and share techniques and strategies. *Guided Writing* (2007), by Lori Oczkus, explores this aspect of writing workshop more closely. Lori gives teachers practical lessons for "guided practice" immediately following modeling and/or shared writing experiences. She defines guided writing as "a bridge between shared and independent writing, a scaffold that supports students with helpful tools as they move into writing on their own" (3). She provides classroom examples of how to turn over the responsibility to writers quickly and shows teachers how they can conduct guided writing lessons for poetry, personal narrative, patterned writing, and expository writing that support each writer at every step of the process.

Independent Writing

> Children independently write a variety of texts, sometimes in the genre currently being studied and other times on topics they choose. Independent writing is an essential component of writing workshop; it's the time for writers to try their wings.

Ben Hart's third/fourth-grade classroom hums with the buzz of independent writers at work while he confers with individual students or meets with a small group. This doesn't happen magically. At the beginning of the year, Ben provides the materials, the time, the structure, and a sense of community that supports writing and promotes independence. He maintains a calm classroom atmosphere and inspires his students by modeling his own writing. Ben realizes the importance of having students internalize the procedures, rituals, and routines of the workshop in September so that writing workshop will run smoothly all year.

Colleen Cruz's *Independent Writing* (2004) focuses on helping intermediate students write independently. She describes in detail the five steps of her month-long, beginning-of-the-year writing unit on independence, in which every student publishes a piece of writing:

- Laying out the supplies
- Getting to know students through assessment
- Studying the writerly life
- Studying writing conventions
- Making sure the foundations are sturdy

Elements of Writing Workshop

Modeled Writing
The teacher composes a piece for the whole class or small groups, all the while thinking aloud and modeling thought processes.

Shared Writing
The teacher and children compose messages and stories together while the teacher scaffolds the children's language and ideas. The teacher demonstrates, guides, and negotiates the craft of writing as well as the conventions.

Interactive Writing
A shared-pen technique in which the teacher and children compose collaboratively, the children writing the letters and other elements they are able to tackle on their own.

Guided/Focused Writing
Children write a variety of texts. The teacher guides the process and provides instruction through minilessons and conferences.

Independent Writing
Children independently write a variety of texts, often based on topics of their own choice and sometimes focused on a specific unit of study.

Figure 1.4 Elements of Writing Workshop, Singapore American School

She writes, "When students learn how to create and navigate their own writing lives through independent work they are able to take the gifts of the writing workshop model even further. The students then have the tools to explore their passions, decide on their audience, design their own writing plans, and set their own pace. They are more able to become lifelong writers because it is their vision they are following" (5). Isn't that our goal?

A chart like the one in Figure 1.4 can be used to explain each of the components of writing workshop. In many of the schools in which I've worked, teachers have crafted "essential agreements" as they've read books together about writing workshop. Interactive read-alouds are often added to these agreements, even though they don't officially take place during writing workshop, since reading aloud and using mentor texts are such critical elements in teaching both reading and writing. I've found that articulating a shared understanding around these essential agreements for writing workshop is one of the most powerful ways to create a shared vision and common approach to teaching writing.

Ponder Box for Teachers

- How comfortable do you feel with the structure of writing workshop in your classroom?

- What is your daily and weekly schedule for writing workshop?

- Which essentials and components of a writing workshop do you already have in place and which ones do you want to learn more about?

- Are there components of writing workshop you would like to observe in another teacher's classroom?

Book List 📖

Resources for Helping You Implement Writing Workshop Components

- ☐ *Writing Essentials* (Chapters 4 and 5) by Regie Routman (2005) (Grades K–8) (modeled and shared writing)
- ☐ *Interactive Writing* by Andrea McCarrier, Gay Su Pinnell, and Irene Fountas (2000) (Grades K–2)
- ☐ *Guided Writing* by Lori Oczkus (2007) (Grades K–5)
- ☐ *Independent Writing* by Colleen Cruz (2004) (Grades 3–5)
- ☐ *Writing Through Childhood* (Chapter 10) by Shelley Harwayne (2001) (Grades K–5)

Ponder Box for Coaches and Principals

- Are all teachers at your school using a writing workshop approach?

- Are writing workshops stronger at some grade levels than others?

- Does the amount of time provided for writing workshop vary between grade levels?

- Can you reevaluate schedules to provide more uninterrupted class time for writing?

Teaching the Writing Process

How do you introduce writing to your students at the beginning of the year? First-grade teacher Eliza Lewis presents a series of introductory minilessons about writing and creates a poster illustrating three things students do as writers (think, sketch, and write). Knowing how quickly students pop out of their chairs saying, "I'm done," Eliza next presents another minilesson about what to do when you are finished writing: "When you are done, you've just begun" (Calkins and Mermelstein 2003, 13). Sherri Ballew created a similar, more detailed chart with her fourth graders based on several minilessons and discussions about "what writers do." You might even want to generate a class chart on which each student writes a strategy or skill they do well and would be willing to share with others, such as "writing poetry," "coming up with interesting titles," or "writing grabbing leads." After this general introduction, both Eliza and Sherri talk about the writing process.

Do you have a strong understanding of the writing process as a teacher *and* as a writer? How do you teach students to move from the rough lump of an idea all the way through to a polished piece? There are ways to provide support for each step of the writing process: prewriting, drafting, revising, editing, and publishing. However, as Ralph Fletcher and JoAnn Portalupi remind us, "We don't want to teach students *the* writing process; rather, we want each one of them to find *a* process that works for him or her. This process will inevitably differ from student to student" (2001, 62). Our goal should be to understand the stages of the writing process from our own perspective as writers and by watching our students, so that we can help them find their own unique, recursive, and sometimes idiosyncratic writing paths.

Almost every writing expert mentions that the best teachers of writing are the ones who see themselves as writers. If you'd like to delve into writing as an insider either on your own or with a group of colleagues, *Inside Writing* (2005), by Donald Graves and Penny Kittle, may be particularly helpful. The accompanying DVD demonstrates "the power of teachers who write with their students and create workshops where the talk is writer to writer" (DVD-1). The authors claim that writing just ten minutes a day can bring about a huge shift in understanding what writers need. "The teacher who writes raises expectations for all students. 'I tried this,' is a powerful invitation for students who admire and respect their teacher. . . . Building this community of writers begins with the teacher's own writing. These teachers model taking risks and allow the students to imagine doing the same. . . . Teachers give students the language to talk about writing with increasing sophistication" (DVD-6, 7).

Shannon Stanton, a literacy coach in Kent, Washington, wrote to me about how her teaching changed once she began to see herself as a writer:

Lucy Calkins [2006] writes, "I do think that in life, all of us try to outgrow ourselves and that we do so by role-playing. And I think that in order to step into new roles, it helps to do so in newly fashioned places, equipped with props that embody the new roles." Teachers College was my newly fashioned place equipped with all the right props: immersion in a writing community; respected authors and mentors to guide the way; colleagues learning and developing alongside me; a new city full of experiences to spark interesting topics; and time to write, think, and practice. The second time I attended the Summer Writing Institute, I was in a section on conferring and writing clubs led by Monique Lopez. We immediately formed writing partnerships and practiced our conferring skills in that dyad. By midweek these partnerships were expanded to writing clubs with four members. I did *not* want to share my writing with my group. But there was no getting out of it, so I read my piece aloud one afternoon. The feedback from the members of my writing club was amazing! They recognized a voice in my storytelling that was nonexistent in my other writing. I could not wait to return to the hotel and work on my piece. On the last day with my writing club, I all but elbowed the other members out of the way so that I could read first. That was the moment I considered myself a writer. Changing my self-identity most certainly changed my teaching. I returned to my work with adults and with children with newfound confidence, inspiration, passion, and understanding for the writing process. I empathize with struggling or reluctant writers; I conjure up opportunities for every writer to be successful; I confer with compassion for the process and rigor toward the product; I write more frequently and talk with others about writing more frequently; and I have more experience and schema to draw on when teaching and learning about writing. Believing I am a writer helps me be a better writer and be a teacher of writers.

Kristen Painter's book, *Living and Teaching the Writing Workshop* (2006), echoes this belief as she walks you through the writing process from start to finish using your own writing. She includes "try its" to get you started and shares examples from her own writing and quotes from successful authors. So find just the right notebook that speaks to you or open up your laptop, curl up in a cozy corner or pull up a comfy chair, and jump in!

Prewriting (Rehearsal)

After I received my teaching degree, I substitute-taught for six months before landing a full-time job. Looking back, I'm embarrassed at how diligently I copied the "journal starters" the teachers in those classrooms used. I was hired to teach second grade in January. A month later I heard Donald Graves speak in our district and those story starters went into the trash. I began to see that when I gave my students writing prompts, I was denying the fact that they already had all the potential topics they could need in their own lives. Vicki Spandel writes, "Every book, film, conversation, ride on the bus, glance out the window, sparks a hundred possibilities for writing—if you have learned to think like a writer" (2005, 21). Our goal is not to collect clever prompts but to help students learn to find and value the threads of writing that are woven into the fabric of their own lives.

Lucy Calkins (1994) and Carl Anderson (2005) both refer to prewriting as "rehearsal." They describe how rehearsal is a way of living with a writer's ears and eyes, rather than a pocketful of *techniques* like brainstorming or creating webs. Carl prefers the term *rehearsal* "because it suggests that writers, like actors preparing for the opening night of a play, have work to do to get ready to draft" (110). Also, this stage sometimes involves lots of writing, so *pre*writing seems a misnomer. Carl explains how rehearsal involves two different kinds of work: finding topics to write about and developing a topic. I'd add organizing topics as a third aspect to rehearsal or prewriting.

FINDING TOPICS

Finding a topic and focus is hard for most kids (and adults). In your first minilessons, you may want to talk about how *you* choose topics, explaining how you usually either write about your own life or about a topic you find interesting. You might also want to create a chart of possible topics with your students. This can sometimes be challenging in kindergarten and at the beginning of first grade since not all students can read, but you can draw pictures or use rebuses.

After many years of exploring how experienced writers choose topics, Katie Wood Ray (1999, 95) describes how their reasons often fall into four categories: a passion or intrigue for a topic or idea; an audience or an occasion; a purpose to fulfill; or the pull of a genre. She goes on to explain how often "young writers do not know yet that it's not what a piece of writing is about but how it's written that makes good writing *good*" (93). Our goal isn't so much finding interesting versus boring topics but helping students find *reasons to write*. Prewriting then becomes far more than a scavenger hunt for topics: it's a way of seeing possible ideas and audiences for writing in their lives. With this broader vision, prewriting becomes a way of seeing and experiencing the world as a writer, filled with possibilities.

DEVELOPING TOPICS

Another challenge during the prewriting stage is how to grow a "seed" idea into a draft. Writer's notebooks are a place to explore topic ideas and to develop what Carl Anderson (2009) calls each student's writing territories, a concept he first encountered in Nancie Atwell's book, *In the Middle* (1998) and in Donald Murray's book, *Write to Learn* (2004). Writers may also want to gather information about a topic or study mentor texts in order to develop a vision for the type of writing they want to tackle. Sometimes, ideas about how to explore a topic happen informally (in the shower, driving to school, before we fall asleep) as we mentally mull over various ways to present what we know.

In *Wondrous Words* (1999, 103–4), Katie Wood Ray has a two-page list of possible ways that authors develop what she calls writing projects before they start drafting. Here are some of her ideas:

- Read books on a topic.
- Search the Internet for more information.
- Talk to an expert or family member about your topic.
- Make a list of questions about your topic.
- Make a list of words related to your topic.
- Gather photographs or objects about your topic.

ORGANIZING TOPICS

Once we've modeled and discussed the many ways writers generate and develop topics, we can also talk about ways they *organize* their writing before they start drafting. Many teachers use graphic organizers such as webs to help students think through possible subtopics. However, very few published writers use webs; most authors talk about their ideas, sketch, or jot down descriptions of characters and snippets of conversation in their writer's notebook. When I wrote most of my professional books, I began by "dumping"—writing everything I knew about a topic. Later, I'd go back and reorganize my writing so that there was a logical flow and sequence. However, when I started writing this book, the staff development rubrics formed a sort of outline and structure for each chapter. The organization for your topic will depend on your personal learning style and the writing task.

Rehearsal for nonfiction writing may require different strategies, since the structure is very different from the beginning, middle, and end format that may have supported students with their stories or personal narratives. Students need to determine their overall topic, break it into smaller components, and write details about each of those subtopics. The type of paper and format can also provide a structure for students to organize their writing. In their primary unit of study *Nonfiction Writing* (2003), Lucy Calkins and Laurie Pessah recommend that students use a separate page for each subtopic and craft their writing on paper formatted with small boxes for drawings, along with accompanying lines on which to describe the details of that subtopic.

Ultimately, we want our students to understand that the more time they spend on the "thinking" stage of the writing process, the stronger their writing will be. Katie Wood Ray reminds us that "we need to spend much more time on helping students with prewriting—thinking through their ideas and how they want to organize them as well as thinking of ways to expand on their ideas. The more we get them to do this *before* they write, the better their drafts will be and the less time they will need to spend on revision" (Literacy Institute at Regis University, Denver, June 2005).

Drafting

A blank piece of paper can be incredibly intimidating. In order to launch students as writers, we need to help them develop confidence, fluency, and stamina. One of the most important things we can do in writing workshop is to provide lots of time and encouragement for students to write and get their ideas down without worrying about correctness. The drafting stage is exploratory; revision and editing come later.

Megan Sloan role-plays and models four aspects of building stamina—write quietly, write the whole time, talk quietly when you need help, and write about what you know. At the beginning of the year, her wiggly second and third graders find it challenging to write for long periods, but once they've had practice and are enjoying writing workshop, they can easily write for thirty or forty minutes. Like runners, students need practice in order to build up their endurance.

Students are able to write independently for longer and longer periods as the year progresses and they build up their "writing muscles." However, you may also occasionally want to ask your students to do five- to ten-minute "freewrites" in response to a prompt in order to build their fluency and get them used to writing spontaneously on an assigned topic. These occasional "freewrites" are sprinting practice; they build stamina and help prepare students for on-demand writing on tests as well as writing tasks down the road in the workplace.

The generative nature of drafting can take us in unexpected directions. In *What a Writer Needs* (1993), Ralph Fletcher describes how sometimes authors don't know where their piece is headed until they begin writing: "It turns out that many writers actually discover what they have to say in the process of writing it" (21). Part of the magic of writing is the potential for surprise and discovery. By sharing our inner talk about what we are thinking as we write, we can help students see how writers sometimes veer from the path mapped out during prewriting.

For me, the key to drafting is to keep my head down and focus on being a *writer*, getting my ideas down without letting my inner editor stand over my shoulder. Good writers learn the intricate tango of moving between being "passion hot" and "critic cold." Of course, even though we often think of drafting and revising as discrete steps in the writing process, most writers end up revising as they reread lines or sections they've just written. It's important to demonstrate the recursive nature of the writing process with our own texts. Since most writers now draft and revise on their PC or laptop, the line between drafting and revising becomes even less distinct, since it's so easy to replace words, delete phrases, and move text around.

Revising

My favorite part of the writing process is revision. I start with a section that feels as messy and tangled as my hair in the morning. By the time I've reread and rewritten a section over and over, all the knots have been untangled, the frizzies tamed, and my writing finally feels smooth. The key is rereading. I read sections over and over, tweaking here and there until they feel right. However, most kids aren't delighted by the prospect of revision, mostly because once they've written something, they think it's quite good! They assume that if you're asking them to revise, it's because something was wrong. It takes a lot of practice for students to begin to see the rewards to be had from polishing a piece of writing.

One of the best ways to model revision strategies to is write every assignment you ask students to produce, sharing how it feels when you're stumped, as well the glow of pleasure when you find just the right image or phrase. Vicki Spandel adds, "Maya Angelou once said that you can learn a lot about a person by the way he or she handles three things: rainy days, lost luggage, and tangled Christmas lights. You can also learn a lot by how someone handles writing. Let your students see how you do it" (2005, 91).

Here are a few tips for keeping revision manageable and even enjoyable:

▶ Model your revision process aloud with your own writing.

▶ Teach rereading as a revision strategy.

▶ Teach revision as part of the process, not something only done at the end.

▶ Have students write and revise short pieces (long ones are too daunting).

▶ Revise only the best work.

▶ Revise for one thing at a time.

▶ Demonstrate concrete strategies for adding, changing, and deleting text (sticky notes, carets, cutting and pasting).

▶ Have students share their revision strategies.

▶ Teach revision as a way of seeing the world.

Cathy Hsu helps her fifth-grade students at Taipei American School remember the revision minilessons she has taught by creating an interactive "revision station" with tip sheets and examples from mentor texts. Each week, students explore a new revision strategy; once the strategies become part of their vocabulary and repertoire, Cathy then adds labeled pockets containing tip sheets and mentor texts to the bulletin board. The station continues to grow throughout the year. During writing workshop, students can walk up to the board, pull down a tip sheet, grab a mentor text they have studied before, and head back to their table. The resources in the revision station help refresh their memory and build independence, inviting students to actively use mentor texts as resources while they are writing.

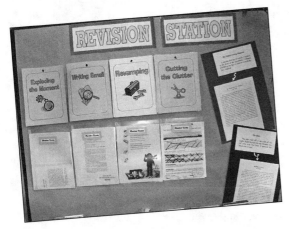

Cathy Hsu's Revision Station

Revision must begin with *vision*. One of my favorite sections in *The Revision Toolbox* is called "That Sinking Feeling." Georgia Heard writes: "One of my writing teachers said that the sinking feeling that a writer gets after she reads a piece of writing and realizes that it's not quite right is actually a feeling to be treasured. Why? Because this disappointed feeling means that we have a vision of how we want our writing to be" (2002, 73).

Editing

It's important for students to understand the difference between revision and editing. Revision is about content; editing is about clarity. When you revise, you revisit your writing to make sure that what's on paper matches what's in your head or heart. Does this piece really say what I want it to say? When you edit, you're making sure readers can easily understand what you're saying. As a writer, I spend 90 percent of my time agonizing over *what* I write and *how* I express myself. I save that last 10 percent for a quick read before I send out a section or chapter for feedback. Even then, my computer does half the work, since I can check for spelling and grammar and even use the thesaurus at the click of my mouse. The computer doesn't catch or solve all my challenges, but I can use all I know about writing to decide which of the red flags I'm going to address.

Many of you probably have memories from high school or college of papers being returned to you with corrections in vivid red pen. Your heart probably sank at the visual evidence of *all you did wrong*. Many teachers, especially in middle school and high school, spend long evenings and weekends correcting student papers. In the meantime, the students are out seeing movies and enjoying being with their friends! Who did all the work? And how much transfer do those teachers see in their students' writing? It makes sense for students to edit their own work, but how do you *teach* editing skills? You can model how you edit your class newsletter or a letter to parents. You can think aloud as you edit what you write with your class on anchor charts. You can also teach editing skills during individual conferences with students' own writing, which is probably the most effective context of all.

The first chapter in *Everyday Editing* (2007), by Jeff Anderson, is titled "Why Do My Students Hate Grammar and Editing?" Jeff's premise is that rather than studying errors in poorly written texts, it makes more sense to share powerful writing, to provide an "invitation to notice" how punctuation and grammar are used, and then to let students dabble with the techniques in their own writing. He asks students to notice, imitate, celebrate, collect, write, combine, edit, and extend their thinking as writers by studying exemplary texts and by looking closely at their own writing. With this inquiry approach, students learn about the mechanics of writing in a constructivist way as part of ongoing conversations about good writing. You can watch Jeff in action in his fifteen-minute DVD *Editing Invitations* (2008) as he invites student inquiry and creates conversations with students about a text he posts on the board, asking, "What do you notice about this sentence?"

We don't want to take over for our students; on the other hand, it's important for readers to be able to read their writing. How much editing can we expect our students to do on their own? Regie Routman states, "By the fall of second grade, I expect students to do most of their own editing" (2005, 233). These students will still need the support of specific, developmentally appropriate editing checklists you have created with them based on your minilessons. By fourth and fifth grade, you should be able to shift most of the responsibility for editing to your students. Regie has high expectations for students and believes they are capable of doing most of their own editing and proofreading. She advises, "Once you establish well-defined editing expectations with the students and require them to do most of the editing work themselves (or with a peer), your editing conferences will be brief, typically about five minutes for one or two pages of writing. Only edit for the student what the student cannot do" (234).

If several students have the same issue, you might want to pull them together into a small group for that particular lesson. You can also create an editing checklist with three or four skills that you've modeled for the class that are within their developmental grasp. Once they have those skills under their belts, you can add further expectations (along with lots of modeling). In first grade, the checklists may include simple skills, such as "I reread my writing to make sure it makes sense" and "I used capital letters at the beginning of each sentence." In primary grades, you may want to help do the final editing after your students have done as much as they can on their own and with peers. (You may occasionally want to publish the work of very young writers in all its developmental glory, but when you do, be sure you note that these are unedited pieces so that parents don't think you don't care or don't know how to spell!)

Published work in the intermediate grades should be mostly error-free, so your checklist will be more extensive. At every grade level, you'll want to show students how they can do a separate pass for each item on the editing checklist. Like so many aspects of teaching, the amount of scaffolding you provide will vary with the purpose, audience, and genre, as well as the developmental stage and personality of each author. In their series *Mastering the Mechanics* (2008), Linda Hoyt and Teresa Therriault have created yearly skills calendars and accompanying three-day lesson cycles focused on capitalization, grammar, punctuation, and spelling in kindergarten through fifth grade (in two-grade increments). The authors state, "Our goal is to develop the understanding that writers integrate conventions into craft rather than seeing them simply as elements of 'correctness'"(8).

One note of caution: One of the disadvantages of drafting and editing on the computer is that unless writers save drafts in separate files or print hard copies, editing changes vanish into cyberspace. If upper elementary students compose on the computer, you may want to have them periodically date and print drafts, save them as new files, or make their revision and editing changes with colored pens on paper copies so that you—and they—have a footprint of their journey. Perhaps it's my age, but I can only edit so far by looking at the screen. Unlike my own children, at some point, I have to print out a draft and do my editing on a paper copy. I catch different types of errors and make different changes than I do on the computer.

Responding to and Publishing Writing

People write for different reasons. Some write just for themselves in a journal (mine in middle school had a velvet cover and a *key*), while other writing is meant to be shared. A fifth grader may draft a letter to the editor about a dangerous school crossing or a second grader may write a poem for his grandfather. These types of writing invite responses from readers. Our challenge as teachers is to find authentic purposes and audiences both within and beyond the walls of our classrooms.

RESPONDING AS READERS IN THE CLASSROOM

Megan Sloan demonstrates how to listen to students' writing when she responds to them as a reader during individual conferences. For instance, she tells Anne Marie, "When you read your story today during author's chair, I thought it was a funny story, but then you talked about your dad and really showed how sad you were." She added, "It reminds me how in *The Sunshine Home* [1994], Eve Bunting wrote about the nursing home being 'painted barf green' that made everyone in our class laugh, but on the next page, she writes about how scared Timmy felt walking into the nursing home to see his grandmother, which was kind of tender." Megan makes those sorts of reading/writing connections during her read-alouds as well as during writing workshop.

Author's Chair in Megan Sloan's Classroom

Megan's students "read like writers" with their ears cocked for an interesting word, a vivid image, or a well-crafted sentence. They can then incorporate what they're learning from mentor texts and their own reading into the poems and stories they craft with an audience in mind. Every day, some of Megan's students have opportunities to share their writing with the whole class or during individual conferences. In addition, because each writer deserves response, teachers like Megan also provide daily opportunities for students to share their work in partnerships. This concept will be explored further in Chapter 4.

Mark Overmeyer (2005) has another way to ensure that all twenty-four students in his classroom have an opportunity for response from their classmates. "I have eight students share something after the first short writing time, eight different students share their revising by adding a detail or two, and the remaining eight students' work I take home, find excerpts that can be used as examples of strong, detailed writing, and use these as discussion starters for the next day's class."

In Chapter 9 of *Writing Circles* (2009), Jim Vopat has a delightful list of ways for students to receive response from fellow writers:

- Nominations (from peers)
- Let Your Light Shine (share a highlight, key phrase, lead, etc.)
- Symphony (like the previous idea, but with kids jumping in to make a whole)
- Post It (display sticky notes on particular aspects, such as strong verbs)
- Open Mike (with microphone to up the ante)
- Gallery Walk (display one page with highlighter to note particular aspect)
- Golden Sentences (display them in a gallery walk or read them aloud)
- First/Last Impressions (read leads or last lines aloud)
- Read Around (each student shares one aspect, such as a lead or visual details)
- Found Poems

SHARING PUBLISHED WRITING

In many schools, the only form of publication is the yearly schoolwide "author celebration." This may be the only time that students ever take a piece through the stages of the writing process, and all too often the focus is far more on the final product than the process. In these classrooms, both teachers and students are often stressed out by the looming deadline and students groan when the event is mentioned. In contrast, students in other classrooms beam with delight as they share their writing throughout the year with peers, with students in other grades, with family members, and with the wider community.

Not every piece that students write is stellar or worth the time and effort required by taking a piece through the writing process (but some of these pieces may still be shared informally with writing partners). Publishing long pieces or every piece that students write can be overwhelming for students (and for you!). It makes more sense to have students do a *lot* of writing in a particular genre, then choose the best poem or vignette to revise, edit, and publish. Regie Routman and Lucy Calkins both recommend that from second grade on, students publish at least one piece each month, connected with your unit of study. Younger students can publish as often as twice a month because they are producing shorter pieces. In classrooms where teachers have been using the Lucy Calkins *Units of Study* (2003, 2006), writing celebrations for peers and parents are often held at the end of each unit. Or one class may invite another to read or listen to their writing and provide feedback. Most often, however, students share their final pieces informally with their classmates. Writers need response, whether they're sharing their writing with us, with a partner, with the whole class from the author's chair, or with families at a celebration at the end of a unit. When the audience responds as *readers*, writers blossom. Katie Wood Ray writes, "We need to respond in ways that shows students we have looked at their writing as *literature*" (1999, 293).

Parents and grandparents are perhaps our young writers' most appreciative audience. In Theresa Marriott's third-grade classroom, family members are invited for an author's tea at the end of the year. Each student is decked out in a crisp white chef's hat and apron. The young authors present their parents with a menu from which they can order an appetizer (a poem), a main course (a fiction or non-fiction piece), and dessert (a personal narrative). After the orders have been placed, students proudly read their pieces to their beaming parents. Ranu Bhattacharyya also has a meet-the-author party in her kindergarten. Her young authors read with "mums," grandmas, siblings, the principal, and their fourth-grade buddies. At the American School in London, teachers hold "literary breakfasts" and "literary lunches" so that children can share their writing with families throughout the year or at the end of each unit of study.

Author's Tea in Theresa Marriott's Classroom

Sometimes school performances can be *a really big deal*. Parents stand in the hallway, pins clenched between their teeth, sewing elaborate costumes. Music teachers lose their sense of humor the week before the performance, and youngsters burst into tears or complain of stomachaches. Parents crowd onto bleachers or uncomfortable metal chairs and zoom in on their darlings with video cameras and rave about the production. If some teachers dare to voice concern about the amount of time spent out of classrooms and the pressure, principals insist, "But that's what we've always done," or "Parents expect it."

Publishing can take on the high-stress aspects of a full-blown full-cast musical when all students are required to take a piece of writing through to publication for a schoolwide contest. Teachers may spend their weekends editing and typing up twenty-eight fifteen-page stories. Shelley Harwayne states, "We need to continually simplify the notion of publishing, taking away the extravaganza feel by creating everyday containers for going public with student work" (2000, 108). If you'd like some tips about how to keep publishing in perspective, Shelley, in *Writing Through Childhood* (2001), presents sixteen authentic, engaging, and low-key ways to make writing public. She explains how publishing becomes a form of parent education as families hear and see the remarkable writing their children have created in school.

It's also important to find an audience for your budding authors in the wider community. Writing can be shared with students at a local college, at a local children's bookstore, or with seniors at a nearby nursing home. Writers can send their persuasive letters out into the world. You can also make writing public by creating a bulletin board on which authors can display their writing to be enjoyed by other students and teachers, as well as parents, administrators, and visitors to the school. Your students' writing not only can be showcased at the time of publication, but can also serve as mentor texts for other students. Classroom and hallway bulletin boards become "free advertising" about the amazing writing your students are producing.

Jennifer Allen has an inspiring article in the May 2008, *Choice Literacy* newsletter about how one school in Maine cele-

Celebrating Writing on Bulletin Boards (Tommy Duncan and Jennifer Abastillas)

brated writing within and beyond their school walls. "We decided that one way to guard against elevating the test scores too much was to make our learning public." The staff agreed to post a piece of writing by every student in the school by the end of March. Sparked by reading *Not Quite What I Was Planning: Six-Word Memoirs by Writers Famous and Obscure* (2008), by Rachel Fershleiser and Larry Smith, teachers launched the writing celebration by posting their own six-word memoirs ("Kids in college and I am broke." "Surprise! Older really does mean wiser!" "It's official. I've become my mother"). After student writing was displayed outside classrooms, tutors from the nearby college teamed up to "read the hallways" and write compliments on colored sticky notes for all three hundred pieces of student writing. Teachers took the same idea into their classrooms and created compliment envelopes. Classrooms signed up for times to read each other's work in the hallways and left positive comments for their peers. Finally, the school hosted a "read our walls" event for parents and the community. "We explained that everyone can read test scores in the newspaper, but what do those scores mean? We wanted everyone to see what writing looks like in the intermediate grades, so community members could understand as we do that you simply cannot capture the heart and emotion of student writing in a test score." The monthly celebration culminated with a visit from guest author Ralph Fletcher. Demonstrating growth and celebrating student work is probably the most effective way you have to garner support from the community and showcase the excellent teaching and exciting learning that occur in your classroom and school.

Chris Weber has written one of the very few books focused solely on publishing student writing. In *Publishing with Students* (2002), he describes student magazines and newspapers, as well as bookmaking techniques. Chris also includes suggestions for and examples of ways students can send their writing out in the world via email, websites, literary magazines, and writing contests. He writes, "I believe that publication is the single strongest way to help encourage students to revise and copyedit" (5).

In addition to the gratifying aspect of sharing my work, I also love when my books are published because it means they are *done*! After the sharing and celebrating, we hope our students will brush off their hands, eager to dig into their next writing project. Before they move on, we can ask students to reflect on how they will apply what they learned to their next project. At the end of their unit of study on realistic fiction, Chris Langdon's intermediate students completed a written reflection. Here's what one student wrote based on the two prompts that Chris provided:

> *As an author,* I think I went through the writing process very carefully and I changed a lot of things as I went along. I also think I showed my voice in my story. I think when I skipped too much it was confusing to my partner.
>
> *I want to make my next writing piece stronger* by foreshadowing and making my author's message clearer to the reader. I also want to show how my character developed more. I think in my next story, I'll try to match the illustrations to the most important bit in the paragraph above or besides it. Also, in my next story, I will try harder to make my cover illustration complement my title. In my story, the title was not bold enough.

Book List

Resources for Helping You Teach the Writing Process

Prewriting and Drafting

☐ *The Art of Teaching Writing* (Chapters 3 and 4) by Lucy Calkins (1994) (Grades K–5)

☐ *Assessing Writers* (Chapter 5), by Carl Anderson (2005) (Grades 3–8)

☐ *The No-Nonsense Guide to Teaching Writing* (Chapter 7) by Judy Davis and Sharon Hill (2003) (Grades 3–8)

☐ *Is That a Fact?* by Tony Stead (2002) (Grades K–3)

☐ *Units of Study for Primary Writing* (2003) and *Units of Study for Writing in Grades 3–5* (2006) by Lucy Calkins and colleagues

☐ *Crunchtime* (Chapters 1 and 2) by Gretchen Bernabei, Jayne Hover, and Cynthia Candler (2009) (Grades 4–10)

Revision

☐ *The Craft of Revision* by Lucy Calkins and Pat Bleichman (from *Units of Study for Primary Writing*) (2003) (K–2)

☐ *The Revision Toolbox* by Georgia Heard (2002) (Grades 2–8)

☐ *Making Revision Matter* by Janet Angelillo (2005) (Grades 3–8)

☐ *Strategic Writing Conferences* (with DVD) by Carl Anderson (2009) (Grades 3–6)

☐ *After the End* by Barry Lane (1992) (Grades 1–5)

☐ *Crunchtime* (Chapters 3 and 4) by Gretchen Bernabei, Jayne Hover, and Cynthia Candler (2009) (Grades 4–10)

Book List *(continued)*

Resources for Helping You Teach the Writing Process

Editing

☐ *Everyday Editing* by Jeff Anderson (2007) (Grades 4–8)

☐ *Editing Invitations* by Jeff Anderson (DVD) (2008) (Grades 3–8)

☐ *Mastering the Mechanics: Ready-to-Use Lessons for Modeled, Guided, and Independent Editing, Grades K–1, 2–3 and 4–5* by Linda Hoyt and Teresa Therriault (2008)

Responding to and Publishing Writing

☐ *Don't Forget to Share* by Leah Mermelstein (2007) (Grades K–5)

☐ *Writing Through Childhood* (Chapter 10) by Shelley Harwayne (2001) (Grades K–5)

☐ *Strategic Writing Conferences* (with DVD) by Carl Anderson (2009) (Grades 3–6)

☐ *Publishing with Students* by Chris Weber (2002) (Grades K–12)

☐ *. . . And with a Light Touch* (Chapters 9 and 17) by Carol Avery (2002) (Grade 1)

☐ *Of Primary Importance* (Chapter 9) by Ann Marie Corgill (2008) (Grades K–3)

☐ *The No-Nonsense Guide to Teaching Writing* (Chapter 7) by Judy Davis and Sharon Hill (2003) (Grades 3–8)

☐ *Is That a Fact?* by Tony Stead (interwoven) (2002) (Grades K–3)

☐ *Units of Study for Primary Writing* (2003) and *Units of Study for Teaching Writing in Grades 3–5* (2006) (interwoven) by Lucy Calkins and Colleagues

Ponder Box for Teachers

● Which aspects of the writing process are solidly in place in your classroom?

● Which aspects of the writing process do your students find most challenging?

● Which aspects of the writing process would you like to explore further?

● How is writing shared with families and other audiences?

● How often do your students publish their writing?

Ponder Box for Coaches and Principals

- How can you support sharing writing workshop processes and techniques between grade levels?

- Is the writing process taught in similar ways in all classrooms?

- How often do students publish their work in most classrooms?

- How often do they share their writing with other grade levels, with parents, and with the wider community?

Before we move on to the next chapter, I wanted to end with one teacher's reflections about his school's journey as they have implemented a new writing program. I asked Ben Hart what his advice would be for schools or teachers just beginning to implement writing workshop and units of study and here are his ten tips:

❶ Provide a clear rationale and purpose for implementing a genre-based writing curriculum. The need for a balanced approach in narrative and nonnarrative writing is a good place to start.

❷ Commit to teaching writing workshop. Don't make it a common agreement; make it an expectation in your school. Every child should be taught specific minilessons in writing each day.

❸ Provide time for writing workshop (at least 45–60 minutes daily).

❹ Have clear grade-level expectations, in writing. We created these after plunging in. Looking back it would have been nice to have had them before we began.

❺ Provide professional development. Teachers' understandings of writing workshop vary widely. We broke up a minilesson into four aspects (connection, teaching, active engagement, link) and expected this structure to be used in our classrooms.

❻ Conferring is a big part of the writing workshop. Professional development also needs to focus specifically on writing conferences.

❼ Start slowly and understand that change takes time. (This was extremely frustrating for me, since I wanted to change the way we taught writing at our school overnight!) It has taken four years from the first pilot group to the end of the first year of implementation. Looking back I am amazed at how far we have come as a school and the way *Units of Study* helped us dramatically change the way we teach writing.

❽ Set up laboratory classrooms. They work and are a great way to involve teachers in professional development. We have learned so much from watching one another teach and confer with students and discussing our reactions afterward.

❾ Use *Units of Study* as a resource to develop your own units. Our teachers now create calendars for specific units, to include teaching points and publishing dates. Grade levels agree on end dates for units.

❿ Design team meetings around student work/samples. Our best conversations have been about student work.

Use one of the rubrics on pages 41 and 42 to ascertain how you have implemented writing workshop in your classroom or school. You may want to list the professional resources that piqued your interest on the log in Appendix A and then use my website to read the annotations about each book and pick one or two to read on your own, with a colleague, or in a book study.

Ponder Box for Teachers

- Have you created a belief statement about writing workshop to include in a parent newsletter or website or distribute at back-to-school night?

- Do you see yourself as a writer? Do you like to write?

- In the writing workshop/writing process rubric, what are your strengths?

- What are your "next steps" in relation to the writing process and writing workshop?

Ponder Box for Coaches and Principals

- Is schoolwide implementation of writing workshop a goal for your school for this year? Next year? Down the road?

- On the writing workshop/writing process rubric, where would you place each grade level at your school?

- Where would you place your school as a whole in terms of writing workshop?

- What staff development on writing workshop has been provided in the past?

- How can you support inquiry about writing workshop and the writing process for a few classrooms, for some grade levels, or for the whole school? Classroom visitations? Book studies? Articles?

- Have you provided time at a staff meeting or workshop for teachers to write and share their own writing?

- How might you offer a differentiated book study about writing instruction using different professional books at different grade levels or based on different teachers' needs or interests?

- Which teachers in your school do you feel could take a leadership role by sharing ideas about writing and inviting colleagues to observe their teaching?

- Which books have teachers already read as a staff about writing workshop?

- Which books and videos/DVDs about writing workshop/writing process do you already have in your professional library?

- Would any of these other professional books about writing workshop/writing process be helpful to read as a staff?

- Are there DVDs or sections of DVDs that would be helpful to share with the whole staff? With just primary or intermediate grade teachers?

- Would any of these resources be helpful in articulating a philosophy statement about the teaching of writing at your school?

Writing Instruction (Teacher Rubric)

Writing Workshop and Writing Process

NOVICE	APPRENTICE	PRACTITIONER	LEADER
☐ I teach writing primarily through whole-group assignments, after which students work independently; I provide writing time once or twice a week; otherwise writing is integrated throughout the day and focuses mostly on other content areas; I determine writing topics and/or provide story starters or writing prompts; I am the primary audience for student writing; as students write, I usually work at my desk; student writing is completed as a draft that is copied neatly into a final draft with little or no revision; I display little student writing in my classroom or hallway	☐ I am beginning to incorporate writing workshop with some instruction and mini-lessons; I teach writing two or three times a week for thirty minutes a day; I direct the writing and occasionally allow students to choose topics or give students free rein during writing workshop; during writing workshop, I monitor student writing or work at my desk; during writing workshop, students occasionally share their writing with peers (author's chair); student writing is taken through the writing process and published a few times during the year, often for a writing contest, class book, bulletin board display, or celebration; I display some student writing in the classroom and hallway	☐ I have implemented writing workshop with minilessons, independent writing, and some sharing; I also teach writing through some modeled, shared, and interactive writing; I teach writing with a predictable schedule three or four days a week for thirty to forty minutes a day; students write independently, often on topics they have chosen themselves; students write in a variety of genres and text types; students regularly share their writing with peers (author's chair) and begin to share in writing partnerships; student writing is taken through the writing process and published and shared often during the year; I display a variety of student writing in my classroom and hallway	☐ I have implemented writing workshop with clear components (minilessons, independent writing, sharing, and some guided writing when necessary); I also teach writing through modeled, shared, and interactive writing; I teach writing with a predictable schedule for forty-five to sixty minutes a day, as well as across the curriculum; students write independently on topics they choose themselves, often within a unit of study; at times they choose their own genres or text types; students share their writing with writing partners, in writing groups, with peers (author's chair), and with authentic audiences outside the classroom; I foster a risk-taking environment in which students are comfortable giving and receiving feedback from me and their peers; student writing is taken through the writing process and published and shared frequently and consistently, often in connection with units of study; I display student writing in my classroom and hallway that reflects range, variety, and the steps in the writing process

Writing Instruction (School Rubric)

NOVICE	APPRENTICE	PRACTITIONER	LEADER
☐ Most teachers teach writing primarily through whole-group assignments, after which students work independently; teachers provide writing time once or twice a week at most; otherwise writing is integrated throughout the day and focuses mostly on other content areas; teachers determine writing topics and/or provide story starters or writing prompts; in most classrooms, teachers are the primary audience for student writing; most teachers work at their desks when students are writing; in most classrooms, student writing is completed as a draft that is transcribed neatly into a final copy with little or no revision; little student writing is displayed in classrooms or hallways	☐ Some teachers are beginning to incorporate writing workshop with some instruction and minilessons; in most classrooms, writing is taught two or three times a week for thirty minutes a day; most teachers direct the writing and occasionally allow students to choose topics or give students free rein during writing workshop; during writing workshop, most teachers monitor student writing or work at their desks during writing workshop; in some classrooms, students share their writing with peers (author's chair); in most classrooms, student writing is taken through the writing process and published a few times during the year, often for a writing contest, class book, bulletin board display, or celebration; teachers display some student writing in classrooms and hallways	☐ Most teachers have implemented writing workshop with minilessons, independent writing, and some sharing; in all classrooms, writing is also taught through some modeled, shared, and interactive writing; writing is taught with a predictable schedule three or four days a week for thirty to forty minutes a day; in most classrooms, students write independently, often on topics they have chosen themselves; in most classrooms, students write in a variety of genres or text types; in most classrooms, students regularly share their writing with peers (author's chair) and begin to share in writing partnerships; in most classrooms, student writing is taken through the writing process and published and shared often during the year; teachers display a variety of student writing in classrooms and hallways throughout the school	☐ All teachers have implemented writing workshop with clear components (minilessons, independent writing, sharing, and some guided writing when necessary); in all classrooms, writing is also taught through modeled, shared, and interactive writing; writing is taught daily with a predictable schedule for forty-five to sixty minutes a day, as well as across the curriculum; in all classrooms, students write independently on topics they choose themselves, often within a unit of study; at times they choose their own genres or text types; in all classrooms, students share their writing with writing partners, in writing groups, with peers (author's chair), and with authentic audiences outside the classroom; each teacher fosters a risk-taking environment in which students are comfortable giving and receiving peer and teacher feedback; in all classrooms, student writing is taken through the writing process and published and shared frequently and consistently, often in connection with units of study; student writing is displayed in classrooms and hallways throughout the school that reflects range, variety, and the steps in the writing process

Writing Workshop and Writing Process

Units of Study for Teaching Writing

Before we begin an exploration of units of study in writing, I think it's important to step back a bit and look at the big picture. In some schools, teachers get so wrapped up in the units and the essence of teaching specific genres that they forget to make the link back to their standards and benchmarks for writing. Standards are helpful by providing:

▶ a focus on the big picture and long-term goals for instruction.

▶ consistency within and between grade levels.

▶ consistency between schools.

▶ reassurance to parents that instruction will be solid and consistent.

▶ a framework for planning instruction.

▶ a way to build on skills and strategies from year to year.

▶ a reminder to keep our expectations high for all our students.

However, we also need to leave breathing room so that we can adjust our instruction to meet the needs of our specific group of learners. We need to keep our eyes on the *learner*, as well as the content of what we are expected to teach. One of the most helpful books about making that link is *Writing Above Standards* (2009) by Debbie Lera. She notes four limitations of standards: politics, poor implementation, presentation, and perception. She explains that unfortunately, one of the results of the government's No Child Left Behind Act is that standards have been inextricably linked to standardized tests and it's important to separate the two issues. Poor implementation can be seen in schools where teachers are required to submit lesson plans or post charts to demonstrate how everything they do is linked to a standard. She also points out that the language and even the binders we are given with lists of state and district standards are almost universally academic and joyless. And they are just lists. "People don't learn in a linear fashion, one skill per day. . . . Teachers know this, which is why they may become overwhelmed when they try to make heads or tails of the standards. It is mind-boggling when we try to marry this linear list to learning theory that states that children learn in a spiral fashion, constantly needing to revisit skills and build on prior knowledge" (53). Standards often have negative connotations and can feel like limitations to our autonomy in our own classrooms and our own sense of professionalism and expertise. Debbie also raises two very fundamental questions that you may also have pondered:

Can standards and workshop coexist in a classroom?

Is there hope for active inquiry in today's standards-based teaching environment? (19)

She believes that the answer to both questions is "yes." She goes on to demonstrate how standards can be helpful and enrich our instruction, using examples from a variety of classrooms. She writes: "When you use standards in a way that makes sense, when you plug these finite skills into units of study in writing that feel rich and appealing to you and to your students, you turn your standards document into a valuable tool. More than that, your standards become a starting point for planning, a foundation on which you will build the part of the writing curriculum that enables your students to soar beyond the standards" (55). She encourages teachers to consider standards as a genre or form of writing that uses specific language to describe the *what* we are to teach, not *how* to teach those skills and strategies. We can use our standards to help us design our curriculum calendars and still leave plenty of room for creativity, serendipity, and joy.

Let me give you an example. In Washington State, one of the fourth-grade standards states that students should be able to do the following:

> 3.1.1 Selects details relevant to the topic to elaborate (e.g., adds detail to each main point using more than one sentence; uses specific words and phrases, reasons, anecdotes, facts, descriptions, and examples).

Kate Norem incorporates that standard in her personal narrative unit, but far exceeds the standards as she immerses her students in the genre. They are not only able to read and write personal narratives, but learn about their community of writers by sharing their stories and discover they carry within themselves stories that only they can share. Many of her students are English language learners and wrote of their lives before coming to the United States. One of her students, who was working on a narrative about his life in Honduras, commented: "I didn't think I had anything interesting that happened to me, but now I know that things that seemed like everyday to me, other people want to know about. Like the way Honduras sounds in the morning, to me that is boring but other people don't know about it so they like it."

Nancy Akhavan (2004) writes: "Standards should guide teachers to create classrooms that encourage the construction of knowledge. Teachers who instruct through the constructivist pedagogy use the standards as connectors to understand their students. They create student-centered classrooms and connect children to learning by actively engaging children in meaning-making activities that encourage students to develop new knowledge and understanding based on their current knowledge" (10).

It's important to plan your units of study and curriculum calendar with your standards and benchmarks in mind, as well as a plan for how learning will be measured. We need to articulate *what* we are going to teach, *how* we are going to teach it, and how we will measure what our students have learned. Standards and benchmarks can provide the framework on which we build our curriculum and specific minilessons within each unit of study.

The unit of study is the "what" of teaching writing, organized in an integrated and logical way. According to Katie Wood Ray, "A unit of study in the writing workshop is a period of time, from a few days to several weeks, when the community of writers turns its attention in a single, focused direction. All of the focus lessons, and sometimes many of the conferences and class sharing times, center around the unit of study" (2001, 130–31). Units of study can be genre based or can focus on process, conventions, or writing strategies.

Book List

Resources about Standards and Writing Instruction

- ☐ *Writing Above Standard* by Debbie Lera (2000) (K–5)
- ☐ *How to Align Literacy Instruction, Assessment, and Standards and Achieve Results You Never Dreamed Possible* by Nancy Akhavan (2004) (K–5)
- ☐ *Reading and Writing Grade by Grade* by Lauren Resnick and Sally Hampton (2009) (K–3)

The Units-of-Study Approach to Teaching Writing

Many classroom teachers have the structure of writing workshop in place but still struggle with teaching writing. In many cases, what's missing is a plan for what units to teach. Teachers need a blueprint of where they want to take their students that is specific to and developmentally appropriate for their grade level. Schools need to build their literacy curriculum both vertically and horizontally so there is alignment both *within* and *between* grades. But even when a school or district develops a "writing curriculum" that lists the genres to be taught at each grade level, there is often little consistency in *how* those genres are taught. Most curriculum documents contain long lists of specific skills ("verb agreement," "onomatopoeia") rather than student-centered and teacher-friendly benchmarks, units, minilessons, and anchor texts. In the meantime, teachers long for something— *anything*—that will help them focus on teaching rather than generating units from scratch. The past six years have seen the publication of several outstanding such resources, from more concrete and specific to more inquiry driven, one of which might suit your situation. Through our work with teachers, Carrie and I have discovered tips for implementing each of these valuable approaches.

Grade-Level Units of Study

I remember opening Pam Allyn's *The Complete 4 for Literacy: How to Teach Reading and Writing Through Daily Lessons, Monthly Units, and Yearlong Calendars* (2007) and gasping at the grade-level charts in Chapter 4; they were in *color* and outlined a unit of study for both reading and writing for each month, September through June. I immediately realized these sample calendars (two different ones for each grade level) could become the foundation for a literacy curriculum. Pam writes, "Teaching inside units of study helps you to organize your thinking and maximize your teaching time" (23). Each monthlong unit of study, augmented by specific minilessons, develops students' expertise in one of four components of writing instruction: process, genre, strategies, and conventions. For instance, if you teach third grade, you might begin in September with "Setting Personal Writing Goals" (process). In November, your class could focus on "Nonfiction Wonderings" (genre). Students would work on "Rereading and Revising for Audience" (strategy) for a week in March, then study "Parts of Speech" (conventions) for a week in April. The book describes a year in the teaching of reading and writing and provides a detailed description of one unit. The last chapter gives teachers an inside glimpse into "A Day in the Teaching of Reading and Writing."

A year later, Pam and her colleagues published a series, *The Complete Year in Reading and Writing* (McNally 2008), with one book for each grade level, K–5. The foldout cover of each book includes an inviting color-coded calendar for the year that outlines reading and writing units for early fall, late fall, winter, and spring.

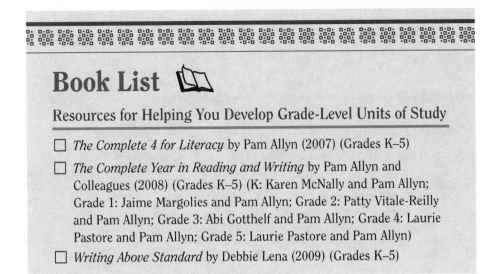

Book List

Resources for Helping You Develop Grade-Level Units of Study

- ☐ *The Complete 4 for Literacy* by Pam Allyn (2007) (Grades K–5)
- ☐ *The Complete Year in Reading and Writing* by Pam Allyn and Colleagues (2008) (Grades K–5) (K: Karen McNally and Pam Allyn; Grade 1: Jaime Margolies and Pam Allyn; Grade 2: Patty Vitale-Reilly and Pam Allyn; Grade 3: Abi Gotthelf and Pam Allyn; Grade 4: Laurie Pastore and Pam Allyn; Grade 5: Laurie Pastore and Pam Allyn)
- ☐ *Writing Above Standard* by Debbie Lena (2009) (Grades K–5)

Reading and writing units are integrated and build on one another. The units are clear and concise, have a predictable structure, and are aligned with the four standards (process, genre, strategies, and conventions). The four standards are further broken down into teacher-friendly benchmarks specific to each grade level. Each unit describes activities for four stages of instruction (immersion, identification, guided practice, and commitment) built on a gradual release of responsibility. Finally, this team of experts provides assessment tools for each unit, a glossary of terms, a list of anchor texts, and sample letters to parents. The accompanying DVDs include all the necessary assessment forms and student response forms, lists of resources, links for publishing, and additional support for professional development.

The Complete 4 for Literacy provides a flexible framework you can adapt to fit your own needs as you develop a writing (and reading) curriculum for your classroom. It is also very cost effective if you and your grade-level colleagues share a book (each book is under $20). Pam honors your professionalism and expertise, recognizing that many of the units she describes are probably ones you already teach. She writes, "The Complete 4 system is meant to simplify your teaching life" (22). That's pretty appealing!

Primary and Intermediate Units of Study

In 2003, Lucy Calkins and her colleagues at Columbia University's Teachers College Reading and Writing Project developed the *Units of Study for Primary Writing: A Yearlong Curriculum* (2003), a series of short books on writing workshop for K–2 classroom teachers (including seven specific units of study). Three years later, Lucy extended the curriculum with six units of study for the intermediate grades, *Units of Study for Teaching Writing, Grades 3–5* (2006). Both boxed resources include a CD-ROM with samples of student work and video clips.

The expertise underlying these texts and their pedagogy is incredible. The books and CDs include mentor texts, minilessons, transcripts of conversations, rich examples of student writing, and information about the structure and philosophy of teaching writing. When they are implemented in classrooms, students produce more and better work. Here are testimonials from two teachers in the upper primary division at Hong Kong International School:

> These units of study have positively changed the teaching of writing in my classroom and at my school. First, they have made writing a defined area of the curriculum. The program requires a commitment to *teach* writing every day of the week. That's quite different from "doing writing" every day. Second, the specific strategies that are taught place control in the students' hands. If they want to be better writers, they can be.
>
> —Kasey, Perry, Grade 3–4 Teacher
>
> These units provide a coherent framework for exploring different genres of writing. Strategies are clearly presented and are easily adjusted to fit the different needs of each class. As a result of the units, my students are much more reflective and have developed a variety of strategies to improve their writing.
>
> —Keith Stanulis, Grade 3–4 Teacher

Lucy's units are not grade specific but are grouped at two general levels, K–2 and 3–5, in keeping with a developmental view that looks beyond grade level to the natural progression of skills and strategies. This open-endedness can be challenging at the beginning, especially for new teachers, as you and your colleagues decide which minilessons and examples to use at each grade level, as well as how to adapt the minilessons to meet your students' developmental needs. One of the strengths of this program is that it includes scripts of actual lessons, along with Lucy's reflections about the reasons the teacher made certain decisions and how those choices affected student learning, which means you can explore the *art* of teaching writing. It's a "coaching curriculum," as if Lucy or one of her colleagues were standing alongside you, helping you make on-the-spot decisions.

Intermediate teachers Kasey and Keith and their colleagues now set aside time for writing on a more regular basis. Their writing instruction is focused and intentional and incorporates learning goals designed to develop skillful writers and hone the craft of writing. These teachers and students are living more "writerly" lives, reading like writers, collecting writing samples as mentor texts, and trying out new strategies in their own writing. For years we have taught our students to "show, not tell" in their writing. Lucy and her colleagues have found a way to "show, not tell" teachers what solid writing instruction looks and sounds like.

If you teach first grade, *First Grade Writers* (2005), by Stephanie Parsons, is so chockfull of specific suggestions and strategies that you could plan your whole year of teaching writing around it. Stephanie structures writing workshop in her first-grade classroom around four goals: writing quality, writing habits, writing conventions, and community. She lays out five units of study—Building a Community of Writers, Pattern Books, Nonfiction Question-and-Answer Books, Personal Narrative, and Fiction—complete with information about how long each will take, how to get ready for the unit, and lists of books for launching the study, as well as lists of specific minilessons and teaching points, revision and publishing ideas, and assessment rubrics.

One of the most helpful aspects is the section in each chapter addressing predictable problems. Stephanie's brilliance and experience shine through as she describes what to do about children who say, "I'm done!" or who are afraid to take risks. Doriane Marvel, a first-grade teacher in Austin, Texas, writes: "I like how the book is organized around different genres. It enhanced my understanding of the characteristics of each type of writing and supported my students' understanding of text structures. This is a great complement to Katie Wood Ray's books and to Lucy Calkins' *Units of Study for Primary Writing*."

The popularity of the first-grade book led to *Second Grade Writers: Units of Study to Help Children Focus on Audience and Purpose* (2007) in which Stephanie maps out a year in second grade, with one unit for each month, directly connected to *Units of Study for Primary Writing*. She goes into five units in detail: Becoming a Community of Writers, Writing for Change, Book Reviews, Writing About Research, and (my favorite) Exploring Humor. The Becoming a Community of Writers chapter will be particularly helpful if you and your second-grade colleagues are implementing writing workshop for the first time. If you're a more experienced second-grade teacher, this gem of a book will help you fine-tune *Units of Study for Primary Writing* for your second-grade curriculum, as well as integrate a few new units.

One of the challenges of implementing Lucy's *Units of Study* is determining which units and minilessons will be taught at each grade level so it doesn't become overwhelming. Figure 2.1 provides a sample curriculum calendar for primary units of study. The intermediate teachers at Hong Kong International School spent several years piloting the units before coming up with plans for how they would be used in each grade level to create a logical and developmental progression for grades K–2. Like many international schools, HKIS has extra subjects (such as the Mandarin language) and other scheduling constraints, so students often have at least one-third less instructional time than is provided in New York City where the original units were developed. Therefore, HKIS chose to focus on a reasonable number of units throughout the year in each grade level. Schools that are just beginning to use *Units of Study* might also cut back the total number of units during their first year or two of implementation.

If you're a literacy coach or teacher leader, you may want to read *A Principal's Guide to Leadership in the Teaching of Writing* (2008), by Lucy Calkins and Laurie Pessah, and give a copy of this book to your principal. If you're a principal, you'll definitely want to purchase a copy for yourself. This book offers a month-by-month plan for schoolwide implementation of both *Units of Study* resources—beginning in March the year before! If you want to make writing a priority, you need to have a clear vision of how you will provide *time* and *resources* and what forms of professional development will help with implementation. Lucy and Laurie even offer a guarantee: "I can promise you that if you make this decision, if your teachers use the *Units of Study* books, if teachers make a commitment to teaching a writing workshop every day (or even just four days a week), and if they plan together and help each other, your children's writing will astonish you" (16).

K–2 Writing Curriculum Calendar

	R2 (KINDERGARTEN)	GRADE 1	GRADE 2
August/ September	Launching the Writing Workshop with Telling and Drawing Stories	Launching the Writing Workshop with Pattern Books	Launching the Writing Workshop
September/ October	Telling and Writing Stories	Small Moments	Small Moments
October/ November	Looking Closely: Observing, Labeling, and Listing Like a Scientist	Writing for Readers— Looking at Conventions	Authors as Mentors
November/ December	Illustrator as Mentor	Authors as Mentors	Persuasive Writing— Book Reviews
January	Nonfiction Writing: How-To Books	Nonfiction Writing How-To Books	Writing and Revising Realistic Fiction
February	Small Moments	Nonfiction Writing All About Books	Nonfiction Writing: Expert Projects
March	Writing for Readers— Looking at Conventions	Poetry	Independent Choice
April	Poetry and Songs	Craft of Revision	Poetry
May	Independent Choice	Independent Choice	Exploring Humor

Figure 2.1 Sample K–2 Writing Curriculum Calendar Using and Expanding on *Units of Study for Primary Writing*

Let me end with Lucy's words in *A Guide to the Writing Workshop*, the introductory booklet in *Units of Study for Teaching Writing, Grades 3–5* (2006): "The most important thing for you to know is that the books are designed to put themselves out of a job. Once you have used this scaffold to support your teaching, you will find you no longer need it. You will see that your students need more help with one strategy or another, and you'll use the principles in these books to help you author minilessons, small-group work, and conferences tailored to the needs of your students" (7). These books and DVDs are not meant to become your entire writing curriculum, but are some of the many resources and tools that can help you improve writing instruction in your classroom.

Book List 📖

Resources for Helping You Develop Primary and Intermediate Units of Study

- ☐ *Units of Study for Primary Writing: A Yearlong Curriculum* by Lucy Calkins (2003) (Grades K–2)
- ☐ *Units of Study for Teaching Writing, Grades 3–5* by Lucy Calkins (2006)
- ☐ *Launching the Writing Workshop* (from *Units of Study for Primary Writing*) by Lucy Calkins and Leah Mermelstein (2003) (Grades K–2)
- ☐ *The Nuts and Bolts of Teaching Writing* (from *Units of Study for Primary Writing*) by Lucy Calkins and Leah Mermelstein (2003) (Grades K–2)
- ☐ *Launching the Writing Workshop* (from *Units of Study for Teaching Writing, Grades 3–5*) by Lucy Calkins and Marjorie Martinelli (2006)
- ☐ *Big Lessons from Small Writers, Grades K–2* by Lucy Calkins (DVD) (2005)
- ☐ *Seeing Possibilities* by Lucy Calkins (DVD) (2007) (Grades 3–5)
- ☐ *First Grade Writers* by Stephanie Parsons (2005)
- ☐ *Second Grade Writers* by Stephanie Parsons (2007)
- ☐ *A Principal's Guide to Leadership in the Teaching of Writing* by Lucy Calkins and Laurie Pessah (with DVD) (2008) (Grades K–5)
- ☐ *Of Primary Importance* by Ann Marie Corgill (2008) (Grades K–2)

Constructivist Units of Study

Study Driven: A Framework for Planning Units of Study in the Writing Workshop (2006), by Katie Wood Ray, is a guide to creating units of study not only for writing but can also be used to construct units of study for reading; it outlines a predictable process you can use again and again. Katie's work is less of a "program," more of a constructivist approach. If you have been using Pam's or Lucy's units in your writing curriculum and are ready to design your own, Katie's framework—reading immersion, close study, writing under the influence (156–60)—aligns well with those resources. However, teachers who are new to writing workshop will probably find this approach very challenging without the support of either a teammate or a literacy coach.

Janet Angelillo, in *Whole-Class Teaching* (2008), states, "Wise teachers use all the tools in their professional toolboxes, knowing what each tool can accomplish and how to use each tool wisely" (100). However, it's also important to be responsive to the needs of your particular group of youngsters. There's always a slight tension between creating grade-level consistency and allowing flexibility and time for choice. Megan Sloan begins the year with the Calkins units on launching writing workshop and writing personal narrative but then allows some "wiggle room." Megan writes, "After the first ten weeks, I am wide open for ideas on which kinds of

Book List

Resources for Helping You Develop Units of Study for
Writing Instruction

- ☐ *Study Driven* by Katie Wood Ray (2006) (Grades K–8)
- ☐ *About the Authors* (Chapter 6) by Katie Wood Ray (2004) (Grades K–2)
- ☐ *The Writing Workshop* (Chapter 12) by Katie Wood Ray (2001) (Grades 3–8)
- ☐ *Wondrous Words* (Chapter 11) by Katie Wood Ray (1999) (Grades K–6)
- ☐ *How to Align Literacy Instruction, Assessment, and Standards* by Nancy Akhavan (2004) (Grades K–5)

writing we study next. I let the students' needs lead me" (2009, 123). If you and your colleagues develop units of study, Lucy Calkins, Pam Allyn, and Katie Wood Ray can be your mentors. However, the order in which you present units, how long you spend on each one, and the anchor texts you use should be based on the needs of your particular group of students. And of course, you still want to give your writers a great many opportunities to choose their own topics.

Zeroing In: Genre-Based Units of Study

By becoming familiar with some genre-based units of study and how these units come to life in real classrooms, you'll be able to ascertain what units you already have in place, which ones you'd like to fine-tune, and which ones you might want to add to your repertoire. The companion website to Regie Routman's *Writing Essentials* (2005), www.heinemann.com/writingessentials, has a detailed list of genre characteristics that includes definitions, lists of frequently found elements, and picture book examples. You may want to refer to this chart as you map out your own units of study (you'll need a copy of the book in order to log on). Before students jump into a new form of writing, you'll want to be sure to first immerse them in reading that genre, and then to use your minilessons to study a few anchor texts up close.

Writing Poetry

Do you write poetry? Do you like to teach poetry? It's my favorite genre, probably because I've been composing poems in my journals since I was little. I realize that not everyone feels this way. In too many classrooms, both teachers and students dread the obligatory April poetry unit in which teachers cling to the predictable structure of haiku and cinquains instead of diving into poetry headlong and paddling around alongside their students.

In *Study Driven* (2006), Katie Wood Ray quotes national poet laureate Ted Kooser: "Before you write one poem, you need to read at least 100" (124). Our students need to be saturated with poetry as readers before they can begin to write poetry with joy and confidence. You'll also want to model by writing your own poems and then composing poems with your students. Some of you are already shaking your head, thinking "but my poems are dreadful." It doesn't matter. In *Writing Through Childhood* (2001), principal Shelley Harwayne explains why she writes what she admits are mediocre poems for her staff and students: "I'm a rather good model, because most people think, 'I can do that.' In fact, they probably think, 'I can do better than that.' The folks at school probably learn more from my pleasure than from my products and that's okay with me. Besides, I don't ask children to do anything I won't do myself" (318). Every time I email Bob Hetzel, the director at the American Embassy School in Delhi, India, about a conference, a workshop, or a teacher, he sends a poem he has found along with his reply. He places poems in teachers' mailboxes and reads them at faculty meetings. Wouldn't you love to work for a principal like Shelley or a director like Bob?

Your students' initial attempts may not be stunning, but with practice, ongoing minilessons, and continued sharing of both published poems and their own, they will soon dazzle you with their writing. Linda Lee starts a chart about poetry and she and her students add to the chart throughout the year as they read and write poems. Once introduced, writing poetry becomes an option students can choose to respond to literature or write in the content areas.

After Georgia Heard's visit to their school, Cathy Hsu created an "amazing language" bulletin board on which students spontaneously celebrate lines of poetry

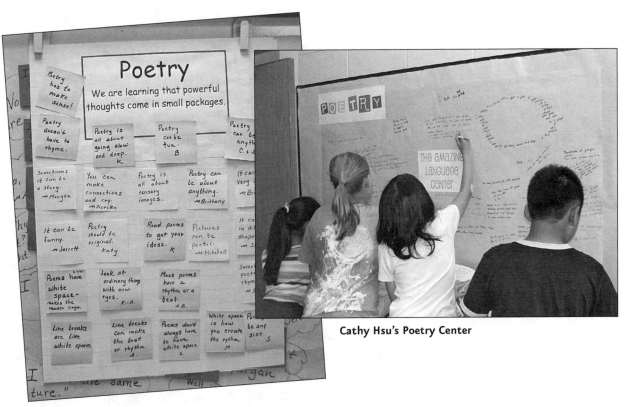

Cathy Hsu's Poetry Center

Linda Lee's Poetry Anchor Chart with Sticky Notes

that jump out at them. The board starts out blank. As kids read poetry during reading workshop, they post words, phrases, or lines for everyone to savor. A basketball lover chose a phrase from Eloise Greenfield's "For the Love of the Game" (1998) that was even more powerful when excerpted. One girl copied an entire concrete poem because she loved the way its circular shape took the reader around a loop. A struggling reader posted a Jane Yolen line about what one should do if one falls: "Just rise—and shine." What a great way to share poetry publicly!

Powerful Thoughts in Tiny Packages, the poetry unit in *Units of Study for Primary Writing* (Calkins 2003), is as much about noticing and delighting in the world around us as it is about teaching poetry. Students begin to "see with poets' eyes." They focus on the concepts of line breaks, rhythm or music, powerful thoughts, and showing instead of telling. After they have crafted a few of their own poems, they choose one and begin to work on word choice and structure. At the end of the unit, the young writers revisit some of their former narrative writing and turn at least one piece into a poem. After they choose a few poems to publish and do the necessary revising and editing, they can celebrate their poetry at a whole-class celebration or invite parents to a "coffeehouse."

One of the things Megan Sloan has discovered over the years is the power of teaching poetry all year long. She writes, "I love to move students into poetry early because often my reluctant and struggling writers find success with poetry. Poems can be short. Students don't have to write in complete sentences. Suddenly, children who don't think they are writers become writers" (2009, 23). She also combines genres, reading *Least Things* (2003) by Jane Yolen and Jason Stemple, who combines short poems with factual information about animals. Her students' poems start to sparkle as they create lists of color words to weave into the poems that accompany their animal research. Every student emerges from Megan's classroom a reader, a writer, and a poet.

If you buy just one book about teaching poetry, I highly recommend *Awakening the Heart* (1999), by Georgia Heard. Since there is no poetry unit in the Calkins units of study for intermediate grades, this book is especially helpful if you teach third, fourth, or fifth grade (although Georgia's ideas can easily be adapted for students in kindergarten through middle school). If you teach younger kids, *Climb Inside a Poem* (2007) is a comprehensive curriculum for poetry in the primary grades. Georgia makes both writing and teaching poetry seem doable. She includes poetry from students and published poets, as well as practical activities for weaving poetry into the fabric of your classroom. Georgia claims that poetry is more a mood than a genre. It's about noticing, slowing down, and savoring language. In the introduction to *Awakening the Heart* she writes, "We all have poetry inside of us, and I believe that poetry is for everyone" (xv). She describes a poem as "a blanket for your heart" or "a place where your heart can rest." It's hard not to fall in love with poetry when you hear Georgia speak or read her books.

Kate Morris often begins the year by having her students create "heart maps," an activity suggested in *Awakening the Heart*. She reads aloud *Wilfrid Gordon McDonald Partridge* (1985), by Mem Fox, then gives students a planning sheet with prompts to help them think of something they will always remember, something that makes them laugh, something that makes them cry, and a secret in their heart. Kate also shares her own heart map (she creates a new one each year) to help teach symbolic thinking—how an object can represent a person or a memory. Inside the shape of a heart, students draw images of all the important events, objects, animals, and people in their lives. As they share their heart maps, they learn a bit about one another and take the first steps in learning to write about things that matter. Later they return to their heart maps and write about a particular feeling or image in more depth.

Anne Klein teaches a poetry unit early in the year, collecting stacks and stacks of poetry books from her own library, the school library, and the public library. Her fifth graders begin each day by browsing in these books and writing down a favorite poem in their poetry journal. They conclude the session with a "poetry pop-up," standing and reading their favorite poem aloud. Anne talks about literary elements and poetic forms and devices, and eventually her students begin adding their own insights. Anne also demonstrates a new type of poetry every day or two and drafts a poem in that form with the class. Then the students experiment with the form on their own. After several weeks, students select one poem of each kind Anne has introduced (anywhere from eight to twelve) to include in a final poetry anthology. They also include one published poem from a book they've read and create drawings to accompany the poems. As a culminating project, the students set out their anthologies, along with a response page, then read and respond to one other's collections.

Kate Morris' Students Create Heart Maps

If we start in kindergarten, we can create an environment in which, even in high school, "poetry is cool." Lucy Calkins writes, "All our effort should go to ensuring that children are invited inside poetry and made to feel at home there" (1994, 377).

Book List 📖

Resources for Helping You Teach Children to Write Poetry

- [ ] *The Complete Year in Reading and Writing: Kindergarten* (Chapter 4, pp. 135–38) by Karen McNally and Pam Allyn (2008)
- [ ] *Kids' Poems: Teaching Kindergartners to Love Writing Poetry* by Regie Routman (2000)
- [ ] *The Complete Year in Reading and Writing: Grade 1* (Chapter 5, pp. 167–69) by Jaime Margolies and Pam Allyn (2008)
- [ ] *Kids' Poems: Teaching First Graders to Love Writing Poetry* by Regie Routman (2000)
- [ ] *The Complete Year in Reading and Writing: Grade 2* (Chapter 5, pp. 153–56) by Patty Vitale-Reilly and Pam Allyn (2008)

Book List *(continued)*

Resources for Helping You Teach Children to Write Poetry

☐ *Of Primary Importance* (Chapter 6) by Ann Marie Corgill (2008) (Grades K–2)

☐ *Kids' Poems: Teaching Second Graders to Love Writing Poetry* by Regie Routman (2000)

☐ *The Complete Year in Reading and Writing: Grade 3* (Chapter 5, pp. 159–71) by Abi Gotthelf and Pam Allyn (2008)

☐ *The Complete Year in Reading and Writing: Grade 4* (Chapter 4, pp. 157–60) by Laurie Pastore and Pam Allyn (2008)

☐ *Kids' Poems: Teaching Third and Fourth Graders to Love Writing Poetry* by Regie Routman (2000)

☐ *The Complete Year in Reading and Writing: Grade 5* (Chapter 4, pp. 138–47) by Laurie Pastore and Pam Allyn (2008)

☐ *Poetry: Powerful Thoughts in Tiny Packages* (from *Units of Study for Primary Writing*) by Lucy Calkins and Stephanie Parsons (2003) (Grades K–2)

☐ *Climb Inside a Poem: Original Poems for Children* by Georgia Heard and Lester Laminack (2007). Includes *Lessons for Climb Inside a Poem,* and *Reading and Writing Poetry Across the Year.*

☐ *About the Authors* (pp. 214–20) by Katie Wood Ray with Lisa Cleaveland (2005) (Grades K–2)

☐ *The No-Nonsense Guide to Teaching Writing* (Chapter 10) by Judy Davis and Sharon Hill (2003) (Grades 3–5)

☐ *Teaching the Qualities of Writing,* poetry section by JoAnn Portalupi and Ralph Fletcher (2004) (Grades 3–5)

☐ *The Art of Teaching Writing* (Chapter 23) by Lucy Calkins (1994) (Grades K–5)

☐ *Awakening the Heart* by Georgia Heard (1999) (Grades K–5)

☐ *Writing Through Childhood* by Shelley Harwayne (2001) (Grades K–5)

☐ *Lifetime Guarantees* (Chapter 5) by Shelley Harwayne (2000) (Grades K–5)

☐ *Mentor Texts* (Chapter 7) by Lynne Dorfman and Rose Cappelli (2007) (Grades K–5)

☐ *The Multigenre Research Paper* (Chapter 4) by Camille Allen (2001) (Grades 4–6)

☐ *A Note Slipped Under the Door* by Nick Flynn and Shirley McPhillips (2000) (Grades K–12)

☐ *Practical Poetry* by Sara Holbrook (2005) (Grades 4–8)

☐ *High Definition* by Sara Holbrook (2010) (Grades 4–8)

☐ *A Fresh Look at Writing* (Chapter 4, pp. 325–42) by Donald Graves (1994) (Grades 1–6)

☐ *Study Driven* (pp. 205–8) by Katie Wood Ray (2006) (Grades K–8)

Writing Fiction

Realistic fiction contains story elements (characters, plot, setting, problem, and solution) that unfold sequentially. *Fantasy* is an even more demanding form of fiction for young writers that contains the same story elements but with the additional challenge of placing the characters and events within a believable imagined world. The seeds for writing fiction grow best when nourished by reading and by storytelling in our classrooms and at home.

Most children have been listening to fairy tales, folktales, and family stories since they were toddlers and love to "make believe." Even older readers have been captivated by fantasy worlds, plot twists, and memorable characters in the Harry Potter books by J. K. Rowling; the Eragon series by Christopher Paolini; and the Twilight series by Stephanie Meyers. Even though my youngest son, Bruce, was heading off to college in the fall, he and I lined up last summer with the thousands of eager fans around the country at the midnight showing of the latest Harry Potter movie as we plunged again into the magical world of Hogwarts and magicians. During recess at any school, you'll see students acting out *A Wrinkle in Time* (L'Engle 2007); *Star Wars*; *The Lion, the Witch, and the Wardrobe* (Lewis 2000); or *The Spiderwick Chronicles* (Black and DiTerlizzi 2003–2004). Bruno Bettleheim (1976) explained how we all wrestle with fears, needs, and challenges through story. The archetypes of good and evil, a hero's journey, and overcoming obstacles are all played out in movies, television shows, plays, and novels.

In *Holding On to Good Ideas in a Time of Bad Ones* (2009), Thomas Newkirk, in a chapter titled "Popular Culture as a Literacy Tool," describes the role of fantasy and the media in children's lives. He explores how teachers often limit writing about the supernatural, humor, danger, and power: "This perspective dismisses children's media-oriented writing as imitative without recognizing the ways children alter, improvise with, and combine popular cultural threads in their writing. To assert that some genres are, by their very nature, 'authentic' and others are 'inauthentic,' is, at its root, simply disguised censorship" (105).

Other children gravitate more toward realistic fiction, enjoying the classic escapades of Ramona (Beverly Cleary) and the funny-yet-touching misadventures of Joey Pigza (Jack Gantos) or Clementine (Sarah Pennypacker). Teachers read fiction aloud in their classrooms every day, and most of you spend a fair chunk of your salary on children's books, most of which are probably fiction. So why is fiction *writing* so neglected in most classrooms? Most teachers nudge children to write about their lives and craft poetry and nonfiction, yet other than twists on familiar fairy tales, the potential for fiction and fantasy writing often remains untapped.

Many teachers simply don't know how to go about teaching fiction. I worry when I see that fiction is the first genre being taught, because this most often results in poor writing. Too often teachers leap into fiction writing without remembering the importance of gradual release. Children need scaffolding and small steps before they can successfully attempt multicharacter, complex fantasy stories. Students often become frustrated when their fiction *writing* lags behind their fiction *reading* and the stories that unfold in their imagination. Lucy Calkins recommends beginning by having students create a short story about *one* character with *one* problem. Regie suggests a similar process, starting in fourth grade.

When she was in fifth grade, my daughter Laura came home chattering about a "lightbulb" experience. She explained that she had been working for weeks on a twenty-page story. The story had many characters, and she kept adding more as it got longer and longer. The thought of editing her piece was daunting, and she was in fact becoming a little tired of it. But that day her teacher, Julie Ledford, introduced Ralph Fletcher's strategy for zooming in on a moment. Laura had crafted a short, powerful piece around an early memory at a swimming pool, the specificity of her dad's tossing her up in the air in her hot pink bathing suit and the ants on the side of the pool. Laura explained, "I finally get it. Every year, teachers talked about details and I kept adding more and more and my pieces got longer and longer. When Ms. Ledford talked about creating a picture in your mind, I *got* it." The breakthrough for Laura was the idea of using details to paint pictures, rather than simply adding to stories that inevitably become overwhelming. Students need plenty of scaffolding before they're able to write effective fiction on their own. We need to hold our students' hands as they take their first short steps before they're ready to run with longer pieces. As with any genre, we need to model how to craft fiction, teach specific strategies, and find just the right authors and mentor texts (picture books and short stories) for our students' developmental stages. We need to craft specific minilessons about how to develop characters, how to map out the plotline of a story, and how to build tension.

Ted DeMille's *Making Believe on Paper* (2008) is one of the few professional books focused specifically on teaching young students how to write fiction. Ted begins with read-alouds and storytelling, then teaches his students how to sketch their ideas. From there, he uses mentor texts to highlight specific characteristics such as clear and memorable patterns, simple but detailed illustrations, and inviting language. Young writers learn to "unpack" these stories and emulate them in their own writing. Ted also provides guided experiences as his students begin to craft their own stories and fairy tales.

The kinds of support Lucy Calkins and Colleen Cruz provide in *Writing Fiction: Big Dreams, Tall Ambitions* (from *Units of Study for Teaching Writing, Grades 3–5*) may be just what you need to jump into a fiction unit with older students. Children begin by collecting possible ideas for stories, going back to their writer's notebook and thinking about everyday moments. They learn that with fiction writing, readers follow along as if they were watching and listening to the events as they unfold. In order to make this rather challenging genre accessible, Lucy and Colleen ask students to focus on realistic fiction with just a few characters close to their own age. The next step is for students not just to undercover the external aspects of their characters but to explore their internal characteristics as well. Fiction writing becomes even more powerful when authors identify the wants and struggles of their main characters. In this unit of study, writers apply a strategy that they worked on in earlier units as they plot out their story using a "story mountain" to sequence a few scenes in order to keep their story short and focused. Students study picture book examples as they learn how to craft enticing leads, describe the setting, and create a climax and final resolution. Their edited and

Book List

Resources for Helping You Teach Children to Write Fiction

- [ ] *Making Believe on Paper: Fiction Writing with Young Children* by Ted DeMille (2008) (Grades K–2)

- [ ] *Writing Fiction: Big Dreams, Tall Ambitions* (from *Units of Study for Teaching Writing Grades 3–5*) by Lucy Calkins and Colleen Cruz (2006)

- [ ] *The Whole Story: Crafting Fiction in the Upper Elementary Grades* by Karen Jorgensen (2001) (Grades 4–8)

- [ ] *First Grade Writers* (Chapter 5) by Stephanie Parsons (2005)

- [ ] *Mentor Texts: Teaching Writing Through Children's Literature* (Chapters 1–6 and 8–10) by Lynne Dorfman and Rose Cappelli (2007) (Grades K–6)

- [ ] *The Complete Year in Reading and Writing: Kindergarten* (Chapter 5) by Karen McNally and Pam Allyn (2008)

- [ ] *The Complete Year in Reading and Writing: Grade 1* (Chapter 3) by Jaime Margolies and Pam Allyn (2008)

- [ ] *The Complete Year in Reading and Writing: Grade 2* (Chapter 3, fairy tales; Chapter 4, story elements; Chapter 4, dialogue and punctuation) by Patty Vitale-Reilly and Pam Allyn (2008)

- [ ] *The Complete Year in Reading and Writing: Grade 3* (Chapter 2, theme and time; Chapter 3, characters) by Abi Gotthelf and Pam Allyn (2008)

- [ ] *The Complete Year in Reading and Writing: Grade 5* (Chapter 4, fiction writing clubs; Chapter 5, historical fiction) by Laurie Pastore and Pam Allyn (2008)

- [ ] *Novel Perspectives* (Part 5) by Shelley Harwayne (2005) (Grades 3–5)

- [ ] *In the Company of Children* (Chapter 6) by Joanne Hindley (1996) (Grades 3–5)

- [ ] *Teaching the Qualities of Writing* (fiction section) by JoAnn Portalupi and Ralph Fletcher (2004) (Grades 3–5)

- [ ] *The No-Nonsense Guide to Teaching Writing* (Chapter 12) by Judy Davis and Sharon Hill (2003) (Grades 3–5)

- [ ] *The Multigenre Research Paper* (Chapter 5, character) by Camille Allen (2001) (Grades 4–6)

- [ ] *Thinking Through Genre* (Chapter 5, short story; Chapter 6, fairy tales) by Heather Lattimer (2003) (Grades 4–12)

- [ ] *Study Driven* (pp. 196–98, realistic fiction, and pp. 199–200, historical fiction) by Katie Wood Ray (2006) (Grades K–8)

- [ ] *The Resourceful Writing Teacher* by Jenny Bender (2007) (Grades 3–8)

- [ ] *The Write Genre* (Chapter 5) by Lori Tog and Paul Kropp (2004) (Grades 4–8)

Book List *(continued)*

Resources for Helping You Teach Children to Write Fiction

☐ *Writing Through the Tween Years* (Chapter 8, historical fiction) by
Bruce Morgan (2004) (Grades 4–6)

☐ *Nonfiction Matters* (Chapter 12, historical fiction) by Stephanie
Harvey (1998) (Grades 3–8)

published stories are then collected in a class anthology. In some classrooms, parents are invited in for a celebration.

Another helpful resource for intermediate teachers is *The Whole Story* (2001) by Karen Jorgensen, with specific chapters about developing plots, settings and characters, and observing like a writer. What's unique about Karen's book is how much she includes actual conversations from students as well as "before and after" examples of how her students' writing improved throughout the unit. She provides demonstrations using her own writing, exercises for practice, and pattern lessons in which students learn more about the craft of writing in this genre. In her introduction, she reminds us that "fiction is the medium; reading, writing, and thinking are the goals" (7).

I'm often asked, "Do you know good examples I can use to teach kids how to write fiction?" *Mentor Texts* (2007), by Lynne Dorfman and Rose Cappelli, is a perfect resource, filled with minilessons and examples from students and published writers. The last chapter, called "A Treasure Chest of Books," lists hundreds of books to support lessons in all categories of fiction and personal narrative.

Writing Nonfiction

The nonfiction writing in many classrooms is often deadly. For instance, in one fifth-grade classroom I visited, children were slogging dispiritedly through reports on crops. Unless they live on a farm in the Midwest, I can't imagine this would be a topic ten-year-olds would choose. Nor would they voluntarily choose to write "state reports" with facts about the population and a list of products. What a shame to turn students off to informational writing with these boring reports, since students naturally gravitate to nonfiction. They love reading books about snakes, soccer, and space. They love being "experts" on a topic, whether it's dinosaurs, medieval armor, or black holes. Kids love to teach their friends how to kick a soccer ball, turn a cartwheel, or make a paper airplane. Young children are natural collectors, whether of baseball cards, rocks, sea glass, or stamps. They are naturally bursting with questions and wonder. We need to support them in understanding how to convey this information through drawing and writing.

My youngest son, Bruce, used to start every question with "So, Mom" or "So, Dad," followed by, "What are the boxes on top of telephone poles?" "How do generators work?" "What's the difference between an implosion and an explosion?" (My response to any technical question was usually, "Ask your dad!") Yet hardly any of his wonderings and questions ever found their way into his classrooms. At nineteen, he fondly remembers his third-grade nonfiction report on deer, still able to recall his diagram of how deer can see 340 degrees (each eye has a 170-degree field of vision). He would have blossomed as a writer if nonfiction had had a more prominent place on his menu of writing possibilities.

In *A Place for* Wonder (2009), Georgia Heard and Jennifer McDonough explain how we can support nonfiction reading and writing best when we create "a landscape of wonder" that builds on young children's interest in nature and their excitement about the world around them, fostering what they call a "ferocious curiosity." They create a classroom in which children's questions and observations, in the form of "wonder centers, projects and clubs," are integral parts of reading and writing workshop. In the second chapter, Georgia and Jen ask children to explore their "three wonders" as they create "wonder boxes" filled with index cards with their questions and explore "research wonders" and "heart wonders." "At the core of all nonfiction writing is often a question, an observation, a passion fermenting in the author's mind and heart" (58). The third section of the book outlines a nonfiction reading and writing unit of study, along with possible minilessons as students craft their own nonfiction books. The descriptions of Jen's classroom and her reflections are so specific and engaging that you'll immediately be persuaded of the value of student-led inquiry as an avenue into nonfiction reading and writing.

Lucy Calkins and Laurie Pessah begin their primary unit of study *Nonfiction Writing* with this statement: "Because young children are avid students of the world, always ready to . . . lie on their backs and study the clouds, they respond joyously to an invitation to write about what they know" (iv). The first part of the unit focuses on "how-to" procedural texts in which children write directions for some activity that they already know well (taking care of a pet, making cupcakes, building sandcastles). After introducing some "how-to" mentor texts, you can provide various types of paper from the CD-ROM that accompanies *Units of Study for Primary Writing*. These specially designed papers help young writers organize the sequence of steps and provide space for their diagrams or pictures.

The focus for the second half of the unit is "all-about" books, in which children write on a topic about which they already know a great deal. For instance, the table of contents of a student in Eliza Lewis' class read:

❶ What little brothers feel when playing Benton

❷ Teaching a little brother

❸ How to stop little brother crying

❹ Playing with a little brother

❺ Things not to do with a little brother

Eventually, students revise and edit their "all-about" books as they learn about periods, parentheses, and colons. During the celebration at the end of this portion of the unit, children love being in a teaching role as they share their knowledge with a small group of peers and parents.

It's important not to view this form of nonfiction writing with our youngest writers as a research project; the writing is based on what students *already know*. The specific paper available on the CD-ROM provides a structure for each page. For instance, if they are writing about making cupcakes, their "different kinds of things" page might be the different utensils a cook would need. Another page might describe (not just list) different occasions on which people bake cupcakes.

After studying mentor texts, students will better understand the purpose of diagrams and how to create their own schematics. The small bit of research they do involves looking through books on their topic and searching for a few other facts they can include. For instance, in Michelle Morton's first-grade classroom, students create posters about their topic with strips of paper indicating what they know, what they learned, and what they still wonder about. It's important, however, that the primary focus for nonfiction writing with young students is on writing about what they know, rather than on finding more information on a topic. They revise by working with a partner to check readability and organization. An alternative would be to create brochures about their topic. Children are so excited about sharing their expertise with others that you may want to make an extra copy of everyone's books or brochures to place in your classroom library. Students can share their expertise with younger grades in small groups as the culminating activity and closure for this unit.

Franki Sibberson, in her article "Rethinking a Study of Nonfiction Writing" (2008), describes how in the past, her nonfiction study focused more on *research* than on *writing skills*. As she shifted the focus to writing, she began to use more mentor texts and encouraged her students to experiment with questions, topics, and formats in their writer's notebook. By wading in using topics students know well, writers can solidify their skills before heading off into the more challenging waters of learning how to research new content and topics.

In the third booklet of *Right-Answer Writing* (2006), Ardith Cole uses examples from two classrooms to show how research writing can become enjoyable and

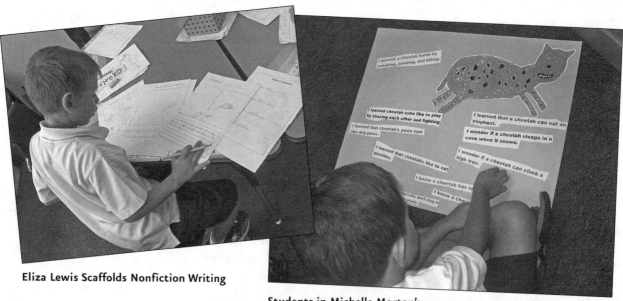

Eliza Lewis Scaffolds Nonfiction Writing

**Students in Michelle Morton's
Primary Classroom Create Posters About Their Topic**

successful for students. (She provides lots of additional examples and resources on the accompanying CD.) She explains how research is most effective when it begins with questions and tells how to scaffold the research process: collect questions, organize and categorize questions, determine final categories, and collect resources. The most fascinating chapter discusses how to deter plagiarism by using "triadic research": one student reads the source out loud, another decides what information to include, and the third takes notes. *Right-Answer Writing* gives intermediate, middle school, and high school teachers a wealth of resources and ideas for teaching research skills and persuasive and on-demand writing.

Tony Stead (2002) writes, "Tapping into the enthusiasm that writing nonfiction inspires in both girls and boys is something that I believe we educators do not do enough, especially in the early years of schooling" (4). In his book *Is That a Fact? Teaching Nonfiction Writing K–3*, Tony includes an extensive list of ways to publish research (including wanted posters, interviews, a book of favorite recipes) that might help you think outside the box. He has amassed an extensive list of resources to help you order children's texts for your classroom library to match each nonfiction unit of study at a variety of reading levels. Mary McMackin and Barbara Siegel provide similar ideas and resources for teaching nonfiction in the intermediate grades and middle school in their book *Knowing How* (2002).

Other types of nonfiction or informational writing that can "hook" authors in your classroom include:

- Question-and-answer books
- Family histories
- Obituaries (for historical character)
- Recipes
- Brochures
- Comics
- Editorials
- Feature articles
- Biographies

In *Nonfiction Mentor Texts: Teaching Informational Writing Through Children's Literature, K–8* (2009), Lynne Dorfman and Rose Cappelli also include a current and comprehensive list of mentor books for teaching nonfiction writing. Lynne and Rose understand the importance of immersing our students in nonfiction: "Today nonfiction writing is more important than ever. After all, it is closely tied with the majority of reading and real-world writing our students will be doing when they leave school to embark on careers and daily living" (278). At the end of each chapter, the authors include the unique feature "An Author's Voice," in which nonfiction authors share how they've used a particular crafting strategy. The concluding chapter of the book, "Treasure Chest of Books," is a goldmine of annotations—about fifty titles for each of the seven chapters. The bibliography for "Nonfiction Writing in the Real World" includes original and inviting examples of almanacs, cookbooks, hero essays, and field guides.

Students' eyes light up and they quickly become engrossed in writing "all-about" books in primary grades or feature articles in the intermediate grades based on their interests and expertise. They can apply all you've taught them in your fiction units about enticing leads, clear organization, strong verbs, and powerful endings so that their nonfiction writing rings with their voices and passions.

Book List

Resources for Helping You Teach Children to Write Nonfiction

☐ *A Place for Wonder: Reading and Writing Nonfiction in the Primary Grades* by Georgia Heard and Jen McDonough (2009) (Grades K–2)

☐ *Nonfiction Writing: Procedures and Reports* (from *Units of Study for Primary Writing*) by Lucy Calkins and Laurie Pessah (2003) (Grades K–2)

☐ *Is That a Fact?* by Tony Stead (2002) (Grades K–3)

☐ *Knowing How* by Mary McMackin and Barbara Siegel (2002) (Grades 3–8)

☐ *Nonfiction Mentor Texts* by Lynne Dorfman and Rose Cappelli (2009) (Grades K–8)

☐ *Time for Nonfiction* by Tony Stead (2004) (DVD) (Grades K–3)

☐ *Nonfiction Matters* by Stephanie Harvey (1998) (Grades 2–8)

☐ *Nonfiction Writing from the Inside Out* by Laura Robb (2004) (Grades 4–8)

☐ *Real Reading, Real Writing* by Donna Topping and Roberta Ann McManus (2002) (Grades 4–8)

☐ *Right-Answer Writing* by Ardith Cole (2006) (Grades 4–12)

☐ *The Complete Year in Reading and Writing: Kindergarten* (Chapter 5, pp. 161–73) by Karen McNally and Pam Allyn (2008)

☐ *About the Authors: Writing Workshop with Our Youngest Writers* (pp. 192–204) by Katie Wood Ray with Lisa Cleaveland (2004) (Grades K–1)

☐ *The Complete Year in Reading and Writing: Grade 1* (Chapter 4, pp. 102–16, all-about books) by Jaime Margolies and Pam Allyn (2008)

☐ *First Grade Writers* (Chapter 3, question-and-answer books) by Stephanie Parsons (2005)

☐ *Second Grade Writers* (Chapter 5, writing about research) by Stephanie Parsons (2007)

☐ *Significant Studies for Second Grade* (Chapter 6, research writing) by Karen Ruzzo and Mary Anne Sacco (2004)

☐ *The Complete Year in Reading and Writing: Grade 2* (Chapter 4, pp. 123–38) by Patty Vitale-Reilly and Pam Allyn (2008)

☐ *Of Primary Importance* (Chapter 7) by Ann Marie Corgill (2000) (Grades K–2)

- [ ] *The Resourceful Writing Teacher* (Chapters 9–14) by Jenny Bender (2007) (Grades 3–8)

- [ ] *The Write Genre* (Chapters 6 and 8) by Lori Tog and Paul Kropp (2004) (Grades 4–8)

- [ ] *The Complete Year in Reading and Writing: Grade 3* (Chapter 2, note taking, pp. 69–71; Chapter 4, science/history, pp. 111–13) by Abi Gotthelf and Pam Allyn (2008)

- [ ] *The Complete Year in Reading and Writing: Grade 4* (Chapter 3, pp. 107–10) by Laurie Pastore and Pam Allyn (2008)

- [ ] *The Complete Year in Reading and Writing: Grade 5* (Chapter 5, research writing, pp. 154–57) by Laurie Pastore and Pam Allyn (2008)

- [ ] *Nonfiction Craft Lessons* by JoAnn Portalupi and Ralph Fletcher (2001) (Grades K–8)

- [ ] *Teaching the Qualities of Writing* by JoAnn Portalupi and Ralph Fletcher (2004) (Grades 3–5)

- [ ] *The Art of Teaching Writing* (Chapters 25 and 26) by Lucy Calkins (1994) (Grades K–5)

- [ ] *Lifetime Guarantees* (Chapter 4) by Shelley Harwayne (2000) (Grades K–5)

- [ ] *A Fresh Look at Writing* (Chapter 4, pp. 305–24) by Donald Graves (1994) (Grades 1–6)

- [ ] *Study Driven* (pp. 1–12; pp. 201–2, historical fiction; pp. 220–21, practical how-to writing; pp. 222–23, informative how-to writing; pp. 215–19, literary nonfiction) by Katie Wood Ray (2006) (Grades K–8)

- [ ] *The Content-Rich Reading and Writing Workshop* by Nancy Akhavan (2008) (Grades 4–8)

- [ ] *Reading and Writing Nonfiction Texts in the Primary Grades* (Chapter 6) by Nell Duke and V. Susan Bennett-Armistead (2003) (Grades K–2)

Writing Persuasive Pieces

If you could write a letter to Barack Obama about education, what would you say? What if you wanted to respond to a letter to the editor in the *New York Times* that was disparaging of teachers? What would you say if you were the person designated to write a letter to the school board asking for funding for classroom libraries or telling them why the school librarian position needs to be retained? In real life, we have many reasons to write persuasively. The media and Internet bombard us with information intended to sway our thinking, and we're deluged with advertisements that try to convince us to buy products. As members of a democratic society, writing persuasively is related to reading critically, looking at different viewpoints, speaking up for what we believe, and taking action.

Even our youngest writers can write persuasively. One year when Ranu Bhattacharyya was taking her kindergartners to the lunchroom at the International School of Beijing, one of her students asked, "Where do our lunches come from?" Their discussion continued after they returned from recess. Ranu decided to weave their inquiry into her unit on community. Students went on a "field trip" to the cafeteria and interviewed the lunchroom cooks, the cafeteria manager, and the food services manager. Their class book, titled *Wr do lngs kum fom?* (*Where do lunches come from?*), revealed that "ISB hs a big ckn" (*ISB has a big kitchen*), as well as many other facts. Ranu bound the students' individual pages into a class book that was sent home each afternoon with a different kindergartner. The kids loved hearing the parents' comments on the response pages. During this inquiry, some of the students had complained about the school lunches. As a result, they created a survey to find out how many of their peers liked the school lunches and how many didn't. Their natural interest paved the way for a simple lesson on reading and interpreting graphs. The students then thought up alternatives to put on the lunch menu. This (tactful) persuasive letter was ceremoniously handed over to the food services manager and rewarded with a special ice cream treat!

Tony Stead (2002) suggests that young children love to weigh in on the best toy in the world or the best sport to play. Real events (like school lunches in Ranu's class) or children's literature can also spark persuasive writing. Doriane Marvel read *Can I Have a Tyrannosaurus Rex, Dad? Can I?* (2000) by Lois Grambling to her first graders, and the next day Kendall used the structure of the text for her own persuasive book about bearded dragons. The students in both Ranu's and Doriane's primary classrooms have discovered the power of writing to persuade.

In *A Quick Guide to Teaching Persuasive Writing, K–2* (2008), Sarah Picard Taylor describes how young children can also write to improve their own lives or the lives of others through posters (kindergartners), persuasive letters (first graders), or persuasive reviews (second graders). In persuasive reviews, students write about their favorite video games, restaurants, movies, and books for their peers. Sarah recommends that you first provide lots of examples, then help students find a topic about which they care deeply. Kids can use conversation and role playing to explore aspects of their topic, then list reasons for their stance. After these prewriting activities, students then move through the writing process, finally displaying their posters or reviews or mailing off their letters.

Cathy Hsu's fifth graders at Taipei American School write about their favorite books in book reviews. Cathy displays three inquiry questions on a bulletin board (*What is a review? Why do people read them? How do you write a good review?*), then launches the unit by playing video clips of Siskel and Ebert's reviews of movies her kids are familiar with, such as *Toy Story* or *Babe*. She also uses clips of Anthony Bourdain's food reviews on *No Reservation*. (Whenever possible, she uses nontextual models to help her English language learners absorb the language, tone, purpose, and feel of a genre.) Once the video clips have filled the classroom with the *sound* of reviews, ignited ideas, and helped generate excitement, the students investigate what makes a review effective. Cathy finds assorted online mentor texts written by children that are kid-friendly, appropriate for her fifth graders, and true reviews, rather than just recommendations. The examples she finds include great voice, technical vocabulary, descriptive words, and both information and opinions to study, highlight, and deconstruct. Then she gives them poorly written reviews to critique and revise. Students choose one of their own reviews to take through the writing cycle and publish as a poster.

Often Cathy invites writing partners to examine the published posters, sharing what they notice. This allows kids to articulate theories they are constructing about reviews (or other genres). There are no right or wrong answers at this point; Cathy wants the kids to *own* their exploration. Cathy loves seeing kids get up from their desk to consult one of the posters. "I like posters to have that open-door quality, inviting kids to scrawl discoveries upon them freely, as well as to use insight from their peers. When kids really use the posters during their writing process, I feel the board is working for us. It's supporting the kids and inviting their participation. It's keeping the conversation alive."

Reviews (about books, movies, games, music, places, or experiences) are the focus of the second booklet in Ardith Cole's *Right-Answer Writing* (2006). She points out that persuasive writing is both fact-based and opinion-based: "The writer makes a claim, but she must then present *grounds* for that claim. Such factual support elevates the writer's persuasive potential—and perhaps her grade" (3). Students learn to construct an enticing lead and a sequence of points, along with supporting facts, and end with a strong conclusion. Ardith writes convincingly about why teachers should replace the ubiquitous book *reports* (just summaries) with book *reviews* (summaries and critiques). Real-life examples abound online, but she finds Teen Ink (teenink.com) particularly helpful, since the reviews are all written and edited by teens. As students look through the examples, they learn how to make connections to their lives and the world, to other texts, and to craft. Once the genre has been introduced, they can publish their reviews for peers in the classroom or school or on websites. Learning to write persuasively also has benefits related to persuasive prompts on state tests: "Students who keep the rubric in their right pocket and the three-part structure (sandwich) in their left should have suc-

cess with persuasive writing, regardless of their state of residence" (43).

Scores on our Washington State tests climbed steadily until the year that the writing prompt was a persuasive one. The sudden dip in writing scores led to a flurry of interest in teaching persuasive writing! Teachers discovered that persuasive writing can be really engaging in intermediate grades, as students learn to hone their ability to argue both sides of an issue.

Students in Cathy Hsu's Classroom Add Their Discoveries About Book Reviews to the Bulletin Board

Anne Klein launched her unit on persuasive writing by listing and thinking out loud about possible topics: the benefits of living in Washington; why she should read instead of watch TV; and why she should exercise more. Her fifth graders then brainstormed a list of possible topics they might like to write about in order to convince someone. Students each selected one topic, then met with a partner or small group to brainstorm a list of all the possible reasons supporting their position. They chose their strongest arguments to include in their persuasive writing. Then they went through the same process in order to anticipate all the "against" arguments, directly addressing them in their writing as well. Alam listed reasons he should get a hamster, and Sadie wrote about wanting a dog—and both were very excited when they got their new pets! Amanda successfully convinced her family to keep their cat instead of giving it away, and C.W. talked his parents into getting a cell phone (it had to stay at home during the day, but he could use it after school). Anne's students really grasped the idea of considering two sides of an issue and learned to address potential arguments and concerns. Once they saw the power of writing to persuade, many chose that form of writing when they were given a choice.

Writing to Persuade (2008) by Karen Caine is a book about teaching persuasive writing in the intermediate grades. She recommends teaching at least two persuasive units each year, starting a third of the way through, once you've established an environment of trust and introduced writing workshop. Karen states that persuasive

Book List

Resources for Helping You Teach Children to Write Persuasively

☐ *Is That a Fact?* by Tony Stead (2002) (Grades K–3)
☐ *A Quick Guide to Persuasive Writing K–2,* by Sarah Picard Taylor (2008)
☐ *Writing to Persuade* by Karen Caine (2008) (Grades 3–8)
☐ *Right-Answer Writing* (Book 2) by Ardith Cole (with CD) (2006) (Grades 4–12)
☐ *Second Grade Writers* (Chapter 2) Stephanie Parsons (2007)
☐ *The Complete Year in Reading and Writing: Grade 5* (Chapter 4, editorials, pp. 104–6) by Laurie Pastore and Pam Allyn (2008)
☐ *Nonfiction Mentor Texts* (Chapters 5–7) by Lynne Dorfman and Rose Cappelli (2009) (Grades K–5)
☐ *Thinking Through Genre* (editorials, Chapter 4) by Heather Lattimer (2003) (Grades 4–12)
☐ *Why We Must Run with Scissors* by Barry Lane and Gretchen Bernabei (2001) (Grades 3–12)
☐ *Study Driven* (1–12; advice, pp. 224–26; editorials, commentary, and op-ed, pp. 235–37) by Katie Wood Ray (2006) (Grades K–8)
☐ *The Write Genre* (Chapter 7) by Lori Tog and Paul Kropp (2004) (Grades 4–8)

writing helps student learn how to express an opinion, support it with evidence, and then convey their ideas with voice and conviction. *Writing to Persuade* contains sample units and a wealth of minilessons for persuasive writing, along with forms and sample texts. In addition to reviews, here are some possible forms of persuasive writing that you might want to consider:

- Persuasive letter
- Political speech
- Advertisement
- Letter to editor
- Advice column
- Petition

As with any unit of study, you'll want to develop your own minilessons, model persuasive writing, and collect examples.

Writing "Small Moments"

It makes sense developmentally to have children write about what they know. In "small moment" writing, the writer zooms in with a magnifying glass on just one event or moment in his or her life, as my daughter Laura did with her vignette about her experience in the pool. Even young students can draw pictures and eventually write a bit about one event. Older students can learn to "paint pictures with words" by including details that make us feel as if we were there.

I went to see my grandparents every summer and vividly remember gathering eggs still warm from under hens, chasing fireflies, the smell of gardenias, the sounds of cicadas, and the feel of the cool, gooey mud at the bottom of the Arkansas River. One taste of a homemade sugar cookie brings back my childhood summers. Each of these memories is a small moment from my childhood I could explore. When you think of your childhood, what smells, sounds, and favorite places come to mind?

The key to writing about "small moments" is that students have to realize that the people, feelings, and daily events in their lives are all worth capturing in writing. In *Writing Through Childhood* (2001) Shelley Harwayne says, "Children don't need to live writerly lives, they need to live lives that are as joyous, playful, and interesting as the grown-ups who care for them can provide" (3). On pages 256–58, Shelley has a great list of writing projects that tap into children's memories that she describes as "grist for their writing mills." She invites students to celebrate their lives as children. She urges teachers to develop lessons around "pretending," secret places, imaginary friends, forts, playing games, and "getting caught."

In *Small Moments: Personal Narrative Writing*, from *Units of Study for Primary Grades* (2003), Lucy Calkins and Abby Oxenhorn write that "what in fact matters most to a child's later literacy are the opportunities children have to take the moments of their lives and spin them into stories" (iv). Ranu Bhattacharyya incorporates some of the ideas from this unit in her kindergarten classroom. Her anchor charts capture the sequence of her minilessons as her students learn to draw and write about their lost cat, their annoying baby brother, their skinned knee, or how they felt when their best friend moved away.

Michelle Morton also implements a "small moments" unit in her first-grade classroom. She launches the unit by reading *A Chair for My Mother* (1984), by Vera B. Williams, and *The Snowy Day* (1962), by Ezra Jack Keats. Michelle and her students talk about how moments in their lives could be stretched into stories. They notice how Vera could have written, "We got home and saw the fire," but instead, she stretched that moment out for her readers. The students notice that Ezra also zoomed in on moments, as he describes Peter walking in the snow, making footprints, and listening to his feet crunch. Michelle talks about how writers delve into the moment by adding details to their pictures and words.

Michelle then crafts a short piece about how excited she was to pick up her violin from the store and start playing again. She and her students next compose a piece together about a small moment they shared when they scared the parents at the pumpkin patch; they use this co-authored sample as a model that the class revisits throughout the unit. (Michelle also finds the "small moments" unit a great place to introduce partner work, so she and the literacy coach model a few partner writing lessons. They demonstrate counting the main events on their fingers as they share their plans.)

The focus of Michelle's minilessons then moves from finding ideas to stretching out ideas with details, getting help from partners, and building writing stamina by writing more. At the end of each writing workshop, students either share with a partner or a few students read their pieces to the whole class. Michelle capitalizes on these wrap-ups to model something new, celebrate successes, or review the skills

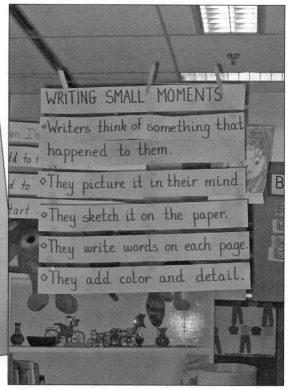

Megan Sloan Brainstorms a List of Everyday Topics for Writing

Ranu Bhattacharyya Creates a Chart About Small Moments

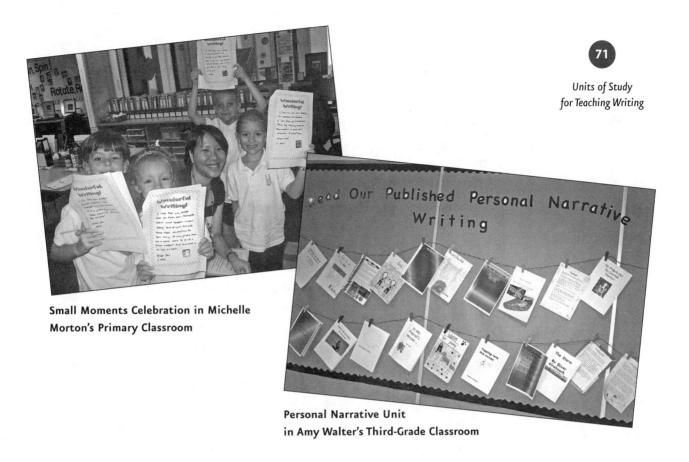

**Small Moments Celebration in Michelle
Morton's Primary Classroom**

**Personal Narrative Unit
in Amy Walter's Third-Grade Classroom**

they worked on that day. The students pick one small moment to publish. At the
end of the unit Michelle invites the literacy coach and principal to listen as students
share their writing in small groups.

Writing Personal Narratives

Personal narratives are also based on the author's life, but are more "storylike,"
usually including a plot with several events and a problem and solution. In these
narratives, tension is resolved or something changes for the narrator. Personal narrative is the perfect springboard into writing for most students, because they gain
confidence by writing about the events, feelings, and people in their lives. It's also
important for us to provide demonstrations by writing about our own experiences
in front of our students. Megan Sloan notes, "Students need to see teachers write
about everyday experience, again and again, before they believe that their own
everyday experiences are worth writing about" (2005, 12).

In *Raising the Quality of Narrative Writing*, from *Units of Study for Teaching
Writing, Grades 3–5* (2006), Lucy Calkins and Ted Kesler begin with a close study of
mentor texts. This is the second unit of study about narrative writing: "We know
that real progress comes not from constantly exposing children to yet another form
of writing but from working long enough within one form to help children write
longer, more significant, more conventional, and more graceful pieces in general"
(vi). You can present ideas for topics, such as the first time your students tried
something new, a time when they learned something, or a time when they felt a

strong emotion. Erian Leishman teaches fourth grade at Shanghai American School and wrote to me about this unit:

> The key element is teaching students to think about getting to the "heart" of the story. Earlier when students are writing step-by-step "small moments," they work to include outside details and inside thoughts that help the reader be in the story or make a "movie in their mind." As they build on this work now, they are focusing on writing a story that their readers can connect to on an emotional level.
>
> This unit guides them to tell a complete story that builds the action, suspense, and/or emotional drama for the reader. These narratives may combine three or four small moments in order to tell the beginning, middle, and end of the story. Students spend time in their notebook capturing entries about first times, last times, people that have changed their lives, places where they have had meaningful experiences. They look for turning points in their lives that helped them learn something about themselves or overcome an obstacle. Mentor texts that work well with this unit are *Fireflies*, by Julie Brinckloe; *Amber on the Mountain*, by Tony Johnston; *The Best Story*, by Eileen Spinelli; and *The Memory String*, by Eve Bunting. Read-alouds that help students learn to create poignant episodes and rising action are *Because of Winn Dixie*, by Kate DiCamillo, and *Poppy*, by Avi. As we read these books we focus on the "pivotal scenes." It helps to have charts of these scenes to reflect back on and motivate entry writing. To find a true "heart" story idea, students need to have many notebook entries to choose from.
>
> In this unit, students begin to get a more developed awareness of their audience. By focusing on experiences that mean something to them or that changed them in some way, students learn to use their life stories to connect to others by writing from their hearts.

Writing Memoir

In intermediate grades, students can move from "small moments" and personal narratives into memoir, which involves a *series* of scenes (rather than just one moment in time) and the added component of *reflection*. The distinguishing feature of memoir is that reflective component. In *Memoir: The Art of Writing Well*, from *Units of Study for Teaching Writing, Grades 3–5* (2006), Lucy Calkins and Mary Chiarella describe how students can "uncover life topics" by searching back through their writer's notebook, with the reminder that "the bigger the topic, the smaller we write" (vii). The emphasis is on slowing down time and writing with depth as they ponder an idea from many viewpoints and search for the significance of their topic. In order to support students, ask them to find mentor texts as a model for the structure and organization of their own memoir. Throughout this study, writers are searching for ways to bring their own voice to their writing as they ask, "What is it I want to show about myself? About my life? How can I bring this meaning out in my draft?"

Colin Weaver talked to his fifth graders about some of his favorite places and memorable moments when he was young. He modeled thinking out loud about when he had to get stitches for the first time, closing his eyes and imagining himself back there. He then wrote about what he saw and felt as a young, very scared boy. Then the students closed their eyes and thought about a strong memory from when they were younger. Colin asked them to turn and talk with a partner about their story before going to find a quiet spot to write.

In following lessons, he and his students looked at some of the patterns in the memories they had listed and started drafting. They looked for recurring themes. The next step was to answer some of the following questions: Why is this a recurring theme for me? What does this theme say about me? Why is this theme important for my readers to understand? That is the key for memoir writing. Students can retell a personal memory story, but the power comes from stepping back to reflect on why the story is significant. Some of the reflections by Colin's students were quite narrow, while others broadened their approach and wrote about the life lesson they had learned.

One of Colin's students was inspired by *All the Places to Love*, by Patricia Maclachlan (1994), which describes the special moments a boy had with his family on a farm. Roheena reflected on moments she shared with nature, those quiet moments when she would just sit and savor its beauty. The message of staying in touch with nature was particularly poignant for her audience—her friends growing up in the concrete jungle of Hong Kong. She wrote, "I sat on the porch listening to the quiet chirping of the birds. I closed my eyes. I thought about the stress in my life, like projects coming up and the test I would have on Monday. I cleared it from my mind and stroked the smooth petals of some daisies and tulips planted close to me. A breeze tickled my cheek and I giggled."

These young writers continued to learn more about creating great leads and using a story mountain to connect ideas. Colin continued to model through his own writing and shared writing experiences. As his students deepened their revision skills, they learned how to bring out the internal story, move forward and backward in time, and weave actions, dialogue, and thoughts together. At the end of this unit, the students' parents came and listened as students read their pieces and described their process and thinking. The parents were struck by how easily these fifth graders were able to articulate their thinking about writing and the life lessons they had learned.

In *Writing a Life* (2005), Katherine Bomer shares a sample yearlong plan for writing instruction in intermediate grades and middle school in which memoir is the concluding unit. She explores the following aspects of writing memoirs:

▶ Reading mentor texts for inspiration

▶ Collecting ideas in a memoir notebook

▶ Selecting, collecting, and layering thoughts to decide on the central idea of a memoir

▶ Structuring the writing

▶ Conferring with the student memoirist

▶ Revising the text

▶ Transferring memoir writing strategies and content into writing to
test prompts

Sprinkled throughout each chapter are examples of published memoirs, both adult and children's literature, as well as numerous student samples. She writes how memoirs help students take the facts of their lives and "breathe life into them" (85). Writing memoirs, personal narratives, and small moment pieces all begin with the author's own life—stories unique to each writer as they look back and inward.

Book List

Resources for Helping You Teach Children About Personal Writing

☐ *Small Moments: Personal Narrative Writing* by Lucy Calkins and Abby Oxenhorn (from *Units of Study for Primary Writing)* (2003) (Grades K–2)

☐ *Memoir: The Art of Writing Well* by Lucy Calkins and Mary Chiarella (from *Units of Study for Teaching Writing, Grades 3–5)* (2006)

☐ *Raising the Quality of Narrative Writing* by Lucy Calkins and Ted Kesler (from *Units of Study for Teaching Writing, Grades 3–5*) (2006)

☐ *Writing a Life* by Katherine Bomer (2005) (Grades 4–8)

☐ *Writing Through Childhood* by Shelley Harwayne (2001) (Grades K–5)

☐ *Novel Perspectives* (Parts 1 and 2) by Shelley Harwayne (2005) (Grades K–8)

☐ *The Complete Year in Reading and Writing: Kindergarten* (Chapter 4, pp. 117–31) by Karen McNally and Pam Allyn (2008)

☐ *Talking, Drawing, Writing* (Chapters 7–8) by Martha Horn and Mary Ellen Giacobbe (2007) (K)

☐ *First Grade Writers* (Chapter 4) by Stephanie Parsons (2005)

☐ *Significant Studies for Second Grade* (Chapters 4 and 5) by Karen Ruzzo and Mary Anne Sacco (2004)

☐ *Craft Lessons* by Ralph Fletcher and JoAnn Portalupi (2007) (Grades K–8)

☐ *Teaching the Qualities of Writing* narrative section, by JoAnn Portalupi and Ralph Fletcher (2004) (Grades 3–5)

☐ *Seeing Possibilities* by Lucy Calkins and Colleagues (DVD) (2007) (Grades 3–5)

☐ *Mentor Texts* (Chapters 1–6 and 8–10) by Lynne Dorfman and Rose Cappelli (2007) (Grades K–5)

☐ *The Art of Teaching Writing* (Chapter 24) by Lucy Calkins (1994) (Grades 3–5)

☐ *Thinking Through Genre: Units of Study in Reading and Writing Workshop* (Chapter 2) by Heather Lattimer (2003) (Grades 4–12)

☐ *Study Driven* (pp. 192–95 and 203–4) by Katie Wood Ray (2006) (Grades 1–12)

Writing Essays

How would you begin a unit of study on essays? What would be some mentor texts you could use? Why are essays an appropriate form for young writers? Third-grade teacher Priscilla Wilson and the school's literacy coach, Jen Munnerlyn, launched an essay unit by using ideas from *Breathing Life into Essays* by Lucy Calkins and Corey Gillette from *Units of Study for Teaching Writing, Grades 3–5* (2006). Lucy and Corey write: "It's important to teach students that their lives are provocative. Writers observe things in the world, recording what they see, and then shift and write their thoughts about them" (vii). This unit helps children learn how to write a personal essay by choosing a topic of personal significance, then advancing their position by providing support for their stance. The authors argue that the scaffolding provided by a thesis statement and topic sentences will help students when they enter middle school and high school.

Jen and Priscilla began their essay unit by having students go through their writer's notebook for ideas, making a list of possible topics. They also used "free writes" as a way for students to explore their topic and begin to amass their arguments. Next they explicitly modeled the language of essays from *Breathing Life into Essays*, exploring how phrases such as *in addition*, *another example is*, and *the important thing is* help readers follow the points in an essay.

As students fine-tuned their arguments, they used 8.5-by-11-inch envelopes (Lucy Calkins uses folders) to separate their supportive ideas, a separate envelope for each argument, which they placed in the side pockets of their folders.

**Students in Priscilla Wilson's Classroom Organize
Their Supporting Points Using Bullets**

Jen and Priscilla next introduced the concrete strategy of creating boxes and bullets to frame the topics and their supportive ideas. One student listed three reasons "Why Life Is Hard"; another listed three convincing reasons "Why You Should Have a Sister." The latter went on to write a four-page essay. Priscilla says, "She absolutely blossomed and used her writer's notebook to work out some difficult feelings." Another parent wrote how this unit had impacted her child: "My son is becoming more compassionate. He thanks me and helps me more than he's ever done. I think writing has changed him!"

Gene Quezada, a fifth-grade teacher at the American Embassy School in Delhi, presented a similar unit on essays, launching the unit by downloading podcasts of essays from National Public Radio's four-year collection, *This I Believe*. (Although this series has ended, you can still download hundreds of examples from the NPR website.) As students read or listened to the essays, they discussed the person's beliefs and whether they agreed or disagreed. Using the ideas from the Calkins unit, as well as ideas from Ralph Fletcher, they went through the following process:

❶ Generate ideas.

❷ Choose an idea.

❸ Stretch that idea.

❹ Create a thesis.

❺ Revise the thesis.

❻ Generate supporting evidence (the "meat" of the essay).

❼ Explore different ways to find evidence.

❽ Organize the evidence.

❾ Write an opening and conclusion.

❿ Revise and edit.

Gene wanted his students to incorporate technology, so his students added photographs and visuals to the podcasts they created using GarageBand software. Next year, he plans to have students post their essays on their classroom blog where they can respond to one another's ideas. For Gene, this unit is much more than learning to write an essay; it's helping kids think through an idea and form it into a thesis that's personal and meaningful. Students also learn to support their ideas—an important concept as they read, write, and talk about books. All this is hard work and takes a lot of time, but the positive results spill over into all areas of the curriculum.

In the second edition of *Better Answers* (2009), Ardith Cole makes a passionate plea to teachers to move past what she calls "a test curriculum" in which we present only those forms of writing that are on the test. To Ardith, writing essays is more than just a test-taking skill. She wants teachers to use models of real-world, authentic essays written by students (and provides websites and resources to find them) and to allow students to write about their passions and ideas so that essay writing becomes a practical and lifelong skill. She writes: "Offer your students real essay writers to emulate. Offer them real issues to question. Offer them real causes for which they feel compelled to write responses. Offer your kids a tool through which they can help change the world. Offer them authentic reasons to write. For indeed, this is what response writing is all about. It's not about tests in school" (143).

Writing Essays About Literature

In addition to writing essays about their lives, their beliefs, and the world around them, students should be able to write about the literature they read. In *Literary Essays* from *Units of Study for Teaching Writing, Grades 3–5* (2006), Lucy Calkins and Medea McEvoy explain how you can begin by providing a selection of short texts to read and then ask students to respond. Eventually, students choose one text from the selection and one idea that will become the focus of their writing. They may choose to write about how a character changes throughout the story or lessons the character learns. Students use the same organizational structure they used to craft their personal essays—folders or envelopes in which they collect their topics and supporting evidence from the text.

Students learn how to use ideas and quotations from the text to support their claims. They learn how to use transition words and literary terms such as *narrator*, *point of view*, and *scenes*. They are encouraged to relate their thesis to their own life or another story. After several rounds of revising and editing, students share their literary essays with another class that has completed the same unit of study. Then each group of students who have read and written about the same text compiles their essays into an anthology. On the day of the celebration, students from both classes who have written about the same text have a literary discussion about the books, using their essays to fuel the conversation.

Jen Munnerlyn found this unit challenging and wasn't sure her third graders could tackle something so "literary." However, she discovered that the unit was fun and that her students rose to the challenge. Jen's class was a typical third-grade group with a wide developmental range in both reading and writing. Students needed a variety of short texts from which to choose, so Jen's first hurdle was to make sure her English language learners had texts they could decode and comprehend but yet were worth discussing. Starting with the list of sample texts in the unit, Jen began to collect and photocopy stories for small ability-based groups. By the time she began the unit, each child had ten photocopied stories to read and consider. For some of the picture book selections, Jen typed the text on to two or three pages. By the end of the first few days, the children had pared the options down to their top five choices. Students worked their way through the unit, learning how to read deeply, paraphrase, write a response, and incorporate quotes.

As the week went on, however, Jen realized these third graders needed a bit more support, so she paired students and asked them to select one text together. These pairs became "literary partners" and bounced ideas off each other. By the end of the unit, each pair has a literary essay that described the author's technique, a character's important point of view, or a big idea. Their literary essays clearly demonstrated how deeply these nine-year-olds had understood their chosen texts.

As a celebration, they invited various teachers at the school to interview pairs of students. The teachers read over the texts in advance in order to be familiar with the stories. During the celebration, the teachers reread each child's essay, then asked the literary essayists questions about the text. The pairs answered as a team, even though there were instances when they didn't agree with their partner or had written about different topics. The result was magic. The third graders had learned how to express their opinions and feelings about a text, and the teachers were deeply impressed with their thoughtful views and insights. Jen wrote:

> I described this unit to a friend who teaches tenth-grade English. He was amazed and asked to see some of the essays. After reading a few examples, he couldn't believe that third graders were capable of such sophisticated thinking and writing. He told me his job would be much easier if his students had started this kind of work (with scaffolding and real instruction) earlier. Until he saw my anchor charts, the texts we used, and some sample student essays, he didn't believe that literary essays were possible with such young writers. For me, the paraphrasing lesson in the unit was particularly powerful, even though it was a very new and therefore a difficult skill for my third graders to grasp. I realized that if we teach kids how to paraphrase in third grade, continuing on into fourth and fifth grade, it will help prevent plagiarism as they learn how to use quotations correctly and how to put their insights into their own words.

Writing About Issues and Taking a Stand

Essays are also a medium for taking a stand, tackling a social issue, and trying to make a difference in the world. After hearing Harvey (Smokey) Daniels talk about inquiry circles at a workshop, Sherri Ballew decided to take a stab at student-selected inquiry with her fourth graders. She began by showing an iMovie she had created that showed images of people, places, and things around the world—everything from volcanoes to aliens. Then she asked, "What do you wonder? What do you want to learn?" and had her students write three questions they had about themselves and three questions they had about the world.

The next day, the students, in groups of five or six, compared their questions and identified what the questions had in common. They then shared their findings as a class and composed a chart of common questions. Sherri asked the students to put their initials directly on the chart next to the question they were most interested in investigating. The third day students interested in the same question formed groups, identified the resources they would need, and checked out materials from the school and public libraries.

The students' research included a wide range of forms and genres. Some groups conducted interviews and one group created a survey for teachers in the building. All the groups did research on the Internet and were eagerly involved in lots of conversations about their topic. After each work session (thirty to forty-five minutes), each group shared what they accomplished with the class and discussed their plans for the following day.

After three weeks of research, each group decided how they wanted to present the information they had gathered about their topic. One group wrote a nonfiction book about the end of the world. Another created a PowerPoint presentation and a model to teach their peers about the inside of the earth. One team wrote an essay about how they hoped to follow their dream careers. Another group decided how they wanted to teach morals at their school (they wrote a play and performed it for the kindergarten classes). The team that investigated the national debt also decided to write a play. The global warming group developed an action plan for their class to follow in order to reduce their carbon footprints. The groups each identified a school audience and shared their projects with those classes one Friday afternoon.

Book List

Resources for Helping You Teach Children to Write About Literature and Social Issues

- ☐ *Breathing Life into Essays* by Lucy Calkins and Corey Gillette (from *Units of Study for Teaching Writing, Grades 3–5*) (2006)
- ☐ *Better Answers* by Ardith Cole (2009) (Grades 3–8)
- ☐ *Literary Essays: Writing About Reading* by Lucy Calkins and Medea McEvoy (from *Units of Study for Teaching Writing, Grades 3–5*) (2006)
- ☐ *Writing to Live* by Lorraine Wilson (2006) (Grades K–6)
- ☐ *For a Better World* by Katherine and Randy Bomer (2001) (Grades 4–12)
- ☐ *Second Grade Writers* (Chapter 3) by Stephanie Parsons (2007)
- ☐ *The Complete Year in Reading and Writing: Grade 2* (pp. 141–42) by Patty Vitale-Reilly and Pam Allyn (2008)
- ☐ *The Complete Year in Reading and Writing: Grade 4* (pp. 181–91) by Laurie Pastore and Pam Allyn (2008)
- ☐ *The Complete Year in Reading and Writing: Grade 5* (pp. 30–33, 78–85, and 95–98) by Laurie Pastore and Pam Allyn (2008)
- ☐ *The No-Nonsense Guide to Teaching Writing* (Chapter 11) by Judy Davis and Sharon Hill (2003) (Grades 3–5)
- ☐ *Seeing Possibilities* (Breathing Life into Essays) by Lucy Calkins and Colleagues (DVD) (2007) (Grades 3–5)
- ☐ *Study Driven* (pp. 209–14, 215–19, 227–29, 239–42, and 245–46) by Katie Wood Ray (2006) (Grades K–8)
- ☐ *Writing About Reading from Book Talk to Literacy Essay* by Janet Angelillo (2003) (Grades 3–5)
- ☐ *The Continuum of Literacy Learning* by Gay Su Pinnell and Irene Fountas (2007) Grades K–2, 3–8, and K–8)
- ☐ *Thinking Through Genre* (Chapter 7) by Heather Lattimer (2003) (Grades 4–12)

After all the presentations, Sherri helped the students develop a rubric so that each group could evaluate their process and final product. Not only had individual students learned more about a topic they found interesting, but they saw how they could use writing in many formats to persuade others and make a difference in their world.

Writing to a Prompt

Teaching writing is a juggling act. We have one ball in the air as we create a writing workshop that includes the writing process applied to many genres. We then toss in student choice in order to provide authenticity and ownership. Then suddenly the district and state throw us another ball—timed writing and high-stakes tests. It's hard to juggle all these challenges and still keep smiling! The obsession in our country with testing all too often drives and narrows curriculum. High-stakes testing often means that teachers feel compelled to spend time teaching students how to write on demand. In *The 9 Rights of Every Writer* (2005), Vicki Spandel wryly points out the limitations of forced writing in which students are required to "write about the prompt, the whole prompt, and nothing but the prompt, so help you God" (30). In Chapter 3, "The Right to Go 'Off Topic,'" she outlines four problems with writing to a prompt: it promotes standardized and often lackluster writing; it's hard to find inviting and authentic prompts; the prompts are impersonal and rarely tap student's passions; and the focus shifts to aspects of writing that can be measured.

One first-grade teacher has this to say about the limits of writing to a prompt: "I feel they are limiting and the kids don't do nearly as well as they do when they're writing in the classroom. Plus, we never sit down to score the papers or even look at them. One time we did sit down and aligned the papers with the writing continuum, but again, nothing was done with the information. I think we need to develop units of study first, then establish prompts based on the units. Right now, my kids are knee-deep in a nonfiction study, and the prompt I have to give them is to write about a time when they felt really happy. It just feels so inauthentic." All too often, what's missing from on-demand writing is a sense of purpose and audience. Students are not writing to anyone in particular and we've eliminated the element of choice, so it's no wonder that the writing we get is often lifeless.

However, testing is a reality, even in the primary grades. Since writing prompts are given on both district and state tests in Megan Sloan's school, she has her second and third graders practice three or four times a year. In addition to the numeric score (1–4) provided by the district, Megan also writes short anecdotal notes that help her see the patterns in one child's writing over time, as well as the patterns within the class. Testing data is most helpful when it leads to improved and targeted instruction and therefore increased student learning.

In addition to grade-level prompts based on your units of study, your school may administer a schoolwide writing prompt in order to examine the developmental stages of writing and provide a focus for staff discussions about instruction and learning. In this case, the greatest value of the writing is not so much about the scores as it is about the schoolwide professional conversations sparked by collaboratively examining student writing.

At Shekou International School, teachers feel their schoolwide prompts *have* been helpful. The genres vary from year to year, according to their writing curriculum and units of study. For instance, this year the prompt was a factual recount (*Write about a time when you felt . . .*), and last year they used a picture prompt. The key to their success has been conducting on-demand writing every year, developing and refining rubrics, and scoring the writing in divisional (K–2 and 3–5) teams.

You can also preface your writing prompt by reading aloud books that exemplify the type of writing you hope to get from students and presenting minilessons linked to these mentor texts. For instance, if you're asking students to write about memorable places, you might want to read some appropriate picture books and explain how specificity and details paint pictures in the minds of readers.

Like the teachers at Shekou International School, the teachers in the Kent school district in Washington State use prompt-writing results to fine-tune their teaching, as well as to collect longitudinal data. The district had used trimester writing prompts for six years, along with rubrics and anchor papers. However, as teachers began to implement the Calkins *Units of Study*, they asked the district for more open-ended and inviting prompts to match the kinds of writing they were doing in their classrooms. Jan Mayes says: "As a result, most of our anchor papers are not as rich and vivid as the writing we are now getting from students. This tells me it's time to collect new anchor papers!" She adds, "We have been moving our teachers away from unrelated prompts to authentic writing about topics that matter to the writer. It's a balancing act with accountability in a standards-based reporting system. Implementing *Units of Study* has certainly helped to tilt the balance as we seek to collect authentic writing samples as a common assessment to use as a basis for discussions about student progress." Figure 2.2 lists the writing prompts used in primary classrooms in Kent, linked to their units of study.

Teachers who attended their district's summer writing institute presented by staff developers from Columbia University's Teachers College suggested they add more non-narrative prompts linked to their social studies curriculum. Primary teachers have the option of replacing one of the trimester writing prompts with one of the following:

Kindergarten:
What is the most important playground rule and why?

First Grade:
Draw or write about a small moment you remember about a celebration in your family.

Create a timeline that shows events or changes in your family.

Draw and write an "all-about" story about your family.

Second Grade:
Create a timeline that shows events or changes in your community.

Draw and write an "all-about" story about your community.

KSD Writing Prompts, Grade K–2

WINDOW	MODE AND FORM	PROMPT
Kindergarten		
Fall	Narrative: Personal Experience and Labeling	**Draw a picture** of your family and **label** each family member.
Winter	Narrative: Personal Experience	**Draw and write** about a favorite place you like to go with your family.
Spring	Narrative: Personal Experience	**Draw a picture** and **write** about a favorite activity that you did in school this year.
Grade 1		
Fall	Narrative: Personal Experience	**Draw and write** a story about an activity you did with your family.
Winter	Narrative: Personal Experience	**Draw and write** about a favorite small moment that happened at school
Spring	Narrative: Personal Experience in a Friendly Letter	Write a **letter** to a friend. Tell about a recent **small moment** you experienced.
Grade 2		
Fall	Narrative: Personal Experience in a Friendly Letter	Write a **letter** to your second grade teacher **telling** about a recent small moment you experienced at school.
Winter	Narrative: Realistic Fiction	Write a **story** about what happened to you you on your way home from school one day.
Spring	Expository: How-To Instructions	**Tell how** to play your favorite game. (math game)

Figure 2.2 Kent School District Writing Prompt, Grades K–2

My favorite writing prompt was one used many years ago in Boulder, Colorado, where I was then teaching. All students, K–8, were told that the librarian had been given $500 to buy books for each grade level. They were asked to write the librarian a persuasive letter about which books she should buy, and justify their choices. Then the librarian took those funds and bought the recommended books for the school. Students had an authentic audience and purpose for their writing, and teachers (and the librarian) had insights into their students as readers and writers.

If we are going to ask our students to write to a prompt, Vicki Spandel challenges us, as teachers, to write in response to the prompt as well and to score our own writing. In her helpful book for intermediate teachers, *Writing to the Prompt: When Students Don't Have a Choice* (2005), Janet Angelillo also states that before we ask students to write in response to a prompt, we also need to provide lots of opportunities for conversations: "Long before asking them to *write* about prompts, teach them how to *talk* about a prompt for a long time" (23). Janet notes that much of the writing students do in school is not personal. They write in many genres about what they think, what they've experienced, what they feel, what they read, and what they've learned. When we teach students how to write to a prompt, what we're really doing is teaching students how to write for others, rather than just for themselves. Janet states that the best thing we can do as teachers is to implement writing workshop and to focus on teaching students how to write well: "Because writing workshops focus on strengthening writing strategies and thereby raise the bar for all writing, they are the perfect way to teach students to write well to prompts. When students learn to write strong beginnings, use specific words, or write about significant details, their writing improves. The challenge for the teacher is to help students transfer knowledge about writing to prompt writing" (9).

Given the current climate of high-stakes testing, part of our job description should be to prepare our student to do well when faced with "on-demand" writing tasks in school. In her booklet on writing to a prompt that is part of *Right-Answer Writing* (2006), Ardith Cole breaks these tasks into self-based responses (describe an experience that changed our life) and text-based prompts (comparing a story and a poem). Furthermore, she explains how this uniquely school-related genre mirrors writing tasks students will encounter in the workplace. After all, students will probably need to write to prompts for scholarships, grants, and job or college applications. As adults, they may be required to use their writing skills in other ways, such as posting information on a website, summarizing company growth, or preparing employee performance reviews. In each case, writers need to learn to support their answers clearly and logically using evidence. Ardith's booklet explores the three steps for on-demand writing—developing an introduction, constructing a body of evidence, and drawing a conclusion—using a sandwich metaphor. (The accompanying CD-ROM includes a wealth of resources.)

In addition to transferring what they've learned about good writing to testing situations, students also need to write every day for long blocks of time so that they have the stamina needed to do well on writing tests. Tommy Thomason and Carol York have written an extremely helpful book for intermediate grades and middle school, *Write on Target: Preparing Young Writers to Succeed on State Writing Achievement Tests* (2000). On the last page of their book, they tell about a famous writer, Dorothy Parker, who was asked if she had any rules to help people write better. "'Oh yes,' Ms. Parker answered. 'I have six.' 'Read, read, read and write, write, write,' she said dramatically" (70). What a great reminder that teaching *to* the test is far less effective than focusing on good instruction. This can be a helpful argument if you're trying to convince administrators about the need for extended blocks of time for reading and writing!

Book List

Resources for Helping You Teach Children to Write to a Prompt

- ☐ *The 9 Rights of Every Writer* by Vicki Spandel (2005) (Grades K–12)

- ☐ *Writing to the Prompt* by Janet Angelillo (2005) (Grades 3–8)

- ☐ *Better Answers* by Ardith Cole (2009) (Grades 3–8)

- ☐ *Right-Answer Writing* (Book 1) by Ardith Cole (with CD-ROM) (2006) (Grades 4–12)

- ☐ *Crunchtime: Lessons to Help Students Blow the Roof Off Writing Tests—and Become Better Writers in the Process* by Gretchen Bernabei, Jayne Hover, and Cynthia Candler (2009) (Grades 4–10)

- ☐ *The Complete Year in Reading and Writing: Kindergarten* (Chapter 3, pp. 94–96) by Karen McNally and Pam Allyn (2008)

- ☐ *The Complete Year in Reading and Writing: Grade 1* (Chapter 2, pp. 46–56) by Jaime Margolies and Pam Allyn (2008)

- ☐ *The Complete Year in Reading and Writing: Grade 3* (Chapter 2, pp. 30–32) by Abi Gotthelf and Pam Allyn (2008)

- ☐ *The Complete Year in Reading and Writing: Grade 4* (Chapter 3, pp. 97–99) by Laurie Pastore and Pam Allyn (2008)

- ☐ *The Complete Year in Reading and Writing: Grade 5* (Chapter 3, pp. 89–91) by Laurie Pastore and Pam Allyn (2008)

- ☐ *Teaching the Qualities of Writing* (Test Writing Practice) by JoAnn Portalupi and Ralph Fletcher (2004) (Grades 3–5)

Off the Beaten Track

Adopting inquiry units as a focus for instruction is a good thing, as long as the units are built on students' interests. However, in many classrooms, the units become must-dos and lose the student-centered focus that makes them so engaging. There's no longer room or time for student-led inquiry. If the curriculum is packed full of "required" units, what happens when a child loses a pet, when someone brings in an old telephone to take apart, or students come in buzzing about something that happened in the news? It's helpful to have the consistency of units of study, but we also have to leave room for spontaneity and serendipity, to teach responsively based on the needs of our students.

COMIC BOOKS

Sherri Ballew noticed that quite a few of her boys were writing comic books in their writer's notebook, but that she couldn't understand their stories without their explanations. So she began a comic book unit, compiling resources (she checked out fifty-one library books in one afternoon!) and immersing herself and the class in the genre. They read graphic novels and comic books and talked about their observations. Sherri developed minilessons about plot structure through the use of thought and speech bubbles, and how to tell a story in images instead of words. Since the school didn't have an art teacher, she also presented several minilessons on specific art techniques. Over the four-week period, Sherri provided lots of time, space, and materials as students worked side-by-side with their yearlong writing partner. Sherri also took a risk and worked on her own comic book alongside the kids.

Since her students were already familiar with the writing process and writing workshop, they embraced this unit with a great deal of independence. They drafted in their writer's notebook (sometimes two or more drafts), as they had done all year. Final comic books were then copied onto white construction paper. Sherri posted a chart where students could sign up for conferences with her during the drafting and revising process. She also met with each student when they thought they were ready to publish. Her students helped create a rubric in order to assess both the process and their final product, using a scale of one to four about five different aspects of creating their comic book.

Sherri Ballew's Comic Book Unit

Sherri commented that some of the more reluctant boy writers felt particularly motivated by this unit and it boosted their confidence. Jake wrote, "I felt good about sharing my comic and I felt a little embarrassed (I thought no one would like it). My family liked it because it has good drawings and I put lots of effort into it." This unit also nudged some of the more confident authors in the class to stretch their repertoire. Spenser said, "It was a fun way to open up a new kind of writing. I learned how to draw more and it really let me experience something new."

LETTERS

Mary Lee Hahn (2009) took a few weeks for an integrated letter-writing unit. The students collected sample letters from their families, and Mary marveled at the glimpses they provided into the lives of her students. She also shared her own letters and anchor texts she'd collected, as well as children's books that incorporate letters, like *Dear Mrs. Larue: Letters from Obedience School* (2002) by Mark Teague, and *Love, Ruby Lavender* (2001) by Deborah Wiles. Students then wrote one business and one friendly letter, but she added a little sparkle to the unit by allowing them to be fictional. One student wrote an imaginative letter of complaint from a deer to a hunter, and another wrote a friendly letter to a video game character. There were persuasive letters and touching letters to coaches, former teachers, and family members. Her students willingly revised and recopied their letters, because writing these creative letters was so enjoyable. She writes: "Never underestimate the power of *fun* in writing workshop."

MUSIC

Since notation is a form of writing, what about collaborating with the music teacher as they did at the International School of Belgrade during the Year of the Writer? Students could compose their own lyrics and write music as another foray into the writing process.

MENUS

Sometimes unexpected writing opportunities arise and you need to follow the enthusiasm of your students. One day Holly Reardon's prekindergarten classroom had a special visitor. A businessman was opening a new restaurant near the school and wanted help deciding what to offer on the children's menu. Holly and her students brainstormed their favorite foods, tried to determine which ones were healthy, and surveyed classmates and other kids at school to see what dishes they liked. They created a sample menu (using models from restaurants) and piloted several versions in the dramatic play area. "Customers" looked at the menus while the students took orders and then voted on their favorite design.

PIRATE JOURNALS

What first grader wouldn't love a pirate unit? Cheryl Perkins and two of her colleagues developed an end-of-year three-week pirate unit (because of recent events in the news, they now call it their *buccaneer* unit!). Cheryl gathers her first graders together on the first day and, as Captain One-Eyed Perk, tells them she has found a treasure map and is looking for sailors to sign on to her ship and go looking for it.

Each day, they look at the map and plot their course (map skills) as Cheryl leads them through an imaginary experience (such as getting stuck in the fog, having a whale ram the ship, and getting seasick). Dressed in their pirate garb, they head for their bunks (desks), take out their log books, and write about their adventures. The sheer glee of these buccaneers when I visited was palpable. Sometimes this sense of adventure and joy gets lost in our focus on standards and testing and the pressure for accountability. But as Cheryl notes, the writing she gets from her students in this engaging unit is incredible. Years from now, it will be their buccaneer days these students remember from first grade.

MULTIGENRE WRITING

The premise of *The Multigenre Research Paper* (2001), by Camille Allen, is that intermediate students love thinking outside the box as they combine genres or try new ones. Jolene Granier, a sixth-grade teacher, used Camille's book to guide her students in writing multigenre research papers. Her student Tony "caught the bug." His topic was soccer and he loved being able to write about it over and over again in different genres. He began with a typical report on the essentials of soccer. Then he moved on to write a personal narrative about one of his soccer games, a poem about the feelings he had as he played soccer, a biography of Pele, a soccer-themed comic strip, a brochure explaining the details of a soccer camp, and a sports newspaper article about a recent professional game. Never had Tony been so energized in his writing. Chapter 10 in *The Writing Genre* (Rog and Kropp 2004) is helpful with multigenre texts.

Through units of study, we can provide models and help students learn to write well in a variety of genres. However, not all your units of study will be genre-based. Depending on your grade level and the needs of your students, you may also want to develop short, specific units on writing process (finding topics or revision strategies) and specific conventions (using punctuation to enhance meaning). You'll also want to incorporate units of study on writing strategies (building stamina, keeping a writer's notebook, or working with writing partnerships). Carl Anderson (2005) reminds us: "What we read about a unit of study is one way the unit *could* go in a classroom. How the unit *should* go with *our* students can only be determined by *us*, by linking assessment to curriculum design" (208).

INDEPENDENT WRITING UNIT

Although it's important to have consistency within and between grade levels, we should also build flexibility into our curriculum so that we can respond to the dynamics, the interests, and the questions of our students. Colleen Cruz writes:

> I'm seeing more and more schools develop grade-by-grade curriculum calendars. They allow for consistency, reinforcement, mastery, and a gradual introduction of progressively more sophisticated skill sets. The curriculum calendars that these schools are developing allow us to make sure we're meeting state standards, preparing students for tests, and, most importantly, giving students rich opportunities to explore and excel in writing. Yet, as with all things educational, many of us have become so focused on our finely crafted units that we've forgotten about the lingering and exploration that allowed us to discover them in the first place. We move from teaching point to teaching point, unit to unit, hardly looking up from our calendars to see what our students are doing. (2008, 62–63).

Partly in response to this challenge, Ben Hart teaches an independent writing unit each year, in which his students explore their favorite genres. Intermediate students choose their own mentor texts (picture books) and identify the features of that genre. Here are reflections from two of Ben Hart's students about their independent writing unit:

> I really love doing the independent writing unit because you get to choose yourself what type of genre you want to write. I think the mentor text from the picture book I chose really helped me with the fantasy story that I'm writing because I could emulate the author. (Sabrina, Grade 4)
>
> I have loved the independent writing unit so much because I get to pick my own genre. I started off by making lists of what other authors wrote in their biography books so I could incorporate them into mine too. (Pranav, Grade 4)

Independent Writing Unit in Ben Hart's Classroom

Ponder Box for Teachers

- What are your strengths related to units of study?

- What units do you teach during the year? Do you have a curriculum calendar?

- Which units are fairly strong?

- What units would you like to explore or add to writing workshop in your classroom?

- Are there one or two professional books about units of study that you would like to read or have as a resource?

- What children's books do you want to purchase as mentor texts for units of study?

Ponder Box for Coaches and Principals

- Where would you place your school on the rubric for units of study?

- What framework are you using schoolwide for implementing and developing units of study for writing (Lucy Calkins, Katie Wood Ray, Pam Allyn, etc.)?

- Do you have a curriculum calendar for units that are taught at each grade level?

- Can you provide time for grade-level teams to explore and create new units?

- Which of the professional books listed in this chapter do you already have in your library?

- Which ones do you most want to add to your collection?

Writing Instruction (Teacher Rubric)

	NOVICE	APPRENTICE	PRACTITIONER	LEADER
Units of Study	☐ My individual lessons may or may not be connected with one another or to a specific genre or unit; I may provide some genre study; my writing instruction often focuses on grammar, spelling, and penmanship	☐ I provide a sequence of skills and writing activities that may or may not be part of a genre study; my minilessons are based primarily on the 6+1 traits or on a pre-determined structure (formulaic writing)	☐ I am beginning to develop some units of study with a sequence of minilessons (e.g., Calkins, Allyn, Ray); my other writing minilessons are based on the 6+1 traits or writing in specific genres	☐ I have developed a clearly articulated curriculum calendar and set of well-developed units of study (e.g., Calkins, Allyn, Ray) with a sequence of focused, connected minilessons; my grade level has developed a calendar with specific units of study within a schoolwide plan to provide consistency

Writing Instruction (School Rubric)

	NOVICE	APPRENTICE	PRACTITIONER	LEADER
Units of Study	☐ In most classrooms, individual lessons may or may not be connected to one another or to a specific genre or unit; most teachers provide some genre study; in most classrooms, writing instruction often focuses on grammar, spelling, and penmanship	☐ Most teachers provide a sequence of skills and writing activities that may or may not be part of a genre study; in most classrooms, minilessons are based primarily on the 6+1 traits or on a predetermined structure (formulaic writing)	☐ Teachers at some grade levels are beginning to develop units of study with a sequence of minilessons (e.g., Calkins, Allyn, Ray); other lessons are based on the 6+1 traits or writing in specific genres	☐ Teachers have developed a schoolwide, clearly articulated curriculum calendar and set of well-developed units of study (e.g., Calkins, Allyn, Ray) with a sequence of focused, connected minilessons; teachers have developed a calendar with specific units of study within a schoolwide plan to provide consistency within and between grade levels

Writing Instruction in the Writing Workshop

Once you have set up a writing workshop, have a solid understanding of the writing process, and have mapped out a calendar of units of study, it's time to consider more specifics about *how* and *what* you will teach. This chapter explores nine aspects of effective writing instruction:

❶ Developing minilessons for teaching the craft of writing.

❷ Using writing folders or writer's notebooks.

❸ Demonstrating with mentor authors and illustrators and mentor texts.

❹ Supporting struggling or reluctant writers.

❺ Examining gender and writing.

❻ Incorporating technology.

❼ Modifying writing instruction for English language learners.

❽ Considering writing and politics.

❾ Communicating with families.

Minilessons

In her introduction to her intermediate units of study, Lucy Calkins describes four components to a minilesson: connection, teaching, active engagement, and a link to ongoing work (*A Guide to the Writing Workshop*, in *Units of Study*, 2006, 57–68). Teachers first identify their teaching point ("Today I'm going to teach you about . . .") and connect the lesson to their students' lives as writers and the ongoing discussions about writing in their classroom. They then launch into the minilesson by either demonstrating with their own writing or providing an example from a student or published writer. Next, teachers actively engage students by asking them to "write in the air" or turn and talk with their partner about the idea or example they just shared. Finally, teachers wrap up their minilesson by reiterating their teaching point and either send students off to use the idea right away or suggest they add it to their writer's toolbox. Lucy says, "These last few sentences need to encapsulate the content of the minilesson in such a way that kids get their hands around it and carry it with them as they head off into the whole of their writing lives" (67). And all this happens in just ten or fifteen minutes!

When I watch great teachers in action, I'm always struck by how artfully they craft these very short, engaging minilessons, weaving together all they know about their curriculum, writing, children's literature, and their particular group of students. Solid writing minilessons are captured in action on two DVDs produced by Lucy Calkins and her colleagues: *Big Lessons for Small Writers* (2005) (grades K–2) and *Seeing Possibilities* (2007) (grades 3–5). You can watch the video clips, then listen as Lucy names the specific teaching moves and reflects on why they're made. Even if you have read about the "architecture" of a minilesson, it's very powerful to watch it unfold in a classroom.

Minilessons needn't take place only at the beginning of writing workshop. They can also be presented in the middle of the workshop, during sharing sessions ("author's chair") or writing conferences, or as part of content area teaching. You can't make up an accurate, comprehensive list of minilessons a month in advance, because you don't know what your students will need. If your unit focuses on personal narratives and the essential qualities and crafting strategies of that genre, you'll of course sketch out some of the critical supporting minilessons. However, you'll still need to fill in the details of your plan once you determine where your students need help. There are often five or six directions you can take; it's up to you to decide the most important tip your kids could use and then how you will present it. Will you use your own writing to demonstrate a strategy, read a piece one of your students has written, or a share a piece by a published author? It's up to you to craft your own minilessons as carefully as you would craft your own poems.

Regie Routman reminds us to "teach it first, label it later" (2005, 195). For example, Anne Klein noticed that many of her students' stories were chronological recountings, beginning to end, so the class conducted a mini-inquiry into picture books and novels in which the narrative begins at other points. Only after that exploration did Anne begin using terms such as *leads*, *foreshadowing*, and *flashbacks*.

Similarly, she asked her students to find examples of memorable characters from their favorite books and they talked about what they liked or disliked. She began using the term *character development* once her fifth graders understood some of the many ways experienced writers reveal how characters change over time.

Charts created with your students during mini-lessons remind them what they've learned and support their independent writing. Early in her teaching, Eliza Lewis found a chart in her classroom closet of "100 words to use instead of *said*," which she hung on a bulletin board. Parents, administrators, and other teachers would comment, "Oh, that's great; it must be helpful," but the students never referred to it. Instead, Eliza and her students discovered and savored alternatives to *said* during read-alouds and shared and independent reading, wrote these words on small pieces of construction paper, and stuck them on a laminated chart. This poster, with its removable words, became one of the most-often-used resources in her room.

**Alternatives to *Said* in
Eliza Lewis' Classroom**

Many schools use the term *traits* in relation to the craft of writing (teachers or administrators sometimes tell me, "We *do* the six traits"). However, the six traits—ideas, organization, voice, word choice, sentence fluency, and conventions—identified by Vicki Spandel and her colleagues at the Northwest Regional Laboratory, in Oregon, are neither a program nor a philosophy of teaching writing, nor should they be taught in isolation. They are simply lenses through which we can examine and learn about craft and assess writing. Vicki writes, "I have struggled all my professional life to help teachers see that the six traits are not a silver bullet, not even a curriculum, but a way of thinking and talking about writing that enormously empowers revision—and therefore, both process and workshop" (in Sloan 2009, x). A discussion of traits or qualities of good writing should be deeply embedded in a writing workshop and interwoven into the writing process.

Cathy Hsu finds the six-trait language helpful in describing aspects of good writing to her fifth graders as part of writing workshop. Instead of buying commercially made six-traits posters, Cathy immerses her students in books as models as they talk about the qualities of good writing; then her students get into small groups and create posters for each trait. Each group presents their poster to the class and the charts go up on the "writer's wall." Later in the year, these posters are joined by study-related charts. Cathy believes that her students are much more likely to understand and refer to charts written in the "kid language" they use during their discussions.

Students Create Six-Trait Posters in Cathy Hsu's Classroom

Megan Sloan's school is near my home, and I'm fortunate to be able to visit her classroom in person and observe a master teacher in action. Even if you can't visit Megan's classroom, you'll get a glimpse into the specifics of her teaching and minilessons through her books *Trait-Based Mini-Lessons* (2005) and *Teaching Young Writers to Elaborate* (2008).

JoAnn Portalupi and Ralph Fletcher have just published a second edition of their book on writing fiction, *Craft Lessons* (2007), which is also filled with mini-lessons grouped by grade level (K–2, 3–4, and 5–8). There's a brief discussion of each lesson and how to teach it and a list of related books or texts to use as examples. Their book *Nonfiction Craft Lessons* (2001) focuses on "all-about" books in K–2; biography in grades 3 and 4; and expository writing (including persuasive and informational writing and biography) in fifth grade and middle school. Ralph and JoAnn believe that nonfiction writing can be as full of voice, humor, and life as any other genre. Rather than dull, dry regurgitation of facts, they believe that readers prefer writing covered with the author's "fingerprints."

JoAnne and Ralph are also the authors of *Teaching the Qualities of Writing* (2004), a professional kit that includes a teacher's guide, over a hundred minilesson cards, and a CD-ROM, all in an easy-to-carry plastic binder. If you already understand the theory behind a writing workshop, are past questions about organization and management, but crave some model lessons to address specific skills, this resource is a gold mine. You can organize the lessons (twenty-plus on each topic) by genre (narrative writing, fiction, nonfiction, poetry, and test writing) or writing craft (ideas, design, language, and presentation). Their appendix is filled to the brim with supports—quotes from published authors about writing, publishing possibilities, a bibliography of children's literature matched to lessons, possible yearly plans, record-keeping forms for instruction and assessment, and graphic organizers. The power of this resource is that it's *not* prescriptive. JoAnn and Ralph trust that you will use your expertise to incorporate ideas and resources in a way that works for you. Ralph's newest book, *Pyrotechnics on the Page: Language Play That Boosts Writing* (2010), provides even more specific and engaging tips about how to have students "play with language" in engaging and exciting ways.

Most minilessons on writing fall into one of these categories:

▷ Traits, craft, or qualities of good writing

▷ Procedures (such as using a writer's notebook, and routines within writing workshop)

▷ Specific genres and text features

▷ The writing process (finding topics, revision, and publishing)

▷ Writing strategies (such as rereading and elaborating)

- Using literature as invitations or examples

- Conventions and mechanics

- Providing feedback (such as during peer conferences, and author's chair sessions)

Minilessons become more powerful when they are sequenced and linked to your units and goals. Janet Angelillo shows how to construct a string of mini-lessons that build on each other in her book *Whole-Class Teaching: Minilessons and More* (2008). Chapter 5, "Studying Whole-Class Instruction to Deepen and Refine It," could spark a yearlong study about the themes of minilessons and how they fold into one another or provide variations on a theme. In the last section of the book, Janet encourages teachers to reflect on their minilessons by videotaping them and evaluating the impact on student learning. She shares several study-group models for exploring the potential for intentional whole-class teaching.

You might want to keep a list of the minilessons you teach throughout the year, along with any model texts, references, or examples. That way, you won't have to re-create your minilessons each year. In some intermediate classrooms, students also keep a list of minilessons in their writer's notebook or binder, including the title, the date, and a page number from their notebook where they experimented with or used the strategy. This list is both an index of students' work and an ongoing record of what students are learning. You may also want to have your students lead the minilesson, sharing their discoveries and insights.

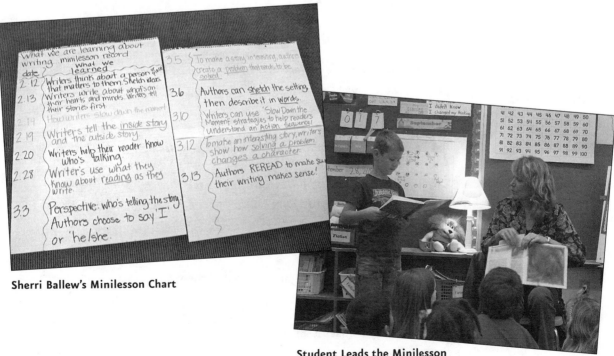

Sherri Ballew's Minilesson Chart

Student Leads the Minilesson in Megan Sloan's Classroom

Ponder Box for Teachers

- Where do you get ideas for your writing minilessons?
- How do you ensure that your minilessons build on each other?
- How do you keep track of the minilessons you have taught?
- What effect do your minilessons have on student learning?

Ponder Box for Coaches and Principals

- How will you provide time for teachers to develop and share minilessons in grade-level and vertical teams?
- What structures can you put in place so teachers can observe one another teaching minilessons, either live or on videotape?

Book List

Resources to Help You Craft Minilessons

- ☐ *Units of Study for Teaching Writing, Grades 3–5* by Lucy Calkins (2006)
- ☐ *Big Lessons from Small Writers, Grades K–2* (DVD) by Lucy Calkins (2005)
- ☐ *Seeing Possibilities* (DVD) by Lucy Calkins (2007) (Grades 3–5)
- ☐ *Trait-Based Mini-Lessons for Teaching Writing in Grades 2–4* by Megan Sloan (2005) (Grades 2–4)
- ☐ *What You Know by Heart* by Katie Wood Ray (2002) (Grades K–8)
- ☐ *The Resourceful Writing Teacher* by Jenny Mechem Bender (2007) (Grades 3–8)
- ☐ *Teaching Young Writers to Elaborate* by Megan Sloan (2008) (Grades 1–3)
- ☐ *Craft Lessons* by Ralph Fletcher and JoAnne Portalupi (2007) (Grades K–8)
- ☐ *Nonfiction Craft Lessons* by JoAnn Portalupi and Ralph Fletcher (2001) (Grades K–8)
- ☐ *Teaching the Qualities of Writing* by JoAnn Portalupi and Ralph Fletcher (2004) (Grades 3–8)
- ☐ *Hidden Gems* by Katherine Bomer (2010) (Grades 3–8)

Book List *(continued)* 📖

Resources to Help You Teach the Craft of Writing

☐ *How to Align Literacy Instruction, Assessment, and Standards and Achieve Results You Never Dreamed* (Chapter 6) by Nancy Akhavan (2004) (Grades K–5)

☐ *The Continuum of Literacy Learning* (pp. 99–173) by Gay Su Pinnell and Irene Fountas (2007) (Grades K–2, 3–8, and K–8)

☐ *Pyrotechnics on the Page: Language Play That Boosts Writing* by Ralph Fletcher (2010) (Grades K–8)

☐ *Whole-Class Teaching: Minilessons and More* by Janet Angelillo (2008) (Grades 4–8)

☐ *Marvelous Minilessons* by Lori Rog (2007) (Grades K–3)

☐ *Creating Writers Through 6-Trait Writing* by Vicki Spandel (2008) (Grades K–6)

☐ *What's Next for This Beginning Writer? Minilessons That Take Writing from Scribbles to Script* by Janine Reid and Betty Schultze (2005) (Grades K–2)

☐ *Reading and Writing Connections in the K–2 Classroom* by Leah Mermelstein (2006)

☐ *Inside Reading and Writing Workshop* (DVD) by Joanne Hindley (2006) (Grades 1–3)

☐ *Creating Young Writers* by Vicki Spandel (2008) (Grades K–2)

☐ *6+1 Traits of Writing: The Complete Guide for the Primary Grades* by Ruth Culham (2005) (Grades K–2)

☐ *6+1 Traits of Writing: The Complete Guide Grades 3 and Up* by Ruth Culham (2003) (Grades 3–6)

☐ *Growing Up Writing* by Connie Campbell Dierkling and Sherra Ann Jones (2003) (Kindergarten)

☐ *Getting Started: The Reading-Writing Workshop* (Chapters 6, 7, and 8) (2007) by Linda Ellis and Jamie Marsh (Grades 4–8)

☐ *Crafting Writers* by Elizabeth Hale (2008) (Grades K–6)

☐ *What a Writer Needs* by Ralph Fletcher (1993) (Grades K–8)

☐ *Snapshots* by Linda Hoyt (2000) (Grades K–5)

Writing Folders and Writer's Notebooks

As students incorporate the strategies you share during minilessons, where do they store their writing? In some classrooms, students write on loose paper that they tuck into a folder or three-ring binder along with notes about potential topics, editing checklists, and other forms. Some teachers color-code the folders by table groups to make it easier to pass out and collect student work. These writing folders are usually kept in students' desks or in magazine boxes on each table.

In other classrooms, especially in the intermediate grades, students keep a writer's notebook in addition to writing folders. Ralph Fletcher and JoAnn Portalupi, in *Lessons for the Writer's Notebook* (2005), remind us that published authors keep something other than a writing folder that they call a "writing diary, notebook, or a daybook. This writer's notebook is a blank book where a writer can engage in the fun, often messy job of being a writer—practicing, listing, playing with language, gathering images and insights and ideas. The purpose of such a notebook is to nourish the writer. . . . [It is] one of the most essential tools of the trade" (4). We can help our students grow as writers by providing writer's notebooks and teaching them how to use this tool. Ralph and JoAnn guide you in this instruction by providing twenty lessons on how to introduce and sustain writer's notebooks and use them as source material.

Alexandra Caso-Gustafson learned about writer's notebooks by attending a weeklong summer institute at Columbia's Teachers College. She writes, "The opportunity to delve into writer's notebooks was an amazing experience! Using a notebook to capture seeds, learning how to grow a seed and then *truly* revise a piece of writing, helped me understand the writing process from the inside out. This year I am hoping to help my colleagues understand the writer's workshop framework, how to use a writer's notebook, and the true spirit of being a writer."

Anne Klein writes, "My kids keep a writer's notebook, though some use it more than others. They have a writer's notebook for our units of study and independent 'choice' writing, but they also have a speckled writer's notebook they use on their own outside of class. There is often crossover—they'll work on a piece of writing at school and continue it at home." When she introduces writer's notebooks, Anne encourages her fifth graders to use their notebooks to record dreams, collect "golden lines" (lovely language from books), and play with language.

Anne also keeps her own writer's notebook so that she can share her entries (and her struggles) with her students. As Anne and her students write in their notebooks throughout the year, she shares quotes by and stories about published writers who jot down ideas, overheard conversations, or images that they later use in poems or stories. For instance, she shares how in *Once Upon a Time* (1995) well-known children's author Eve Bunting writes, "Always, though, I write my stories out first in a notebook. That works best for me. Pencils are easy to carry and I can take them any place I go. I have written in dentists' waiting rooms, in my car during a traffic jam, and in a floating chair in our swimming pool. Sometimes I get an idea when I don't have my notebook with me. What a disaster!" (20–22). She also reads Ralph Fletcher's definition from his book, *Breathing In, Breathing Out: Keeping a Writer's Notebook* (1996): "A notebook can be a clearing in the forest of your life, a place where you can be alone and content as you play with outrage and wonder, details and gossip, language and dreams, plots and subplots, perceptions and small epiphanies" (5).

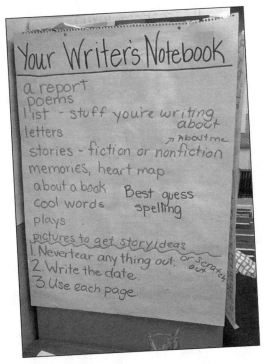

Sherri Ballew's Minilesson Chart About Writer's Notebooks

In *Authors as Mentors* (from *Units of Study for Primary Writing* [2003]), Lucy Calkins and her colleague Amanda Hartman share a strategy for introducing even very young writers to the concept of a writer's notebook. Each child is given a very small (one-inch by two-inch) notepad formed when a small spiral notebook is cut into thirds. The teacher models how to use the notebook to capture small moment ideas at home as well as in school. Yarn or plastic lanyards are threaded through the spirals so that the children can wear their writer's notebooks all day and into the evening. They learn that many published authors use writer's notebooks to capture ideas from life experiences.

Shelley Harwayne says that learning how to keep a writer's notebook is almost a genre in itself. If you're a coach looking for a way to introduce writing notebooks to a group of teachers or your whole staff, the list of six key writing lessons on page 81 in Shelley's book *Writing Through Childhood* (2001) would be a perfect handout to launch conversations. In Chapter 3 of the book, Shelley provides helpful tips on and examples of how writer's notebooks can help children lead "writerly lives" in and outside of school.

An example of using a writer's notebook within a unit of study comes from Ben Hart. Using one of Lucy Calkins' strategies in *Raising the Quality of Narrative Writing* (from *Units of Study for Teaching Writing, Grades 3–5* [2006]), he teaches his students a series of minilessons about how narratives include instances in which a character faces a dilemma or a problem is introduced. He reads *The Miraculous Journey of Edward Tulane* (2006) by Kate DiCamillo as a model, discussing how Edward changes throughout the book. Then, using other read-alouds and their own writing as examples, the class discusses the points at which characters change their thinking or the way they react to a situation. They discover how a turning point in a story can occur when the problem is resolved and the characters learn something new about themselves or others. Then, in their writer's notebooks, students explore the turning points in their own lives.

Intermediate teacher Carol Dulac describes her journey using writer's notebooks over the past few years: "My students keep writer's notebooks each year, and I have struggled with how to encourage them to work in the notebooks and also write drafts and publish pieces. Katie Wood Ray's book *Study Driven* (2006) and the *Units of Study* by Lucy Calkins (2006) have helped me see how you can use these notebooks to plant seeds and play with ideas that students can later pull out and develop into drafts." For example, during her personal narratives unit, Carol asked her students to think about people and list some small moments they remember in connection with these people. Here is Rahel's list:

▶ Girl day with mommy—I was 6 and we went to Margret Island for a picnic.

▶ My dad's birthday in May—picnic in Normafa Park.

▶ When I was two, Mom took me everywhere in her convertible.

▶ Grandma Joan: when we visit her we always go to my favorite shop (American Girl).

▶ My sleepover at my friend Sarah's house.

Later, Rahel chose an idea from her list for a notebook entry and explored it:

> Me and my grandma are sitting in her car, driving to the American Girl shop! I am so excited I can barely sit still. I have two out of five of my dolls, Nellie and Jennifer. When we get there there's so much to do!! What first?!? So we decide to first put our coats in the coat check, then we pick out some clothes for my dolls. Matching clothes, so me and my dolls can wear the same clothes! We try to reserve lunch, but we'd have to wait for a long time until we can eat, so instead we go to TGIF. I eat fried mac and cheese and my grandma eats a hamburger. When we get back to her apartment I say, "Grandma Joan, this was the best day of my life!" Then we relax on her bed and watch TV.

Carol adds, "I have had more success and I'm enjoying teaching writing more this year as all these pieces have started fitting together."

Another book that explores the power of writer's notebooks is Aimee Buckner's *Notebook Know-How* (2005) and the accompanying DVD, *Inside Notebooks* (2006). She describes how she often launches writer's notebooks with oral storytelling in which students talk about the events, places, and people in their lives. At other times, she begins by sharing her own notebooks, which inevitably sparks the request, "Can we write in a notebook, too?" Two teachers from the Kent School District, in Washington State, share the impact Aimee's work has had on their teaching:

> Aimee Buckner's book makes teaching writing easy. *Notebook Know-How* is a resource that you can pick up and use right away. After reading it, I was pumped with ideas and excited to teach writing. I started the very next day working on the lessons I read about in her book. I also encouraged my second-grade teammates to read it, and now we are all writer's notebook converts. This is one book you should definitely have in your lap, not on the shelf!
>
> —Tina Criste, second-grade teacher
>
> Thanks to the inspiring guidance and minilessons contained in *Notebook Know-How*, I have kids punching the air with their fists and saying, "Yes! It's writing time!" It's amazing to watch kids fill their writer's notebooks and proudly share their writing, knowing they have accomplished something of significance with these notebooks that will last for the rest of their lives.
>
> —Colleen Oliver, sixth-grade teacher

Aimee Buckner's ideas about writer's notebooks continue to evolve. In a December 2009 posting on the Choice Literacy website, Aimee describes how she recently reread several books about writer's notebooks (including her own) and tried to articulate her core beliefs about this form and container for writing, followed by the implications for teaching:

My Core Beliefs About Notebooks

❶ A writer's notebook is a place where writers explore their thinking.

❷ A writer's notebook is a reflection of who that writer is at a point in time of her life.

❸ Notebooks are tools that require writers to make decisions.

❹ Rereading their notebook helps writers explore topics more deeply or in a new way.

❺ As a writer becomes more diligent about keeping a notebook, his notebook will evolve in its purpose.

From Belief to Practice: Teaching with Notebooks

❶ I refer to notebook writing as entries, not drafts or stories.

❷ By drafting outside the notebook, my students are forced to make decisions about their writing and to refocus their efforts for the different stages of the writing process.

❸ Students need guidance and support in establishing and maintaining a writer's notebook.

She explores each of these statements in her article, but what struck me was how, even for an expert on this topic, she continues to read and reflect on her beliefs and practices.

Writer's notebooks are places in which students can generate topics, analyze different points of view, and reflect on their own learning. This skill of reflecting through writing also spills over into other curricular areas. In the past, some teachers asked students to write throughout the school day in learning logs; however, this often evolved into a dull regurgitation of activities. Donna Topping and Roberta Ann McManus, in *Real Reading, Real Writing* (2002), use the term *jotting* as they encourage students to use writing during reading workshop and content area classes. Students can jot down notes they want to remember, as well as reflect in writing about their understanding of new concepts and ideas.

Lil Brannon and other authors in *Thinking Out Loud on Paper: The Student Daybook as a Tool to Foster Learning* (2008) share another version of a writer's notebook, which they call a daybook. "Daybooks for us are thinking tools. As teachers we use them throughout our day to reflect and to research, and we ask our students in our classrooms to use them to research and think about their worlds. . . . We ask students to use them to write about their lives, to keep track of their thinking, and to notice all the world around them with open eyes, and ears, and hearts" (2–3).

I use writing in different ways every day. I jot things to remember on sticky notes, create "to-do" lists, take notes during workshops, and reflect in my journal.

Even the process of writing this book clarified my thinking as Carrie and I took notes on the books we read, wrote drafts, emailed questions back and forth, and revised each chapter. I learned from both my reading and my writing.

As your students begin using writer's notebooks, the process of writing to learn can spill over into content areas so that they can begin to understand the life-long skill of using writing as a tool for learning and reflection.

Book List

Resources to Help Support Students' Use of Writer's Folders and Writer's Notebooks

- ☐ *Breathing Out, Breathing In* by Ralph Fletcher (1996) (Grades 3–12)
- ☐ *Lessons for the Writer's Notebook* by Ralph Fletcher and JoAnn Portalupi (2005) (Grades 3–8)
- ☐ *Authors as Mentors* (from *Units of Study for Primary Writing*) by Lucy Calkins and Amanda Hartman (2003) (Grades K–2)
- ☐ *Launching the Writing Workshop* (from *Units of Study for Teaching Writing, Grades 3–5*) by Lucy Calkins and Marjorie Martinelli (2006)
- ☐ *Writing Through Childhood* by Shelley Harwayne (2001) (Grades K–5)
- ☐ *Study Driven* by Katie Wood Ray (2006) (Grades K–8)
- ☐ *Notebook Know-How* by Aimee Buckner (2005) (Grades 3–6)
- ☐ *Inside Notebooks* (DVD) by Aimee Buckner (2006) (Grades 3–6)
- ☐ *Using the Writer's Notebook in Grades 3–8* by Janet Elliott (2008)
- ☐ *Inside Reading and Writing Workshop* (DVD) by Joanne Hindley (2006) (Grades 1–3)
- ☐ *Thinking Out Loud on Paper* (Chapter 3) by Lil Brannon and colleagues (2008) (Grades 4–8)
- ☐ *Of Primary Importance* (pp. 34–39 and Appendix) by Ann Marie Corgill (2000) (Grades K–2)

Ponder Box for Teachers

- Are you using a writer's notebook yourself? If not, what would help you get started?

- Are you using writer's notebooks in your classroom? If so, are there challenges you'd like to overcome and read more about?

Mentor Authors and Illustrators and Mentor Texts

It feels like standing on one foot to talk about writing without discussing reading as
well. What better way to learn about effective writing than to examine the work of
writers we admire? As Katie Wood Ray says, at any grade level "The read aloud is
the single most important tool we have in the teaching of writing." (Workshop April
17, 2010) Here are a few questions to consider as you select mentor authors and
mentor texts:

▶ Who are your favorite adult writers?

▶ Who are your favorite children's authors and illustrators?

▶ Who would you most like to hear speak at a conference?

▶ If you could pick one author to invite to dinner, who would you choose?

▶ Have you read all the books that some authors have written?

▶ Is there one author or illustrator whose work you know really well?

Mentor Authors

I wish I could write like Regie Routman, Lucy Calkins, Ralph Fletcher, Brenda
Miller Power, and Katie Wood Ray. These are my mentor authors for writing professional books. I look closely at the way they weave in classroom stories and research,
how they use memorable language, and even the way they craft their acknowledg-
ments. Students need to apprentice themselves to published authors as mentors in
this same way.

When I taught elementary school and even when I taught children's literature
to college and university students, I always conducted author studies. I used to collect author pamphlets at conferences; I bought biographies of authors; and I still
have an entire filing cabinet drawer filled with the articles I collected about children's authors and illustrators. (This was before this information could be accessed
so easily on the Internet!) However, when I read this statement by Lucy Calkins, I
realized I had usurped the joy of inquiry:

...when I conducted elaborate author studies, immersing my students in a sea of trivial details about my favorite authors, I was probably learning more than were my children. I was the one who had all the fun of choosing a favorite author, of beginning to make a collection of that author's work, of digging up information on the author. How much better it would have been if I had invited each of my students to find a book that mattered enormously to him or her, and then to search for a second book by the same author, and finally, to put those two books together, asking, "What does this author tend to do?" and "Can I borrow any of these techniques in my own writing?" (1994, 275)

She's totally right. With the Internet at their fingertips, students can learn about an author whose writing they admire. Why not let them lead their own journey of discovery?

Ranu Bhattacharyya and her kindergartners fell in love with books by Mem Fox. Ranu read Mem's books aloud and students listened to her books on tape, making a list of what they knew about Mem through her books. They read her autobiography, *Memories* (1992). Ranu's students begged her to read *Possum Magic* (1985) over and over; they were so captivated that they created their own middle and ending to the story.

Lucy Calkins and Amanda Hartman begin their primary unit of study *Authors as Mentors* (2003) with a focus on Angela Johnson's writing. Students then choose

their own author to study, applying the process they just learned. The final portion of this unit is all about publication, as children edit their pieces and write "about the author" blurbs for their own work. During the celebration, children are placed in small groups with visitors—often parents and grandparents. They read a small portion of one of Angela Johnson's stories and then share how they emulated one of her crafting techniques. They then read their piece of writing and their "about the author" blurb.

Megan Sloan's second and third graders apprenticed themselves to Valerie Worth after hearing some of the poems from *All the Small Poems and Fourteen More* (1996). As they listened, students could clearly see how even tiny images such as a dog lying down for a nap, daisies growing along a path, or a tractor sitting in a shed could be interesting to write about. In her minilesson, Megan first talked about how during spring break she saw a butterfly flitting through a tulip garden, an experience that lasted all of thirty seconds. Then she wrote in front of students, stretching out the moment by describing what she saw, smelled, heard, and felt. Megan explained to students how, like Valerie Worth, they could craft small, powerful writing that paints a picture in their readers' minds.

If you developed an author study for your classroom, who would you choose as the focus? Which authors do your students most enjoy? You might want to check out the books in the

An Author Study of Mem Fox in Ranu Bhattacharyya's Kindergarten Classroom

Meet the Author series published by Richard C. Owen. These books have stories and interesting information about the lives of thirty-five children's authors and illustrators, as well as photographs from their childhood and pictures of where they write. For instance, Tommy Duncan read some of Ralph Fletcher's picture books, poetry, and novels to his students and showed video clips of Ralph sharing advice about writing. He read Ralph's autobiography, *Marshfield Dreams* (2005), and *Ralph Fletcher: Author at Work* (2007) from the Richard C. Owen series. This short book includes pictures from Ralph's childhood, examples from his writer's notebook, and information about what he does as a writer at each stage of the writing process. Soon students were talking about Ralph as if he were a member of the class.

To help you plan your own author studies, there's a really helpful K–3 planning guide by Gayle Brand (November 2006), complete with monthly grids, available through the Choice Literacy website. Learning alongside experienced authors and illustrators gives students a lens they can use to explore writers' craft for years to come.

In her book *In Pictures and In Words* (2010) Katie Wood Ray explores how children's thinking deepens as they examine the decisions that illustrators make about their craft. Her book includes over fifty ways you can use illustrations to help students internalize key aspects of craft through their love of picture books. Katie writes that, "If teachers show children how an illustrator's decisions about pictures are a lot like a writer's decisions about words, they form a bridge of understanding that nurtures children as writers." Katie's book is guaranteed to spark some ideas about how you could incorporate a study of illustrations by multiple artists into your units of study.

Mentor Texts

Many ideas for things to write about come from our own lives and experiences; others are sparked by the books we read. Mentor texts are pieces of literature we use numerous times with our students to teach and model the crafting strategies of published authors or illustrate an aspect of writing we want to showcase. The idea of mentor texts has been growing in recent years as teachers help even young students learn to "read like writers."

Katie Wood Ray's books shine a light on how to help students learn to write as apprentices to mentor authors. In *Wondrous Words* (1999), Katie writes, "We want our students to have 'full checking accounts' as writers, and our attention to reading aloud in our classrooms will help to ensure that they have access to all the 'funds' available in the texts around them" (69). Even young children can learn to notice both how texts are organized and each author's unique way with words. Katie writes about how knowing the work of a few authors has strengthened her teaching:

> Before I started studying the craft of writing, I didn't know any texts as a writer, I didn't know with any explicitness any techniques that writers use to make their writing come alive, so I wasn't in a position to suggest very much. It wasn't that I was holding back; I just didn't have anything much to hold back. . . . Studying the craft of writing has expanded my knowledge base exponentially in

> what I know about how good writing happens. I now know a whole repertoire of techniques for good writing that I didn't have in my first years of teaching. I now have a stack of texts that I know like the back of my hand. (247)

Katie describes the study of craft as a "curriculum of possibilities" and suggests a predictable format for a series of minilessons scaffolding students as they learn to "read like writers":

- *Notice* something about the craft of the text.
- *Talk* about it and *make a theory* about why the author used that craft.
- Give the craft a *name*.
- Think of *other texts* you know ("Have you seen this craft before?").
- *Envision* using this crafting in your own writing. (136)

Like Lucy Calkins, Katie recommends ending each lesson with a "reader's digest" version in which you sum up what you've taught, reiterating the steps involved so that students can picture exactly how they will incorporate this new strategy. Then, they're off to write! What students need next is the opportunity to dabble with the new strategies that you've so carefully demonstrated as your students learn to "read like writers."

Immersing students in the types of texts we want them to write helps them learn to envision what they hope for their writing. Katie offers this pearl of wisdom: "If a person ever hopes to write well, there may be no more important question for him or her to answer than this: 'What have you read that is like what you are trying to write?' For the recursive process of drafting and *re*vision to lead to good writing, writers have to have a clear vision of the good writing they want to do" (2006, 36).

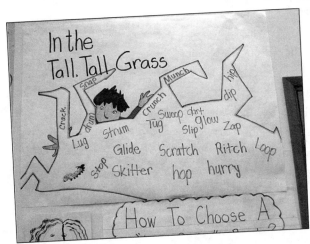

**Using a Mentor Text
in Megan Sloan's
Classroom**

Picture books are a great resource for mentor texts. Megan Sloan read *In the Tall, Tall Grass*, by Denise Fleming (1991), and her students listed "energetic verbs" and acted them out. They then examined their own writing to see whether they could add strong verbs. As part of your interactive read-alouds, you can have students "turn and talk" or "stop and jot" as they learn to listen as writers. The body of shared literature in any classroom becomes a well of resources from which teachers and students can draw all year long.

Anne Klein explores examples of strong writing in novels with her fifth graders. Last year, she read aloud a delightful book by Ingrid Law called *Savvy* (2008). The book brims over with great descriptions, similes, and memorable language, such as, "The woman wore a long, coat-like, belted sweater that hung down past the hem of her old-fashioned green and white waitressing uniform. She was bigger and broader than Lester with his narrow chest and caved-in shoulders, and they made a funny pair standing there" (130–31). One of Anne's fifth graders immediately used a similar descriptive style for one of the characters in the story she was writing. Anne finds that her read-alouds often have an impact on students' writing, so she chooses books for an author's use of language, description, or dialogue.

Lester Laminack examines his own writing in his book *Cracking Open the Author's Craft* (2007). On the accompanying DVD, Lester reads one of his picture books aloud, highlighting a few ways we can help students think about an author's craft. He demonstrates seven "audible craft moves" and seven "visual craft moves." In the book, he expands his ideas into detailed lessons designed to help elementary students see and hear an author's intentional use of language and form. Lester approaches these lessons through the lens of *why*: "Why did the author do that?" He implores us not to zip through a series of preplanned craft lessons but instead to linger as students learn how to make their writing sing. You may want to share snippets of the DVD with your students, along with the anchor texts he recommends at the end of each lesson.

Lester recommends that we read, study, and really come to know a handful of books with our students. As our instructional focus shifts, we can revisit these "old friends" using different lenses. When kids already know a book well, we can zoom right in on our teaching point. Shelley Harwayne once said that great writing teachers teach with a vision of helping each student write not just "this" piece but all kinds of writing. Lester lives those words. The lessons he includes in *Cracking Open the Author's Craft* can be incorporated anytime we want students to notice craft that they can apply to their own writing. Lester's book and DVD will make you want to gather a stack of good books, roll up your sleeves, and explore the craft of writing alongside your students.

Which books that you love and know well could serve as the anchor texts in your classroom? In her May, 2009, Choice Literacy article, "Planning to Teach with Mentor Texts: Two Examples," Karen Terlecky describes how she used Lester Laminack's picture book *Saturdays and Teacakes* (2004) for lessons on inferring, onomatopoeia, dialogue, and word choice. Karen also used *Marshfield Dreams* (2005) by Ralph Fletcher as a mentor text for inferences, "small moment" writing, and how to sequence a group of short stories. Karen first reads these books to her students simply for enjoyment, then dips back into them throughout the year to tease out more about the author's craft. You might think about which three or four books (of the many that you love) would be rich enough to warrant multilevel excavations like this. In the same issue of the Choice Literacy newsletter, Franki Sibberson has a two-page article, "New Mentor Texts for Word Choice," that includes a great list of picture books she uses for word choice, similes, idioms, verb choice, and content-specific words.

Mentor Texts (2007) by Lynne Dorfman and Rose Cappelli is a fabulous resource for examples of great writing. This book identifies mentor texts for writing personal stories, discovering the inside story, focusing on a moment with descriptions, creating powerful beginnings and endings, using various organizational structures and poetry techniques, choosing the right word, and using (and sometimes abandoning) grammar and other conventions. The last chapter, "A Treasure Chest of Books," includes an annotated list of hundreds of titles, organized by topics, such as "Creating Powerful Beginnings and Satisfying Endings." The same authors also wrote *Nonfiction Mentor Texts* (2009), which includes a current, comprehensive list of books for teaching the process and the craft of nonfiction writing.

In *Writing Anchors* (2004), Jan Wells and Janine Reid provide exemplars in four genres—personal recounting, nonfiction, poetry, and narrative writing—for grades 2 through 7. The book includes rubrics, examples from published writers, student examples, and teaching tips. A reflection component is built into each anchor lesson: "This metacognitive awareness is one of the major goals of the anchor lessons. We want students to be more mindful of the techniques they are using, to select words with care and to be aware of the choices they can make as writers" (6).

Graham Foster and Toni Marasco explain how in recent years most teachers use rubrics for writing assessment. They argue that rubrics are far more powerful when combined with examples. Their book *Exemplars: Your Best Resource to Improve Student Writing* (2007) will save you hours and hours of time looking for examples to use with students in the intermediate grades and middle school. In addition, they've provided exemplar-based minilessons for writing strategies, content, organization, sentence variety, word choice, voice, and conventions. The activities and examples in this book "challenge students to think about a writer's options and to transfer what they learn to their own writing" (6).

Book List

Resources to Help You Use Mentor Authors and Illustrators and Mentor Texts

☐ *Wondrous Words* by Katie Wood Ray (1999) (Grades K–8)

☐ *Authors as Mentors* (from *Units of Study for Primary Writing*) by Lucy Calkins and Amanda Hartman (2003) (Grades K–2)

☐ *Mentor Texts* by Lynne Dorfman and Rose Cappelli (2007) (Grades K–6)

☐ *Nonfiction Mentor Texts* by Lynne Dorfman and Rose Cappelli (2009) (Grades K–8)

☐ *The Allure of the Author: Author Studies in the Elementary Classroom* by Carol Brennan Jenkins (1999) (Grades K–8)

☐ *Nonfiction Authors Studies in the Elementary Classroom* by Carol Brennan Jenkins and Deborah White (2007) (Grades K–8)

☐ *In Pictures and In Words* by Katie Wood Ray (2010) (Grades PreK–4)

☐ *Cracking Open the Author's Craft* by Lester Laminack (with DVD) (2007) (Grades 1–5)

☐ *Exemplars: Your Best Resource to Improve Student Writing* by Graham Foster and Toni Marasco (2007) (Grades 4–9)

☐ *Writing Anchors* by Jan Wells and Janine Reid (2004) (Grades 2–7)

☐ *I Can Write Like That!* by Susan Ehmann and Kellyann Gayer (2009) (Grades K–6)

☐ *Using Rubrics to Improve Student Writing, Revised Edition* by Sally Hampton, Sandra Murphy, and Margaret Lowry (2009) (separate books for K, 1, 2, 3, 4, 5)

Susan Ehmann and Kellyann Gayer (2009) have done your homework for you in *I Can Write Like That!* They describe twenty-seven craft elements and suggest five children's books you can use to illustrate each craft. In addition to providing ideas for minilessons and annotated lists of anchor texts, they list the craft elements found in each book. The titles are presented in alphabetical order so you can easily scan the chart for your favorite books.

All of these resources contain teaching ideas and helpful exemplars; however, you and your students will also want to collect your own examples from the books, magazines, newspapers, the Internet, and other materials you read.

Ponder Box for Teachers

- How are you using mentor texts in your classroom?
- Which books would be helpful mentor texts for your current unit of study?

Ponder Box for Coaches and Principals

- How will you provide time for teachers to collect mentor texts and to share ideas about using mentor texts in grade-level teams and vertical teams?
- What structures can you put in place so that there is diversity in mentor texts across grade levels?

Struggling or Reluctant Writers

Even when you have writing workshop in place around specific units of study and have provided mentor texts as examples, do a few hesitant or reluctant writers still struggle with some aspect of writing? In *Writing Essentials* (2005), Regie Routman provides an extensive list of strategies to help struggling writers during modeled, shared, interactive, and guided writing, as well as tips for helping those students in different genres and contexts (169–72).

In *A Classroom Teacher's Guide to Struggling Writers* (2009) Curt Dudley-Marling and Patricia Paugh describe how best to help writers who flounder from time to time: "The key to meeting the instructional needs of struggling writers—in fact, of meeting the particular needs of even the most successful students—is individualized support and direction, informed by appropriate, ongoing assessment. To support struggling writers, teachers must be able to organize their classroom with structures that permit them to collect routine, in-depth assessment data and to work with students individually and in small groups" (3).

Your first step will be to determine the cause of the problem. Is the child new to English? Has the child had previous negative experiences with writing? Is the student struggling with the physical act of writing? Lucy Calkins recently edited a series of "quick guides," tiny books the size of a big index card. It only took me an hour to read *A Quick Guide to Reaching Struggling Writers K–5* (2008), by Colleen Cruz, but I picked up lots of helpful tidbits. Colleen provides six short chapters on the most common reasons that writers struggle:

"I'm not a good writer."

"My hand hurts."

"I don't know how to spell."

"I never have anything to write about."

"I never get to write anything I want to write."

"I'm done."

Colleen assumes that you already have writing workshop in place in your classroom so that you are able to work with individual students and small groups. In each of the chapters, she includes concrete suggestions for what you can do to help those students. I love her idea of creating a "help wanted—help offered" bulletin board where students can post both their strengths ("I'm good at punctuation") and needs ("I need help with a lead").

In *Reclaiming Reluctant Writers* (2007), Kellie Buis writes, "We can support reluctant writers and challenge them in the right proportion at the right time. We don't have to cajole them or remediate them. We don't have to blame them for the lack of success. Rather, we can build on their strengths and teach them what it takes to be authentic writers" (6). Process writing demands that writers take risks, and struggling writers may be easily defeated by tasks that other students tackle with ease. Instead of complaining about our students or giving up, we should examine our teaching and consider what we can do to make writing successful and enjoyable for *all* kids. We need to show students that writing is challenging for all writers, and we need to help them see the potential poems and stories in their own lives. Kellie claims that teachers don't need to be cheerleaders or to "motivate" students. Our job is to help reluctant writers find their own motivation for writing: "It is all about reviving them with the freedom, choice, and responsibility to record what they decide to know and care about. It demands that our reluctant writers discover their topics and flow of ideas from the inside out, not outside in" (35).

For many students, resistance comes from having to reveal themselves too soon, so Kellie encourages teachers to start the year with "safe" genres such as descriptive writing or free-verse poetry until they build up their confidence and trust. In the third chapter, Kellie presents some fabulous ideas for reclaiming writers by building fluency. She recommends writer's notebooks and freewrites as safe forums: "Reluctant writers need psychologically safe environments where they can

Book List

Resources to Help You Work with Struggling Writers

☐ *Reclaiming Reluctant Writers* by Kellie Buis (2007) (Grades 4–8)

☐ *A Quick Guide to Reaching Struggling Writers* by Colleen Cruz (2008) (Grades K–5)

☐ *A Classroom Teacher's Guide to Struggling Writers: How to Provide Differentiated Support and Ongoing Assessment* by Curt Dudley-Marling and Patricia Paugh (2009) (Grade 2–6)

☐ *Supporting Struggling Readers and Writers* (Chapters 2 and 9) by Dorothy Strickland, Kathy Ganski, and Joanne Monroe (2002) (Grades 3–6)

express their ideas in writing without concern for adult standards of correctness. Some of them don't read much, have trouble with simple spelling and punctuation, and have limited vocabularies. Frequently, they worry about where to begin because they don't want to reveal their inadequacies with the printed word" (32). If we push them too soon to revise and share their writing, these students often shut down. Kellie also suggests that revision be active and social rather than solitary.

Lucy Calkins and her colleagues, in each of their units of study for both K–2 and 3–5, also provide helpful suggestions for working with struggling or reluctant writers in side boxes labeled "Assessment" or "Tailoring Your Teaching" or "If Children Need More Time." They provide specific student writing samples and suggest things you might try. The key is to create situations in which those students can be successful.

Ponder Box for Teachers

- Who are the struggling or reluctant writers in your classroom?
- What might be the most likely causes for their difficulty with writing?

Ponder Box for Coaches and Principals

- How might you provide time for teachers to analyze the patterns of reluctant and struggling writers in your school?
- How might you provide time for teachers to brainstorm ideas about how best to meet the needs of the reluctant or struggling writers at your school?

Sometimes the solutions are as simple as letting students compose on the computer. At other times, it means helping writers find a topic that sparks their interest or letting kids write with a partner. Most often, what reluctant writers need is to develop stamina and confidence.

Gender and Writing

My daughter has always loved to write—she learned to write before she formally learned to read. She kept journals, wrote reams of letters and stories, and is still a fluent and confident writer today. The same is not true of my two sons. Oh, they learned to write and were successful in school, but neither enjoyed writing. As a teacher, I was usually successful in hooking most of my students on writing.

However, there were always a few students (often boys) who never seemed to catch the spark or engage in writing with the same enthusiasm they displayed for reading, science, math, or computers.

Thomas Newkirk's ground-breaking book *Misreading Masculinity: Boys, Literacy, and Popular Culture* (2002) sparked heated discussions when it was first published, as he challenged widely held practices and asked teachers to think carefully about the choices of topics we provide for the boy writers in our classrooms. Tom writes, "By defining, teaching, and evaluating literacy in narrow ways—even under the banner of 'choice' and a student-centered curriculum—we have failed to support, or even allow, in our literacy programs the tastes, values, and learning styles of many boys. More specifically, we have discouraged, devalued, or even prohibited the genres of reading and writing that are most popular with many boys, stories that include violence, parody, and bodily humor" (xvi). He adds that "humor, managed effectively, is the gold standard in children's writing" (167), because it brings celebrity to the writer and often affirms male friendships. He also describes a clearly identifiable group of boys found in most classrooms who love to draw and how we can capitalize on that passion through the use of storytelling and storyboarding. From interviews with one hundred boys, Tom learned that the reading and writing they do in school is often removed from their interests and passions. He urges us to bring these boys into the "literacy club" by widening the circle of acceptable writing in our classrooms.

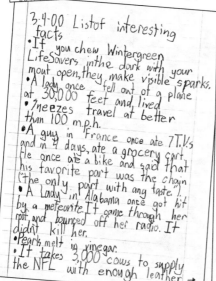

**Bruce Hill's Nonfiction Writer's
Notebook Entries**

Luckily, my son Bruce had a teacher one year, Cindy Flegenheimer, who let him write about things he found interesting. Instead of writing poems or stories, Bruce demonstrated his propensity for nonfiction in his writer's notebook entries about dog years, interesting facts, and directions for making paper airplanes. I believe that more boys would enjoy writer's notebooks and writing if we allowed them to include facts, collections, and aspects of their lives outside school.

As one of six boys in his family growing up and with four boys of his own, Ralph Fletcher provides additional insights in his book *Boy Writers* (2006). Like Tom Newkirk's book, *Boy Writers* has sparked plenty of lively conversations and reflection by teachers and coaches who have used his book to explore how to make their classrooms and teaching more "boy-friendly." A few of Ralph's ideas might make some teachers squirm. As he notes, 90 percent of elementary teachers are women, so it's natural that classrooms reflect women's ways of knowing and seeing the world. Ralph asks us to question what types of writing we value in our classrooms and to allow room for boys to express who they are. "Many boys find that the choice coupon in the writing workshop contains a great deal of small print listing many types of writing they are *not* allowed to do. Boys get an unfriendly response from their teachers when they try to write about high-interest boy topics, such as hunting, favorite movies, comics, outer space adventures, video games, war" (42). In addition to topic choice, Ralph's book addresses wait time, conversational style differences, the role of drawing, and the use of humor. With Ralph's permission, I've included some of his tips for creating boy-friendly classrooms that you may want to share at a staff meeting (see Figure 3.1). This list and his book always spark animated discussions.

If I'd had *Boy Writers* all those years ago, I know I would have devoured it, combing each chapter for insights about my own sons and the boys I taught. In her book *Into Writing* (2009), Megan Sloan describes some of the modifications she has made in her classroom after reading *Boy Writers* and listening to Ralph speak. She has allowed a wider range of topics and writing forms, honors boys' desire to draw, and provides comfortable spaces for boys (and girls) to read and write. When they want to write about videos or movies, she uses shared writing to work on craft elements (clarity, organization, word choice, dialogue, and voice) within these action-packed retellings.

By tossing out a wider net of writing genres, we catch more writers. When Anne Klein expanded the topics students could write about in her classroom, she saw significant changes for some of her more reluctant boy writers. I brought a group of teachers to visit her classroom last spring, and we watched as Anne conferred with Blake about the video game manual he was writing. Blake's face lit up as he explained that he was trying to break new ground by writing a manual with a sense of humor. He flipped through page after page of his draft and described how the feedback from some of his friends had led him to make changes. This was a huge breakthrough for Blake, who for the first time was deeply engaged in drafting and revising a piece for a real audience and purpose.

Anne also led a book study of *Boy Writers* in her school. As a result, her colleague Susan Lockhart presented a parent workshop called "Encouraging Reading and Writing for Boys." In addition to her PowerPoint presentation, Susan provided a list of books for parents about boys and literacy, as well as a list of the boy-friendly books Ralph recommends in his book. The parent response was extremely positive:

> Mrs. Lockhart,
> I wanted to thank you for the great presentation last night. I gained a lot of information, ideas, and approaches to encourage my fourth grader and first grader.
> I also put your teachings into action today at work. I work at a construction company in Edmonds full of "boys." I recognized that a list would be a much more effective way of communicating some very detailed instructions. Worth a try!

Ralph Fletcher's Tips for Creating Boy-Friendly Classrooms

- Get boys excited about writing. Worry about their engagement first; the quality will come later.
- Give real choice about *what* to write and *how* to write it.
- Show an interest in what your boys are passionate about. These things often make great subjects for writing.
- Be more accepting of violence in writing (within commonsense limits).
- Celebrate the quirky humor in boys' writing (humor = voice).
- Give boys specific praise during writing conferences.
- Don't insist that students revise everything they write.
- Make room for genres that engage boys: fiction, fantasy, sports writing, spoofs and parodies, comics/graphic novels, and so on.
- Allow upper-grade students to draw while composing.
- Messy handwriting is a developmental issue for many boys. Don't take it personally. Allow students to keyboard when possible.
- Talk about the writer's notebook as a place to collect important "stuff," including odd facts, artifacts, quotes, lyrics, and drawings.
- Show an interest in the writing kids do at home, for fun.
- Be inclusive about the writing you allow kids to read out loud. If only sincere, realistic, emotional pieces get shared, boys will turn off.
- Don't be surprised if boys view other boys as their main audience.
- Take the long view. Don't expect great writing right away.

Figure 3.1 Ralph Fletcher's Tips for Creating Boy-Friendly Classrooms

Ralph Fletcher also has a DVD titled *"Dude, Listen to This!" Engaging Boy Writers* (2008) that is a perfect complement to his book. In the first section of the video, literacy coach Jennifer Allen and Ralph meet with a writing club for boys, eager writers who voluntarily meet every Monday during lunch and recess to share the writing they're doing in and outside school. Jen and Ralph respond to the voluntary writing of these boys and their obvious delight in writing. Jen says how stunned she is at how much writing these boys are doing outside of school. When Ralph asks the boys about their favorite part of school, they immediately respond that it's writing in class and in their club. Ralph comments that girls often write for the teacher; boys most often write to entertain other boys. This snapshot of a writer's club demonstrates the power of a supportive writing group: in the DVD, these boys cheer one another on but also make helpful suggestions as they voluntarily explore a wide range of topics and genres. In the next clip, Ralph asks a group of fourth-grade boys to sketch a map of a favorite place (a strategy he mentions in *Marshfield Dreams*). He comments that many stories are rooted in places and that allowing boys to draw as part of the writing process often results in stronger writing. The final section eavesdrops on a group of teachers as they study *Boy Writers*. Ralph notes that teachers often work in isolation and appreciate the opportunity to share ideas and talk about important issues.

Ponder Box for Teachers

- What changes are you considering that might make your classroom and writing instruction more boy-friendly?

- How could you explore this issue on your own or with a colleague or grade-level team?

Ponder Box for Coaches and Principals

- What structures can you put in place to allow more time for teachers to brainstorm ideas for supporting boy writers at your school?

- Would this be a helpful topic to explore at a staff meeting, in a workshop, or as a book study?

Book List

Resources to Help You Understand Gender in Relation to
Writing Instruction

☐ *Boy Writers* by Ralph Fletcher (2006) (Grades K–6)

☐ *"Dude, Listen to This!" Engaging Boy Writers* (DVD) by Ralph
Fletcher (2008) (Grades K–8)

☐ *Conferring with Boys* (DVD) by Max Brand (2006) (Grades 3–5)

☐ *Misreading Masculinity: Boys, Literacy, and Popular Culture* by
Thomas Newkirk (2002) (Grades 3–8)

☐ *Raising Cain: Protecting the Inner Life of America's Boys* (PBS video)
by Michael Thompson (2006) (Grades K–12)

Technology and Writing

When I sent an email to teachers asking how they use technology in connection
with teaching writing, the responses were fascinating. Cheryl Perkins uses a
SMARTBoard to make morning attendance rituals go smoothly and as a way to promote independence. Each morning when the children enter the room, their first
stop is her SMARTBoard, which displays a small picture of each child along the
side. On the board is a yes-or-no question or a question to which they respond on a
graph. Her first graders move their picture into the yes/no column or into the
appropriate column on the graph. Everyone can tell at a glance which students are
absent, and they discuss their responses at Cheryl's morning meeting.

Many teachers have begun using their digital cameras to capture learning. These photographs of students
sharing their writing in the author's chair or at a poetry
reading for family members can be included in their
portfolios. Pat Barrett Dragan uses digital photographs
to spark learning in and out of school, to connect with
families, and to support English language learners. Her
book *Kids, Cameras, and the Curriculum* (2008) provides fascinating ways to incorporate photography into
all areas of the curriculum in primary classrooms.

In her first-grade Texas classroom, Doriane Marvel
integrates technology into her writing minilessons by
using webcasts (most recently, from www.readingrock-
ets.com and the Library of Congress) in which authors

**Cindy Curtis Uses her Interactive Whiteboard to Help Her
Prekindergarten Students Understand Directionality**

read their own work and writers and illustrators talk about their creative process. Marc Brown's comment that he gets all his ideas by thinking back to when he was in third grade validates Doriane's minilessons about writing from experiences. When David Shannon explains that *No David!* (1998) was a book he wrote as a child, Doriane's students feel they too could be real authors. Doriane has used author webcasts to support minilessons on small moment stories, adding detail, editing, and more, as well as to model how to match illustrations to the text.

Anne Klein just finished a successful writing project that integrated social studies, reading, writing, and technology. In pairs, her fifth graders read several books about life during the American Revolution. Anne then combined three pairs together to form groups that had read three different books. Each group logged on to the Library of Congress website and studied newspapers and political cartoons from the period, then created their own newspaper on the computer, including highlights of what was happening, along with political cartoons. The students decided on the title and location of the newspaper and the point of view (loyalist or patriot). History came alive much more than if they had merely read a textbook, and students loved the chance to incorporate technology in their research and final products.

Tommy Duncan's excitement about using technology in classrooms is contagious. He loves using interactive whiteboards (or SMARTboards) for minilessons and likes the fact that he can save what he and the students have written together. They often refer to the saved interactive whiteboard (IWB) file during another lesson, and students instantly remember where they were in their discussion or concept. Tommy often talks with his students while revising on the computer or using the "digital ink pen" on the interactive whiteboard. He has also saved all his introductory writer's notebook lessons based on Ralph Fletcher and JoAnn Portalupi's *Lessons for the Writer's Notebook* (2005) as interactive whiteboard "notebook software" files. Each lesson contains a "photo message." There is some text, but the students have to figure out the message using photos. They get better at figuring out the message, and the visual symbols help them remember the concepts. Plus it's fun! Tommy also uses the interactive whiteboard to share author stories and interviews that he finds on the Internet. He's also been able to find videos of authors reading their own work.

Tommy likes being able to scan and save student work, then project their writing on the interactive whiteboard during minilessons as students revise and edit in front of the class. For one lesson, Tommy typed up the text from *Mr. George Baker* (2007) by Amy Hest into one long paragraph without any breaks. Students tried to guess where the author would have placed the page/paragraph breaks. Tommy then read the picture book aloud and the students were delighted that they had predicted almost every break correctly.

In addition to interactive whiteboards, Tommy also has his students distribute their writing using his school Gmail account and Google's file-sharing sites. As part of a poetry unit, Tommy's students found kid-friendly websites for poetry that everyone can access. Here are just a few they discovered:

www.gigglepoetry.com

www.poetry4kids.com/poems

www.poemhunter.com/poets

www.funnypoets.com

www.poetrykid.com

www.shelsilverstein.com/play.asp

Eventually, he hopes to have students collaborate on assignments via shared documents.

Tommy also uses technology when publishing books. His class just finished making an ABC book about the country of Oman (the site of his international school) using Publisher software, which makes it easy for students to move text around and create stunning final products.

Recently when Tommy knew he was going to be absent, he recorded an audio clip. The substitute teacher clicked on the photo of Tommy on the interactive whiteboard and he was able to tell his students exactly what they were expected to do. When he returned to school the next day, his students told him how much they loved it. His "virtual" appearance really got their attention!

Teachers like Cheryl, Doriane, Anne, and Tommy are just beginning to tap into the potential of technology as part of teaching. A current topic on blogs and discussion boards is how most teachers use an interactive whiteboard as a fancy overhead projector rather than as an interactive teaching tool that can engage students as part of reading/writing workshop. A great website that will help you maximize the learning potential of the whiteboard is http://sn.im/ning-iwb-community.

Whether you're an experienced "techie" or feeling tentative about how to use technology in your classroom, *I Have Computers in My Classroom—Now What?* by Bob Johnstone (2006) will show you how technology can enhance your students' learning and engagement in very doable ways. Bob offers hints about what to do and not do in your classroom, as well as solutions for common problems and engaging ways to weave in technology. He presents tantalizing ideas about how to incorporate clay animation; how to use Inspiration software for graphic mapping

Technology and Publishing in Tommy Duncan's Classroom

and TimeLiner software for slideshow presentations; and how to use interactive whiteboards, online discussion boards, and blogs.

Bob claims that since computers are part of learning for all of us, the challenge is to figure out how technology can fit into our teaching. He suggests that we start with our curriculum, *then* figure out how technology might enhance the activities and student learning. He includes ten specific suggestions:

1. Take baby steps.

2. Give choices.

3. Have a backup plan if the technology fails.

4. Watch the screens (set up the classroom so you can always see the students' screens, or use Microsoft Remote Desktop to monitor computer use).

5. Hands off the mouse and keyboard (let the students learn by doing).

6. Get to know your tech support people.

7. Teach kids to use the Help function.

8. Teach cut-and-paste.

9. Save often.

10. Don't overdo the use of computers.

He points out that most of our students know a lot more about technology than we do and encourages us to work *with* our students and learn from them. Bob has a bulletin board in his classroom on which he posts challenges he can't solve as a teacher. For example, when one of his students left Caps Lock on and typed his whole document in uppercase, Bob couldn't remember how to highlight the whole document and change it to mixed case; he posted a note on the board and a student figured out how to solve the problem, then shared his solution with the class. Bob also has a monthly pizza lunch during which kids show him new things they've discovered with technology that can be useful in their classroom. He writes, "I can't tell you how much I've learned through the years from those lunches" (19). Their school had an outdated website run by an overloaded teacher, so Bob started an after-school class in which he and his students explored web design. The kids created new pages and Bob uploaded their "new and improved" version; he learned a great deal by working with students for whom technology is so intuitive. Their school also has an "e-learning team" of computer-literate teachers who get training, try out ideas, help solve problems, and provide professional development for the rest of the staff.

In the previous section, I mentioned that my daughter was a writer. However, my older son, Keith, created my website, and my younger son, Bruce, developed the database of annotations and photographs for this book. They do write but in a different language—not fiction, but code. Students are quickly surpassing us with the many ways in which they use technology outside the classroom—web pages, blogs, twitter, Facebook, and instant messaging. They can download pictures and music and insert video clips. We can make writing even more relevant and exciting by inviting our students' expertise and the exciting potential of technology into our classrooms.

Book List

Resources to Help You Integrate Writing and Technology

☐ *I Have Computers in my Classroom—Now What?* by Bob Johnstone (2006) (Grades K–12)

☐ *Literacy, Technology, and Diversity* (with CD-ROM) by Jim Cummins, Kristin Brown, and Dennis Sayers (2007) (Grades K–12)

☐ *Kids, Cameras, and the Curriculum* by Pat Barrett Dragan (2008) (Grades K–3)

☐ *Supporting Content Area Literacy with Technology* by William Brozo and Kathleen Puckett (2009) (Grades K-8)

☐ *Literacy Moves On* by Janet Evans (2005) (Grades K–6)

☐ *Family Literacy Experiences* by Jennifer Roswell (2006) (Grades K–8)

Ponder Box for Teachers

● How comfortable do you feel about integrating technology into your writing program?

● What are some ways you incorporate technology into teaching writing?

● What are some ways you can collaborate with colleagues to discuss the developmental appropriateness of various technology strategies at your grade level?

Ponder Box for Coaches and Principals

● How much training have you provided for teachers on developmentally appropriate and instructionally sound ways to incorporate technology in the teaching of writing?

● What structures can you set up to provide time for teachers to brainstorm and share ideas for using technology in writing instruction?

● Would this be a helpful topic to explore at a staff meeting, in a workshop, or as a book study?

● Does your technology teacher have some strategies to share with the staff on using technology for the teaching of writing?

English Language Learners and Writing

Writing is a challenging task for all students, but even more so for students who are writing in their second (or third) language. English is not the first language for some of Doriane Marvel's first graders in Austin, Texas, so she makes sure to keep picture dictionaries handy. During instruction, she always models the concept in a number of ways and makes sure she thinks aloud, providing as many visual clues as possible. When her young students are prewriting, Doriane confers with them and helps them talk through their ideas. Together they make a picture plan or record words that the students might want to use.

In *Writing Between Languages* (2009), Danling Fu makes a convincing argument that students who are just learning English should be allowed to write in their first language in all subject areas starting on their first day of school. This allows students to be active participants in the classroom and to build on what they can express in their first language. They can share their writing with writing partners who speak their language. At the beginning, they may begin to sprinkle in a few words in English and share their drawings with the class. Later, they may write primarily in English, using their first language only for the words they don't know.

She goes on to show how code-switching (mixing languages) is as developmental and natural in written language as it is in spoken language: "I believe that in teaching ELLs to write, code-switching is not only a necessary transitional stage, but a useful strategy in promoting the growth of their English writing. When ELLs try to write in English, their thinking is often blocked due to their limited vocabulary. Code-switching can serve as a borrowing strategy by using the native language to fill in the English words they don't know so they can continue their thinking process" (49). When students are limited to using the words they know in English "the writing can be pedestrian and flat, but if allowed to use their own language to express themselves, they can write vivid pieces" (52). We can help students feel like members of a community of writers by allowing them to write in their first language, then gradually incorporate more English as their confidence and vocabulary grows. In addition, mixed writing is a window into the language skills students need next. We can examine their response journals and writing to determine the vocabulary words and grammar that students most need and teach them bit by bit so that students don't become overwhelmed.

Many of the students in Tommy Duncan's class at the American International School in Muscat, Oman, are nonnative English speakers. So that all his students will feel successful and be able to tell the stories they bring with them to fifth grade, Tommy gives them the option of writing in their native language. When Tommy first introduced the idea of writer's notebooks, NaYoung did not have the vocabulary to express herself in written English, so Tommy encouraged her to write in Korean. Being able to draft her thoughts in her native language allowed NaYoung to participate fully in writing workshop.

You may want to encourage students who are just learning English to write in their own language, then either translate it into English or talk about it in English.

If they are not literate in their home language, they can draw a series of pictures to tell their story. Asking English language learners to read their work aloud during individual writing conferences reinforces their confidence in speaking English. If they make grammatical errors, start with a positive comment about content, then help them with conventions.

In *Becoming One Community* (2004), Kathleen Fay and Suzanne Whaley share helpful tips on how to support ELLs with few prior literacy experiences:

- Engage them in conversation.
- Write for them or share the pen with them.
- Have them draw.
- Ask them to write about a shared experience.
- Model writing in English.
- Have them make pattern books.
- Have them compile a personal dictionary.
- Ask them to write or draw about their weekend.
- Use nonfiction books as springboards.

Writer to Writer (2007), by Mary Lee Prescott-Griffin, has some great ideas for how writing partnerships and collaboration can support English language learners. She recommends creating partnerships or triads of students who speak the same language but who might not be comfortable speaking up in whole-group settings. Texts created in collaboration with other students are often richer and more complex than any of the students could create alone. Mary Lee explores the power of four different types of writing partnerships:

- Writing buddies: editing, fluency, research
- Small-group collaboration: peer editing, research, group story and study groups
- Cross-age writing buddies: dialogue journals, writing projects, research projects, collaborative story writing
- Home writing partnerships: literature response journals and book bags, dialogue journals, buddy biographies, word hunts, resource buddies

Pat Barrett Dragan, in *A How-To Guide for Teaching English Language Learners in the Primary Classroom* (2005), finds that her students blossom when they are interviewed by the class. She teaches her young students how to ask helpful questions; take notes using letters, words, lists, or pictures; and then turn the information into a class story through shared writing. Paula Rogovin (1998) also provides detailed information about how interviews with students, parents, and community members help create a sense of community and are a springboard for learning to read and write. Interviews are the focus of inquiry in her primary classroom.

ELL Scaffolding Techniques

SUPPORTING ORAL LANGUAGE DEVELOPMENT	SUPPORTING WRITING DEVELOPMENT
• Slow down your speech and extend your wait time.	• Use peer tutors or partners for group work, allowing ELLs to contribute whatever they are able.
• Model correct usage rather than correct pronunciation and grammar errors, especially at early stages.	• Use drawing as a communication tool; label drawings in English; add phrases, then sentences.
• Use gestures, drama, objects, and pictures to help students understand word meanings.	• Allow some pieces to remain unpublished and modify expectations about how much revision and editing ELLs can do.
• Honor the language of students by asking them to teach the class words in their language.	• Make charts during minilessons and keep them up for extended periods.
• Use picture books to teach vocabulary.	• Encourage students to continue reading and writing in their own language.
• Bond through music.	• Only assign homework that requires students to practice what they are learning.
• Use graphic organizers.	
• Build confidence by highlighting successes in content subjects like math or science.	• During conferences, start with positive comments, then respond to content before helping with conventions and grammar.
• Encourage children and parents to teach the class about their home country as soon as they are comfortable doing so.	• Let them practice reading their writing with you or other students before they share their writing with the whole class.
• Provide time for play and incorporate drama, music, and art.	• Examine their writing to determine what vocabulary and grammar students need, then teach a few skills gradually and provide lots of opportunities for practice.
• Allow down time for students new to English.	
• Ask parents and older students to provide language support and serve as translators.	• Celebrate learning.
• Create a key word bank for all content areas as a reference (include small pictures as support).	
• Provide dual-language dictionaries.	
• Have kids design a personal picture dictionary with English words, a picture, and the word in their own language (ask parents for help).	

Figure 3.2. ELL Scaffolding Techniques from The American School of Muscat

The American International School in Muscat designates one class at each grade level to host most of the emergent/intermediate ELLs. The other class at each grade level includes more proficient ELLs and students who receive support from reading or resource teachers. This "sheltered immersion" approach has proved an effective strategy for providing cohesive support. Literacy coach Kerry Harder and ELL resource teacher Ken Ingram collaborate with classroom teachers to help them modify materials and instruction for their ELLs (some of the scaffolding techniques they use are listed in Figure 3.2). They have also trained four ELL assistants in literacy who collaborate with classroom teachers.

Amanda Hartman and Lucy Calkins have produced a DVD, *Up Close* (2008), containing clips of seven writing conferences, one strategy lesson, and three story-telling lessons with English language learners. You can watch the lessons as presented or with Amanda Hartman's voiceover describing her intentional use of language and her teaching points. She bases many of her decisions on each student's knowledge of English as she provides scaffolding for their language and writing skills and creates a risk-taking environment in which these students can flourish.

One of my favorite descriptions of a primary classroom that is home to English language learners is found in Chapter 4 of *"The Words Came Down!"* (2006) by Emelie Parker and Tess Pardini:

> Jesse acts as though he has ants in his pants. Mohammad wants to chatter in Arabic to his best friend. Jebin's straight face isn't giving Emelie many clues to what she is thinking. Ana still looks shell-shocked. Emilie thinks Ana's state is a combination of being separated from her twin, Jasmin, and the "noise" of all the English. Emelie pats the floor next to her, smiles, and slips her arm around Ana. Ana snuggles up to Emelie. Emelie feels Ana's body relax as she continues with her lesson. (60)

As she gets to know her students, Emelie is better able to match her teaching to each child's needs. She has high expectations that each day her students' writing will be a little better than it was the day before.

We need to be sensitive to the endurance levels, emotional responses, and general adjustment of students who are learning English. Speaking a new language all day can be exhausting and frustrating. Parent communication is a key component in making things go smoothly the first few months, so we need to keep in very close touch with parents. It's also helpful to notice if writing and reading can be a tool for developing speaking and listening, or vice versa. Some kids control the written aspects of English sooner, while other kids control speaking more quickly. You may want to encourage ELLs who are more confident about writing than speaking to read their own writing or participate in small-group shared reading. Finally, it's always important to celebrate small successes and approximations.

We also need to be aware of the home literacy practices of the ELLs in our classroom. Katharine Davies Samway (2006) advises:

English language learners come from homes that have established ways of learning and transmitting cultural and literacy knowledge. Sometimes, these practices and experiences are hidden from teachers, who then mistakenly assume that families do not value literacy. We need to find out what children do at home around literacy and what their areas of expertise are, through observing them, through talking with them and their family members, and through visiting them in their community and home environments. (100)

As classrooms become more and more diverse, it's important to examine how to modify our materials, expectations, and our classroom environment to best meet the needs and value the contributions of the English language learners in our classrooms.

Book List

Resources to Help You Modify Your Writing Instruction for ELLs

- ☐ *"The Words Come Down!"* (Chapter 4) by Emelie Parker and Tess Pardini (2006) (Grades K–2)
- ☐ *Up Close* by Amanda Hartman and Lucy Calkins (DVD) (2008) (Grades K–2)
- ☐ *Becoming One Community* by Kathleen Fay and Suzanne Whaley (2004) (Grades 3–6)
- ☐ *Writer to Writer* by Mary Lee Prescott-Griffin (2007) (Grades K–5)
- ☐ *A How-To Guide for Teaching English Language Learners in the Primary Classroom* by Pat Barrett Dragan (2005) (Grades K–2)
- ☐ *When English Language Learners Write* by Katharine Davies Samway (2006) (Grades K–8)
- ☐ *Writing Sense* by Juli Kendall and Outey Khuon (2006) (Grades K–8)
- ☐ *English Learners, Academic Literacy, and Thinking* by Pauline Gibbons (2009) (Grades 4–8)
- ☐ *Balanced Literacy for English Language Learners, K–2* by Linda Chen and Eugenia Mora-Flores (2006) (Grades K–2)
- ☐ *English Language Learners Day by Day, K–6: A Complete Guide to Literacy, Content-Area, and Language Instruction* by Christina Celic (2009) (Grades K–6)
- ☐ *Literacy Instruction for English Language Learners* by Nancy Cloud, Fred Genesee, and Else Hamayan (2009) (Grades K–8)
- ☐ *Writing Between Languages: How English Language Learners Make the Transition to Fluency* by Danling Fu (2009) (Grades 4–12)
- ☐ *Smart Answers to Tough Questions* by Elaine Garan (2007) (Grades K–5)
- ☐ *How to Align Literacy Instruction, Assessment, and Standards* (Chapter 8) by Nancy Akhavan (2004) (K–5)

Ponder Box for Teachers

- How many students in your classroom are English language learners?

- What are some ways that you already modify your writing instruction for ELLs?

- What other strategies are you considering to modify your teaching of writing for ELLs?

Ponder Box for Coaches and Principals

- How many students in your school are English language learners?

- What structures could you implement to provide time for teachers to brainstorm ideas for modifying writing instruction for ELLs?

- Would this be a helpful topic to explore at a staff meeting, in a workshop, or as a book study?

- Does your ESL/ELL teacher have some strategies to share with the staff on modifying writing instruction for these students?

Politics and Writing

It's easy to get caught up in the day-to-day details and drama of classroom life and forget the big picture. Sometimes we need to step back and remind ourselves what's most important in our teaching.

In the last chapter of *Classrooms That Work* (2007), titled "Beyond the Classroom: Ten Things Worth Fighting For," Pat Cunningham and Richard Allington state: "Research and experience tell us that what the classroom teacher does, day in and day out and minute by minute, has the greatest effect on what children learn. . . . Whereas the major efforts of a classroom teacher are rightfully expended within one classroom, we feel that you should know which beyond-the-classroom suggestions are worth whatever crusading efforts you are able to make" (285). Backed by research, here are the ten battles the authors think are worth fighting (284–92):

❶ Smaller class size

❷ Early intervention

❸ Better school libraries and better access to books

❹ Responsive special programs

❺ Extending the school day or year

❻ An end to retention and tracking

❼ Head Start/Even Start

❽ Family and community involvement

❾ Fairness in funding

❿ Teacher input on the business of running schools

In *The 9 Rights of Every Writer* (2005), Vicki Spandel devotes one chapter to each of nine rights she believes belong to every writer:

❶ The right to be reflective

❷ The right to choose a personally important topic

❸ The right to go "off topic"

❹ The right to personalize the writing process

❺ The right to write badly

❻ The right to see others write

❼ The right to be assessed well

❽ The right to go beyond formula

❾ The right to find your own voice

Most teachers know Vicki's name in connection with six-trait writing, which has had a huge impact in classrooms around the world. In this book, she speaks more broadly about what's important (and often lost) in writing instruction in the current climate of accountability and testing. At the end of the chapters, experts in the field (Thomas Newkirk, Jim Burke, and Barry Lane, among others) add their voices to Vicki's clear soprano solo. If you're a teacher, you may want to weave some quotes from these writers into your parent newsletters. Principals and coaches may want to pluck some quotes or pages from this gem of a book to share with your staff around testing time as a reminder to "smell the roses" and keep focused on what matters in the teaching of writing.

Tom Newkirk begins *Holding On to Good Ideas in a Time of Bad Ones* (2009) with an introductory chapter called "The Curse of Graphite," in which he bemoans the current climate of accountability in which "if you can't count it (preferably with a machine), it doesn't count" (4). He claims that our schools are still using the factory model of public education popular a century ago. He discusses how appealing a centrally controlled, uniform system is to politicians and administrators even though this conformity rarely leads to excellence. He links this model to "educational clutter— the piling on of objectives and requirements—that makes any form of sustained work difficult. . . . This proliferation of objectives (and programs designed to meet these objectives) contributes to one of the key features of the contemporary classroom—and I believe one of the major sources of stress for teachers" (11).

Tom asks, "Why can't we be more like doctors?" When doctors "do rounds," they share information with colleagues, pool their expertise, and both diagnosis and treatment become situational and nuanced. In contrast, "The life of the classroom is often so hectic, the teacher's attention is so consumed by minute-to-minute decisions, that there is no time or support for reflection, no opportunity to stand back and think" (39). Tom devotes one chapter to each of these six key principles:

❶ Parity between reading and writing

❷ Expressive writing

❸ Popular culture as a literacy tool

❹ Reading and writing for pleasure

❺ Uncluttering the curriculum

❻ Finding a language for difficulty

All three of these books are wide-ranging, and the ideas are bound to spark conversations and reflections about the potential for writing (and reading) to transform lives.

Once you know what's worth fighting for, you need some concrete ammunition. Every educator should have a copy of *Smart Answers to Tough Questions* (2007) at her or his fingertips. Elaine Garan gives you research, quotations, even PowerPoint slides and handouts, based on some of the most difficult questions that parents and community members raise when they challenge us about phonics and handwriting, invented spelling, and high-stakes testing. For example, when parents ask about the lack of weekly spelling lists, she lists research to share in response showing that "traditional spelling instruction requiring students to memorize words for spelling tests is ineffective and inefficient" (127). Her responses are so respectful, thoughtful, and well researched that you could dip the entire book in yellow highlighting!

In her introduction to *Literacy at the Crossroads* (1996), Regie Routman writes that "unreasonable voices outside our profession are clamoring to tell us how and what to teach" (xv). The public wants easy answers and quick fixes and a return to what they often view nostalgically as "the good old days." However, Regie pleads with teachers to become informed consumers of research, more political, and more outspoken advocates for literacy practices that will help our children.

In Seattle, it's cloudy most of the time. I'm not a native, so I still struggle with all that grayness. When the sun does poke out of the clouds for a few hours every month or so, it's amazing how much my heart lifts. That's how I felt encountering the much needed perspectives provided by these five resources. They remind me that writing is the *heart* of teaching. These days, reading, math, and standardized tests are filling up our classrooms. It sometimes feels as if writing has been stuffed into a closet, a seasonal item like gardening shorts and bathing suits. We need to give writing its rightful place in the sun.

Book List 📖

Resources to Help You Understand the Politics of Writing
Instruction

☐ *Classrooms That Work* by Patricia Cunningham and Richard
Allington (2007) (Grades K–5)

☐ *The 9 Rights of Every Writer* by Vicki Spandel (2005) (Grades K–12)

☐ *Holding On to Good Ideas in a Time of Bad Ones* by Thomas Newkirk
(2009) (Grades K–12)

☐ *Smart Answers to Tough Questions* by Elaine Garan (2007) (Grades K–5)

☐ *Literacy at the Crossroads* by Regie Routman (1996) Grades (K–8)

Families and Writing

The way you teach writing is probably quite different from the way that writing was
taught (or just assigned) when your students' parents were in school. (My definition
of parents and families includes stepparents, grandparents, guardians, older siblings,
and extended family.) How do you explain how you teach writing to families? Katie
Wood Ray and Lisa Cleaveland have some advice about communicating with parents
who want to know why kids are writing in kindergarten or why we're not using work-
books: "We can't ask them to please just read a little Brian Cambourne and Frank
Smith, a little Sandra Wilde and Lev Vygotsky so they'll understand what we're doing
with their children. We can't ask them to do the homework we've done to come to
understand this teaching. We need clear, articulate explanations for why we're doing
the work we're doing that will make sense to parents (and any other interested con-
stituents)" (2004, 49). It's part of our job to communicate with families about how we
teach writing and what parents can do to support writing at home.

In *Beneath the Surface* (2008), Ken Pransky describes how he and some of the
teachers in his district had asked parents to read to their children (or tell them stories), make sure they finish their homework independently, and come to parent
conferences. When they didn't get much response from the Cambodian families in
their school, they started asking these families about what they wanted for their children and their expectations from the school. They learned that in Cambodia, many
parents show support by deferring to the school. They teach their children to be
respectful and never question a teacher. It's the grandparents' or the monks' job (not
the parents') to tell stories, and older siblings are expected to help the younger children with their homework. They also liked parent conferences to be conducted at their
home. "It turned out that almost everything we had been telling the parents they
should do ran counter to the norms, values, and beliefs of their discourse community!
In other words, in our patronizing certainty, we had inadvertently been giving families

this message: Your ways are wrong" (27). What a powerful reminder that we sometimes need to question our viewpoint and values and actively elicit feedback so that we can become true partners in the education of the children in our community.

Research clearly shows a link between parental involvement and student achievement. I heard Patricia Edwards speak years ago and was impressed by her passion and commitment to building bridges between school and home. In her new book *Tapping the Potential of Parents* (2009), Pat recommends developing a philosophy statement for parent involvement, then presents examples. This slender book includes tips for creating a welcoming environment for parents, how to deal with the challenges some families face, and various ways in which families can become involved with their children's education. She has appealing, concrete suggestions, such as creating "traveling friends" (books that travel back and forth from school to homes, along with a companion journal). She also describes "traveling science boxes" and "parent bags" with parent information and activities.

Here are a few more ways you and your colleagues can inform families and increase parental involvement:

- Parent surveys
- Home visits
- "Good news" phone calls, notes, and emails
- Back-to-school night
- Curriculum nights or coffees
- Newsletters and websites
- Involving parents in the classroom
- Writing celebrations
- Getting dads on board
- Getting to know the community
- Using assessment as communication
- Student-led conferences

In *Literacy at the Crossroads* (1996), Regie Routman claims that reforms in the teaching of reading and writing will only be successful if we enlist parents as partners:

> We have not done our homework in keeping parents and communities informed. Parents, accustomed to weekly spelling tests, phonics drills, and worksheets, do not understand why fewer papers are coming home, why misspellings are permitted at times, and why handwriting is not necessarily being formally taught. Whenever teachers and schools change practices without informing the community of the whys and hows of that change, there is likely to be a backlash. By contrast, when parents are included in the change through parent-teacher meetings, curriculum nights, periodic letters from the teacher and/or students, open classroom doors, and open communication, the problems are minimal. (64)

Ponder Box for Teachers

- How do you provide ongoing communication with families about how writing is taught and how they can support writing at home?

- Do you have a weekly or monthly classroom newsletter?

- What aspects of your weekly or monthly classroom newsletters seem to be effective? Are there other ideas you could incorporate?

- Do you have a classroom or grade-level website where you post information for families?

- How can you provide additional information for families about your writing program at a back-to-school night or a curriculum night?

- What types of questions about writing might you include in a parent survey?

- What types of accommodations can you provide for families whose cultural values and traditions differ from those in your classroom/school/community?

- How might you provide training for parent volunteers to help during writing workshop?

Ponder Box for Coaches and Principals

- How do you provide ongoing communication with families about how writing is taught at school and how they can support writing at home?

- What information about writing in your school do you presently provide for families? What additional information could you include in the future?

- Do you have a school website where you could post information about writing for families?

- How can you provide additional information for families about your writing program at back-to-school nights, curriculum nights, or daytime meetings?

- How can you improve communication with families so that they feel welcome at school?

- What types of accommodations can you provide for families whose cultural values and traditions differ from those in your school/community?

- Would you like to explore ideas as a staff about how to involve families more in writing instruction?

We can be more successful in supporting our students as writers at school and at home when we share information and welcome parents as partners.

It's hard to be an expert in all the aspects of writing instruction! Take a few minutes to skim through this chapter again and then answer the questions in the ponder boxes. Use a highlighter to note on the appropriate rubric what aspects of writing instruction you're already doing in your classroom or school. Read the annotations on my website (bonniecampbellhill.com) for any professional books you may want to read and record the author and titles of those books you most want to read on the reading log in Appendix A. You may want to choose the two books that sound the most intriguing and see whether any of your colleagues would be interesting in forming a book study group. It's easy to become overwhelmed; remember that these ideas are a synthesis from many, many professional books and many teachers. Take a deep breath, pat yourself on the back for all you're already read and incorporated into your writing program. Then pick one or two books and one or two new ideas that you can add to your repertoire.

Book List

Resources to Help You Communicate with Families About Writing Instruction

- ☐ *Beneath the Surface* by Ken Pransky (2008) (Grades K–6)
- ☐ *Tapping the Potential of Parents* by Patricia Edwards (2009) (Grades K–5)
- ☐ *Parent Power* by Brenda Power (with CD-ROM) (1999) (Grades K–5)
- ☐ *Becoming One Community* by Kathleen Fay and Suzanne Whaley (2004) (Grades 3–6)
- ☐ *Parent to Parent* by Gerald Oglan and Averil Elcombe (2001) (Grades K–5)
- ☐ *The Parent's Guide to Literacy for the 21st Century* by Janie Hydrick (1996) (Grades K–5)
- ☐ *Supporting Your Child's Literacy Learning* by Bonnie Campbell Hill (2007) (Grades K–8)
- ☐ *Getting Dads on Board* by Jane Baskwill (2009) (Grades K–5)
- ☐ *Family Literacy Experiences* by Jennifer Roswell (2006) (Grades K–5)
- ☐ *Parents and Teachers Working Together* by Carol Davis and Alice Yang (2005) (Grades K–5)

Ponder Box for Teachers

- Where would you place yourself on the writing instruction rubric?

- Which areas do you feel are your strongest?

- Which area would you like to improve or learn more about?

- Which professional books about writing do you most want to read and discuss with colleagues?

Ponder Box for Coaches and Principals

- How can you support the teachers in your building in the teaching of writing?

- Where do you see your staff on the writing instruction rubric?

- How can you provide support for the next steps of individual teachers, grade-level teams, or the entire faculty?

- Which books about writing instruction do you want to add to your professional library?

Writing Instruction (Teacher Rubric)

Writing Instruction

NOVICE	APPRENTICE	PRACTITIONER	LEADER
☐ My instruction focuses on conventions rather than on writing strategies and the writing process; I often assign rather than teach writing	☐ I provide some instruction about writing strategies and the writing process; my students keep writing journals	☐ I explore the writing process and writer's craft, as well as teach revision and editing strategies through minilessons; I am beginning to modify my instruction for ELLs and learners with special needs; I am beginning to use mentor texts to teach writer's craft; my students keep writing folders; I provide some explanation of writing instruction and writing workshop to parents at Open House and in newsletters	☐ I provide intentional, focused minilessons (five to ten minutes) about the writing process, writer's craft, and revision and editing strategies based on my planned curriculum, as well as on assessed student needs; I use engagement strategies like "turn and talk"; I modify my instruction for ELLs and learners with special needs; I often use mentor texts and teach students to read like writers; my students keep writing folders (K–5) and/or writer's notebooks (3–5); I provide clear, ongoing communication with parents about how I teach writing and what they can do to support writers at home

Writing Instruction (School Rubric)

Writing Instruction

NOVICE	APPRENTICE	PRACTITIONER	LEADER
☐ In most classrooms, instruction focuses on conventions rather than on writing strategies and the writing process; in most classrooms, writing is assigned rather than taught	☐ In most classrooms, teachers provide some instruction about writing strategies and the writing process; a few teachers are beginning to modify instruction for ELLs and learners with special needs; in most classrooms, students keep writing journals	☐ Most teachers explore the writing process and writer's craft, as well as teach revision and editing strategies through minilessons; some teachers modify instruction for ELLs and learners with special needs; some teachers are beginning to use mentor texts to teach writer's craft; in most classrooms, students keep writing folders; in most classrooms, teachers provide some explanation of writing instruction and writing workshop to parents at Open House and in newsletters	☐ Teachers in all classrooms provide intentional, focused minilessons (five to ten minutes) about the writing process and writer's craft, as well as revision and editing strategies based on the planned curriculum as well as assessed student needs; teachers in all classrooms use engagement strategies like "turn and talk"; all teachers modify their instruction for ELLs and learners with special needs; all teachers use mentor texts and teach students to read like writers; in all classrooms, students keep writing folders (K–5) and/or writer's notebooks (3–5); all teachers provide clear, ongoing communication with parents about how writing is taught schoolwide and how families can support writers at home

Writing Conferences

Writing conferences are the lifeblood of writing instruction. But what does a writing conference look like and sound like? Quite a few books have been written about this topic, but thanks to the many DVDs of writing conferences now being produced, we can finally see and hear conversations between children and their teachers.

In *A Fresh Look at Writing*, Donald Graves states, "A rough profile of a good conference shows the child speaking about eighty percent of the time, the teacher twenty percent" (1994, 61). He recommends that we tape our conferences to monitor the balance of talk and how well we prompt students to talk about their writing. The more we know about our students as individuals, the better we know their work; and the more we know about the craft of writing, the more effectively we can use that 20 percent of a writing conference for intentional teaching.

Conferring with Students Effectively

Lucy Calkins was one of the first educators to highlight the intentional teaching that occurs during individual writing conferences. Her classic book *The Art of Teaching Writing* (1994) devotes two chapters to conferring and includes the often-quoted reminder that "we are teaching the *writer* and not the *writing*" (228). This tiny sentence contains an ocean of wisdom. Our goal is bigger than improving the title or one line or one section of a piece of writing; we're hoping to add to the pool of strategies that our students will be able to dip into for the rest of their lives as writers. We're so programmed to look for what our students *don't* know that it's often hard to look at student work through a different lens. However, if we're teaching what they *don't* know, we're often outside Vygotsky's (1978) "zone of proximal development." It's a major shift to zero in on what our students know and do well in order to help them do it better.

**Anne Klein Holds a
Writing Conference**

In the last few years, Lucy and her colleagues at Columbia Teachers College have crafted books, units of study, and DVDs that make writing conferences come to life. (The annotations on my website provide more information about these excellent resources.) *Big Lessons from Small Writers* (2005) helps you see and hear what solid writing minilessons and conferences look like and sound like in primary classrooms. You can watch video clips of writing conferences with or without voiceover commentary in which Lucy identifies the rationale for the instruction, names the specific teaching moves, and tells why those moves were chosen. You can also read about conferences in *The Conferring Handbook*, part of *Units of Study for Primary Writing* (2003). In this booklet, Lucy introduces three kinds of conferences—content, expectation, and process goals—and explains her method of teaching through guided practice, demonstration, an explanation of a strategy, and an example.

Another helpful book for primary teachers is *One to One: The Art of Conferring with Young Writers* (2005), by Lucy Calkins, Amanda Hartman, and Zoë White, which also explores the art and craft of writing conferences. The first chapter explains different kinds of conferences, includes how to set the tone of a conference, and how to structure the conference for success. Subsequent chapters delve into the specific challenges of conferring with kindergartners and English language learners. The book includes transcripts you can use to craft and revise your own conferences.

Primary teacher Doriane Marvel finds *One to One* a great resource for conferring because it not only breaks the conference down into manageable stages but also includes transcripts of each stage. Doriane says she now feels more comfortable exploring what her students need in the research stage: "Extending these conversations in such an intentional way has allowed me to have a clearer view of each writer's needs. I now feel I am providing my students with the feedback they need to immediately improve their writing. Conferences have become so much more than just a check-in."

Intermediate grade teachers and literacy coaches have begged for video clips of strong minilessons and writing conferences. We finally have them from Lucy Calkins and her colleagues on the DVD, *Seeing Possibilities: An Inside View of Units of Study for Teaching Writing, Grades 3–5* (2007). This DVD includes clips of seven writing conferences in classrooms in which teachers and students are fully engaged in writing workshop. Watching these conferences, you see how the writers do most of the talking as the teachers make eye contact, listen carefully, then leave the authors with strategies they can apply to future writing.

Lucy outlines four types of conferences focused on content, design (about format or genre), process, and evaluation. She also outlines the four essential parts of a conference: research, decide, teach, and link. In the *research* phase, the teacher watches the child write, asks some probing questions to find out what the child is doing well, and identifies some possible next steps. Then the teacher *decides* on one teaching point that will move the child forward as a writer. Next, the teacher compliments the child on a specific skill or strategy she or he is demonstrating as a writer, then *teaches* one new point with examples or through explanation and/or demonstration. Often the teacher may ask the child to practice the new skill or strategy on the spot. The teacher concludes the conference by *linking* the teaching point to the child's independent writing with the reminder that from now on the child will be able to use this new skill or strategy in his or her writing. All of this occurs in just three to five minutes!

Carl Anderson, the author of *How's It Going?* (2000), noted quite emphatically in a recent workshop that as he observes in schools across the nation, he rarely sees teachers *teach* writing strategies to students during a conference. Instead, most teachers evaluate the student's work and provide compliments. They miss the powerful next step of intentionally teaching the writer something new.

Keeping Records

Katie Wood Ray identifies record keeping as a necessary writing conference component: "Records of what we teach in each conference—the tracks of our teaching—are absolutely essential. . . . Close to an extra minute is added to each conference when we stop to record it, but it is worth the investment" (2001, 169).

Many teachers keep a notebook or clipboard and jot down what they've taught students, as well as their goals. Megan Sloan finds it more helpful to keep individual records so that all her comments about each student are in one place. She keeps a notebook (with a section for each student) organized in a simple three-column format on which she records the date, her observations, and notes about goals or next steps. She tries to confer with each of her twenty-eight students once every week and a half. She provides a detailed description of her writing conferences on pages 196–215 in her book *Into Writing* (2009). (A copy of Megan's conference form is included in Appendix D.)

Whatever sort of record you decide to use, you'll want to note three things:

▶ What the writer is doing well

▶ What strategy you taught

▶ The student's goal

Carl Anderson (2005) thinks that four or five goals are plenty for the first half of the year and that most of these goals will be about initiative, writing process, or writing well. As you glance at your notes and each student's goals, you'll be able to target each conference to what that student needs next.

Asking Questions and Deciding What to Teach

At the heart of conferring is listening intently in order to find just the right teaching point. After students have shared parts of their writing and talked about their process, it's helpful to turn their papers over so you can focus on each writer. Many teachers want to know just what to say during a writing conference. When Anne Klein sits next to a student, she begins by listening and asking open-ended questions such as "Tell me about this piece" or "Talk to me about how your writing is going." Students may not initially offer in-depth responses; it's only after modeling, opportunities to role play, thoughtfully crafted minilessons, and lots of practice that students learn how to reply to these conversation starters about their work.

Carrie tells about learning from a student during her first year of using a writing workshop:

> During writing workshop, I approached one of my first graders and asked her, "So, how's it going, Shawna?" She immediately launched into an explanation of how she had written about a time that her baby sister had thrown something at her. Then she showed me in her writing how she had added more details about what had happened and how she felt about it. I listened in amazement and then, genuinely curious, asked, "So how did you know how to do that?" She looked at me with an expression that clearly said, "You're the teacher; you should know this!" Patiently, she explained: "Well, every time you come and talk to me or anyone else about our writing you always ask us 'How's it going?' Then you start asking questions about something in our writing and we answer the questions and that helps us to know what else to write to make it even better. So I did the same thing with myself. I reread my writing and asked myself, 'What else happened and how did I feel about it?' That helped me to add these parts."
>
> I smiled at Shawna—and at how much she had taught me that day about the power of conferring with children as well as the power of being predictable in my conferring routine. I had taught several minilessons about how students might respond to my opening question in a conference and

how they could explain what they were working on. But I had not yet presented a minilesson about how good writers ask themselves questions as they write and reread their work.

The very next day, Shawna helped me begin teaching that string of lessons. Shawna's internalization of the process caused me to listen intently to what she was saying so that I would still have something new to teach her as a writer. I discovered that the next step for Shawna was to use more emphatic words when she wrote about her feelings in order to strengthen her writer's voice—a powerful lesson for a young six-year-old writer. I was learning quickly that year what Joanne Hindley states in her book—that "conferring has more to do with learning how to listen, than it does with learning what to say" (1996, 104). I needed a student like Shawna to reveal the power of open-ended questions like, "How's it going with your writing today?" I cringe to think what I would have missed if I had gone into that conference with a set agenda without listening to the insights and reflections of this wise young writer!

The hard truth is that even though we try to have meaningful and practical one-on-one conversations with our students, they sometimes ramble on and we get sidetracked. It's easy to become so worried about "doing conferences right" that we either avoid or overstructure them. We get bogged down asking, "What should I do during conferences?" What are some good questions to ask?" and "How do I decide on my teaching point?"

In *Crafting Writers* (2008), Elizabeth Hale writes, "Conferring is not about *knowing* what to teach, it's about *deciding* what to teach" (152). Our decisions about *what* to teach will be based on our curriculum and standards, the focus for our unit of study, and what we know about each individual writer. Here are a few tips for effective conferences:

- Ask open-ended questions like "How's it going with your writing?"
- As you listen, look at the student, not the paper.
- Always start with a compliment about the writer's strengths.
- The pen stays in the hands of the writer.
- Be a *reader* first, not a *corrector*.
- Teach only one or two things during a conference.
- Increase your wait time.
- Celebrate approximations.
- Give the student an opportunity to try the strategy while you're there or to tell you where he or she might apply the tip.
- Take notes about the conference.
- Leave the student with a goal and a plan of action.

Individual conferences are very short and focused—two to five minutes. The rest of the time you circulate through the classroom helping students who are stuck, providing encouragement or suggestions, and taking anecdotal notes. Most teachers confer with students at their tables, allowing other students nearby to listen in and benefit from the conversation. In most classrooms, students may also request a conference when they need help. The reason conferences are so powerful is that you're individualizing your instruction—teaching just the strategy or concept (often linked to your unit of study) this particular student needs on this particular day. Conferences also help you really know each and every one of the writers in your classroom.

One of the best ways to figure out what to teach is to get together with other teachers and examine a few writing samples, talking about what each writer did well and what your teaching point might be. As you share ideas and confer with students in your classroom, predictable patterns will emerge. For instance, once they've broken the length barrier, second graders often write bed-to-bed stories, filled with "and then . . . and then . . . and then. . . ." For many of these students, learning to find a focus and zero in on one specific moment might be the next logical teaching point. One of the most helpful parts of *Assessing Writers* (2005), by Carl Anderson, are his two-column charts, "If I see this . . ." next to "I might . . . ," in which he lists ideas for next steps about writing with detail, developing writing territories, structuring writing, and more.

Anne Klein and her colleagues used Carl's first book, *How's It Going?* (2000), as one of their book studies, and everyone in the group became much more comfortable with writing conferences. Reading the book and talking about it with colleagues helped them realize how a conference provides focused instruction, whether it's short (popping in) or long (focusing on a specific skill). Carl reminds us how important it is to be "real" so that your students know you as a person and that you know and care about them. He describes the conversation-like nature of a writing conference: "You probably hear a certain kind of talk—it's intimate, personal, shared. This is the kind of feeling I want to create as I talk with students about their writing" (7). Anne Klein adds, "There's a very human side to what he's talking about—it's more than just teaching. I think one of the things I like best about Donald Graves, Ralph Fletcher, and Carl Anderson (among others) is their focus on students as individuals—more than just students to be taught. It's the relationship teachers have with their students that matters most."

Creating a Teacher-as-Writer Notebook

Since a critical part of the conference is to teach each student one new tip for writing, it's helpful to have some tools at your fingertips to use as you model new strategies. As we were editing this book, I was fortunate enough to hear Carl Anderson speak at a workshop in Seattle. He showed a video clip from *Strategic Writing Conferences* (2009) in which he uses his own writer's notebook as a teaching tool, dabbling with various strategies students might find helpful. He explained that he creates this notebook each year for just this purpose.

For years I've kept black spiral-bound journals and have tried sharing excerpts with students, but the writing I do has a specific purpose. I jot down ideas I learn from books and speakers like Carl Anderson, record insights gained from my travels, and keep lists of the books I read (along with pertinent quotes). But since most of my writing is professional and I don't have my own classroom, my writing seldom provides an appropriate model for writing conferences. What I needed was a teacher-as-writer notebook in which I could address issues that all writers encounter with examples that would be helpful to elementary students. I decided to start a notebook like Carl's in which I could demonstrate how I make a chart listing possible people, places, events, and ideas I might want to explore. I could draft a few pieces and use various revision strategies, such as "nudge paper," an asterisk (*), or arrows. I could model Georgia Heard's idea of a heart map (1999, 108–16) and draft a few poems and "small moments." I used to model my own writing with kids on chart paper or the whiteboard for whole-class minilessons; Carl inspired me to also create my own teacher-as-writer notebook to model and share my writing during individual conferences.

Creating a Conferring Notebook or Writer's Toolkit

You might also want to collect a handful of mentor texts based on various genres and your units of study to keep at your fingertips. Sparked by ideas she encountered at a summer training session presented by Columbia Teachers College's Reading/Writing Project, Trudy Nelson set up a conferring notebook filled with plastic sleeves and tabs for each of her units of study in which she includes copies of her favorite anchor texts. When she gathers her children's writing folders, Trudy often finds pieces in which her students have used strategies or skills that she taught during a writing minilesson. With their permission, she makes a quick copy and tucks it into her conferring notebook to use as a mentor text to help support children who might need extra coaching or examples. During writing conferences, she keeps her eyes out for student work she can use to demonstrate effective techniques. Trudy says, "The notebook has been really beneficial for those students who learn best from a visual prompt of how they could improve their writing. They can see examples of what I am teaching. I also use the notebook with students who need reminders of previous minilessons they've missed or are ready to tackle—I can show them the 'target' they're aiming for. The conferring notebook is a quick and easy way to reinforce teaching points and provide concrete examples as models."

Cheryl Perkins has created what she calls a "writer's toolkit." She carries this three-ring binder

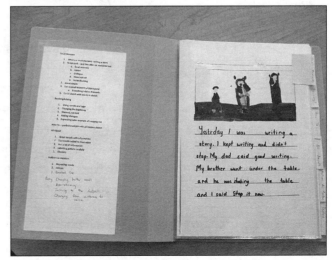

Trudy Nelson's Conferring Notebook

around as she confers with her first graders during writer's workshop. Since Cheryl recognizes the importance of *showing* (not just *telling*), the plastic pockets in her toolbox hold a variety of things she can use for her teaching points:

> ❫ Mentor texts (student writing or a selection from a piece of children's literature) marked with sticky notes highlighting examples of what she wants to show a child (such as incorporating dialogue, adding details, using speech bubbles)
>
> ❫ Copies of posters she has used during a minilesson
>
> ❫ Topic possibilities (for when students are stuck)
>
> ❫ ABC grids, word wall words, or other tools
>
> ❫ Various stages of a story (just a picture, a picture with labels, pictures with labels and a sentence)

Cheryl uses these mentor texts and examples based on what her students are working on and what they need next, and she doesn't have to hunt them down—they're right at her fingertips. Does the idea of a teacher-as-writer notebook, a writer's toolkit, or a conferring notebook sound intriguing? What would you include?

One of the things that strikes me when I watch videos of master teachers like Regie Routman, Carl Anderson, Ralph Fletcher, and Lucy Calkins conferring with students is the clear gradual release of responsibility as they first demonstrate a strategy with an anchor text or their own writing, then provide guided practice before sending the writer off to try the technique in her or his own writing. It's this "we do it" aspect that makes new learning "doable" for writers.

Cheryl Perkins with Her Writer's Toolkit

Whole-Class Conferences

Regie Routman (2005) believes strongly in the power of whole-class sharing that occurs when an individual conference is conducted publicly. When students listen in on a conference, they pick up strategies for effective questioning, as well as tips on writing. This whole-class conference can occur either at the beginning or end of writing workshop. It's important to keep track of who has shared in this way so that all your students have this opportunity. Regie always begins by celebrating what the student did well, then identifies one strategy that the child could incorporate into his or her repertoire of writing techniques. She writes, "Always start with a compliment for something the writer has done well. We have the power to encourage the writer for the whole year or destroy his desire and energy to write with one negative comment" (224). She reminds us that we want students to internalize the questions we model so that they can eventually ask those questions of themselves as they become independent writers, much like Shawna demonstrated in Carrie's classroom.

Small-Group Conferences

In Chapter 1, I discussed guided writing as a structure in writing workshop in which the teacher meets with one or more students to provide support for common specific needs. A number of authors have written about this structure as small-group conferences. As a classroom teacher, Holly Slaughter tried to confer with four or five kids each day in order to touch base with all her students at least once a week (and more often with some students). However, despite her best intentions, each week she fell short of her goal. So she decided to keep the number of daily conferences the same, but to hold some of them with small groups of writers. In *Small-Group Writing Conferences: How to Use Your Instructional Time More Efficiently* (2009), Holly describes how her small-group conferences now fall into two categories. She conducts *skill-group conferences* when several students need help with the same thing. She also holds *table conferences* when she wants a small gathering of students to notice a strategy (often from her minilesson) that one of them has successfully attempted. She groups students with common needs in order to teach more efficiently based on three questions: Who in the class is doing this *now*? Who in the class is *almost* doing this? Who in the class is *not* doing this?

Another way Holly forms groups is to list all her students' names down the left side of a piece of paper and then list the skills she's taught in unit minilessons across the top of the page. She then rates each student using a simple rubric (1–4) or a symbol (+, ✓, or –). By scanning the chart, it's easy to form temporary groups of students who need further instruction or support. Since her small-group conferences last about ten minutes, she is able to hold two individual conferences and one group conference each day. Other teachers might prefer to confer with one student each day in addition to holding two group conferences. Some teachers conduct individual conferences two days a week and group conferences the other three days. Within any of these structures, you'll be able to meet with eight to ten students in just one day.

In her Choice Literacy article "The Five-Minute Solution: Mini-Groups After Mini-Lessons to Maximize Conferring Time" (2006), Aimee Buckner describes how she uses voluntary minigroups as a bridge between her minilessons and individual conferences. After a minilesson, she invites any students who want more explanation or extra help to linger with her for five or ten minutes for more focused instruction. Sometimes only a few students need help, while at other times ten or more students get that extra boost as she thinks aloud, provides more examples, or answers questions. She can then follow up during individual conferences. Aimee's minigroups allow her to differentiate her teaching more efficiently.

Eliza Lewis Confers with a Group of First Graders

Another technique for working efficiently is what Mark Overmeyer calls "stacking the deck" (2005, 93–97). Mark finds he can be more effective and efficient if he reads one sample from each student in advance. On a sheet of paper, he lists each student's name and one specific positive comment, one content suggestion, and one recommendation. Reading the pieces in advance saves time, and his lists help him note common needs, which he can then address in a whole-group minilesson or in a needs-based small-group conference.

If you're a teacher in the intermediate grades (or in middle school) and are already comfortable with writing workshop, Carl Anderson's new product, *Strategic*

Book List

Resources for Helping You Conduct Conferences

☐ *The Art of Teaching Writing* (Chapters 13 and 14) by Lucy Calkins (1994) (Grades K–5)

☐ *Conferring with Primary Writers* (DVD) by Lucy Calkins, Amanda Hartman, and Zoë White (2005) (Grades K–2)

☐ *Big Lessons from Small Writers* (DVD) by Lucy Calkins and colleagues (2005) (Grades K–2)

☐ *One to One* by Lucy Calkins, Amanda Hartman, and Zoë White (2005) (Grades K–2)

☐ *The Conferring Handbook* (from *Units of Study for Primary Writing*) by Lucy Calkins (2003) (Grades K–2)

☐ *Seeing Possibilities: An Inside View of Units of Study for Teaching Writing, Grades 3–5* (DVD) by Lucy Calkins and colleagues (2007)

☐ *How's It Going* (pages 146–50) by Carl Anderson (2000) (Grades 2–8)

☐ *Writing Essentials* (with DVD) (Chapter 9) by Regie Routman (2005) (Grades K–8)

☐ *Small-Group Writing Conferences* by Holly Slaughter (2009) (Grades K–5)

☐ *Strategic Writing Conferences* (with DVDs) by Carl Anderson (2009) (Grades 3–6)

☐ *Reading and Writing Connections in the K–2 Classroom* (Chapters 10 and 11) by Leah Mermelstein (2006) (Grades K–3)

☐ *Inside Reading and Writing Workshop* (DVD) by Joanne Hindley (2006) (Grades 1–3)

☐ *Collaborative Conferences* (DVD) by Linda Dorn and Carla Soffos (2007) (Grades K–6)

☐ *In the Beginning* (DVD) by JoAnn Portalupi and Ralph Fletcher (2006) (Grades K–1)

☐ *Talking About Writing* (DVD) by JoAnn Portalupi and Ralph Fletcher (2006) (Grades 3–5)

Writing Conferences (2009), will help you take writing conferences to a new plateau. This collection of four books and DVDs could be titled *Everything You Wanted to Know About Writing Conferences But Were Afraid to Ask!* In the introductory book, Carl outlines a philosophical foundation for conferences based on the gradual release of responsibility. He then provides individual books about three stages of writing (identifying topics, crafting drafts, and polishing finished projects), along with diagnostic guides to help you identify each student's needs and annotations of over a hundred conferences. He models how to assess students, diagnose their needs, and then scaffold their next steps as he focuses on the writer, not just the writing. For example, when one student is stuck and unsure of what to write, Carl asks the boy to revisit his writing and identify topics to which he continually returns. He explains how even published authors write about the same topics over and over in new ways so that this developing writer comes to understand he doesn't have to start a new topic every day. Rather than "fixing" the immediate problem, Carl has given this young writer a strategy he can apply to many writing tasks down the road. At the heart of *Strategic Writing Conferences* is the belief in the responsive nature of teaching and conferring.

Supporting Effective Writing Partnerships and Peer Conferences

Someday I want to follow Katie Wood Ray around for a week and listen to her talk to children. She has a gift for genuinely appreciating and celebrating writing, from the earliest scribbles of young children to the knock-your-socks-off writing of older students. I've found that peer conferences in the intermediate grades are fairly easy to put into place, as long as I do a lot of modeling. However, I've struggled with how to make peer conferences with younger students work. I've browsed stacks of professional books on writing, but it was Katie's unit "How to Have Better Peer Conferences" in *About the Authors* (2004) that provided the key to what I was missing. I love her honest acknowledgment that "most six-year-olds joyfully and quite innocently don't really care that much about what other people think about their writing. They still live happily in their own egocentric world" (188). So true! Rather than focusing on what the *listeners* should say, she flipped the notion of conferences upside down to put the focus on what the *writer* can get from a conference. Katie demonstrates how powerful it can be to get help from another writer as she models six different purposes for peer conferences (189):

I need some "wow!" in my writing.

I'm just stuck.

I have a question that I'm wondering about in my writing.

I need to test-drive my piece.

My ideas need to be bigger—ask me some questions.

I need someone to look at my illustrations and make sure they match my text.

These prompts are cast in "kid language," yet they're so universal that I found myself emailing Carrie with just those same needs as we wrote this book! During Katie's role plays, students see the power of learning from each other.

When you see students seek out a peer for a conference on their own, you know you're not the only teacher in the room. Let's now explore how students can learn from one another in three different formats: writing partnerships, peer conferences, and writing groups.

Writing Partnerships

In Chapter 1, I listed *sharing* as one of the components of writing workshop. One of the significant ways in which the work of Lucy Calkins and her colleagues at Teachers College have impacted the teaching of writing in the last few years is their recognition of the critical role of daily sharing through the use of writing partnerships. As with any learning, it's helpful to build your students up slowly to the point of independence. Carl Anderson, in *How's It Going?* (2000), notes that classrooms have begun using "writing partnerships" as a beginning step in the process of peer response. Right after the teaching part of the minilesson, partners have a brief opportunity to turn and talk about how they might use that teaching point in their writing for the day. These same partners respond to each other's work after independent writing. In some classrooms, students may co-write pieces of work, one as author, the other as illustrator. Some teachers create "help wanted" and "help offered" boards as a way to build on the strengths within a writing community.

In *Launching the Writing Workshop*, from *Units of Study for Primary Writing* (2003), Lucy Calkins and her colleagues recommend providing this kind of support, beginning in kindergarten. Youngsters sit next to designated long-term partners each day during the minilesson. The teacher prompts these partners to do a quick task directly connected to the lesson. For instance, if the lesson is on choosing a "small moment" for their personal narrative, you might ask partners to turn and talk to each other about a moment they remember. This brief engagement is the precursor to learning how to confer with peers independently. Most primary students crave the opportunity to *talk* to a peer but find it harder to *listen*. That's where explicit teaching and modeling come in.

In the *Launching the Writing Workshop* unit of *Units of Study for Teaching Writing, Grades 3–5* (2006), Lucy and her colleagues explain that you can also launch writing partnerships on the first day of writing workshop in intermediate classrooms. After your minilesson, students make plans for how they are going to work as effective writing partners. For the rest of the year, these partnerships become an embedded and predictable part of writing workshop. Every day, students engage with their partners right after the teaching point in the minilesson and again when they share their work at the end of the writing workshop. They examine mentor texts together and coach each other about their writing. Over time, some of these partnerships evolve into true peer conferences in which writers give and incorporate specific feedback (not an easy skill!). If you create this type of scaffolding and gradual release of responsibility from the very beginning of your writing workshop and do lots of modeling and role playing, students will soon be eager to get feedback from their writing partners.

As he's studied Lucy Calkins' books over the last three years, writing partnerships have become an essential part of writing workshop in Ben Hart's classroom of third and fourth graders. He says, "I couldn't teach writing without them!" In his classroom, the writing partnerships change with every new unit, and students work closely with their partners each day during writing workshop. They sit next to each other and turn "knee-to-knee and eye-to-eye" during the student engagement portion of the minilessons. The interactions deepen learning, keep kids actively involved, engage English language learners, and provide a chance for Ben to listen in to their conversations.

Cathy Hsu is an incredibly knowledgeable and articulate fifth-grade teacher at the Taipei American School. Last year, she chose partnerships and peer conferences as her professional goal. In this section of her journal, she reflects on this topic (you can read more about her journey in her article in the October 2009 issue of *The Reading Teacher*):

November 21: Students using partnerships productively and independently!

I have been thrilled to see the students seeking out their writing partners independently. Several partnerships surprised me with how fruitfully, seamlessly, and pleasantly they have been working together these past two days. Today, especially, I didn't give a reminder to talk to their writing partner, but there they were, eagerly going to their writing partners for response and feedback.

Charlotte and Phillip explored Shel Silverstein and Jack Prelutsky mentor texts together, read each other's poems, and constantly conferred during revision. Charlotte specifically directed Phillip to think more about word choice. In the middle of the workshop, Justin and Pauline popped out of their seats to read their drafts to each other, laughing and interacting freely. Vergil was done "exploding the moment," so he walked over and presented his revision to Louisa for review. Harrison shared his revised draft with Xiao Yang, explaining that he wanted the chance to get his partner's feedback since he was absent yesterday. Irene and Celine were working closely on their respective plays, sitting side by side, discussing their writing softly, filling their pages. Jenny and Rejina have also conferred with one another frequently, explaining that they have been revising based on what doesn't make sense to their partner. I am pleased with how several writing pairs are seeking each other out without prompting, giving each other specific feedback as we've modeled the past months, and

A Writing Partnership in Cathy Hsu's Classroom

enjoying the rapid peer response (as opposed to having to wait for my attention).

I should have been assigning writing partners all along! All those years of writer's workshop and now I see that giving kids writing partners, especially when dealing with fifth graders, is not high maintenance—it's high impact!

In *Writer to Writer* (2007), Mary Lee Prescott-Griffin also explores the power of writing partnerships, small-group writing collaboration, and cross-age writing buddies, ending each chapter with tips on how to support English language learners. She explains how texts created in collaboration with other students result in writing that is richer and more complex than either student could create alone. In addition, she writes that "writing partnerships provide a bridge between shared, modeled, and interactive writing, and the sometimes daunting task of solo composing" (3). This collaborative context can be particularly helpful for learners of English as they write, revise, edit, and talk with their peers. Mary Lee provides examples of editing buddies, fluency buddies, and research buddies. She demonstrates how charts, bookmarks, and checklists that *students* help create can remind writing partners how to support each other. I love her example of "strategy gloves" that have reminders written on each finger! Chapter 3 on cross-age writing buddies may spark some ideas about how to pair older and younger students using dialogue journals, structured writing projects, research projects, and collaborative story writing. Mary Lee extends these ideas into writing partnerships at home through literature response journals and book bags, dialogue journals, buddy biographies, word hunts, and resource searches.

Peer Conferences

How do writing partnerships evolve into true peer conferences? In *How's It Going?* (2000), Carl Anderson suggests that if you feel your students are ready to give each other specific feedback in peer conferences, the best way to teach them how is to place two students in a "fishbowl" in the middle of a circle, with the rest of the class watching. First provide a small amount of background information, then ask the two students to begin. Throughout their peer conference, periodically stop and name the techniques they are using and offer one or two suggestions.

On pages 51–59 of the *Finished Projects* booklet from *Strategic Writing Conferences* (2009), Carl provides the script of a video clip (included on a DVD) in which he coaches two students who are just learning how to provide and use feedback in a peer revision conference. Carl, using his own writing as a model, explains a strategy for giving and using peer feedback and then coaches the pair in their first wobbly attempts.

A Peer Conference in Jemma Hooykaas' Classroom

Writing Groups

In his book *When Writing Workshop Isn't Working* (2005), Mark Overmeyer explains how he transforms literature circles into what he calls revision circles. His students meet in groups to share their work and then explain one thing they revised and why. They then ask the group for advice about other possible revisions and record their changes on a revision form.

Mary Lee Prescott-Griffin, in *Writer to Writer* (2007), also describes how after you have established a sense of community and trust in the first month of school, you can launch small-group heterogeneous writing groups of four to five students in intermediate classrooms. She describes four types of small-group collaborations: peer response or editing groups; research and special interest groups; story composing groups; and study groups.

Chapter 4 of *Independent Writing*, by Colleen Cruz (2004), contains the most thought-provoking ideas I've found in any book about writing conferences; I'm still mulling them over. Colleen begins by discussing how writers need feedback—from people who provide deadlines, who have more expertise about the topic or about writing, or who can help solve problems. As I wrote this book, my publisher set (and reset) deadlines that kept me at my computer well past the time when the rest of my family went to bed. When Carrie and I felt bogged down by our ever expanding to-do list, we divided up tasks in our back-and-forth emails. I bombarded all the teachers and coaches I knew with questions and requests for examples and clarification. I relied heavily on Sandy Figueroa's expertise about English language learners and my editor's ability to tighten my sentences and rein in my verbosity. I wrote within the warm embrace of a writing community, which is exactly what we want for our students. Colleen provides four forums for the student writers in her classroom, which she describes in detail:

❶ Writing colony (the whole class)

❷ Writing salon (permanent or semi-permanent group of six to eight students)

❸ Writing club (group of three to five students that meets for a specified number of weeks)

❹ Writing partnership (two students become partners for a brief period or all year)

Colleen doesn't expect peer conferences to happen automatically. She provides lots of modeling in which she uses her own writing to demonstrate what sorts of changes are possible and how to receive feedback gracefully. Students learn to start with a compliment that is honest but kind, then make specific suggestions and provide examples from other authors' work. She describes how "salons" sometimes spring up naturally when a group of kids choose to collaborate as they bounce ideas off one another and talk through the hard parts. She writes, "Salons are often jumping-off points for other relationships such as partnerships and clubs; however,

I believe this particular configuration of students cannot be teacher-created. . . . It must come naturally from the students" (113).

Writing clubs, like writing salons and literature circle groups, are student-led and based on common interests or needs. Some writing clubs study specific genres or mentor authors. In addition, each Friday, Colleen provides "seminars" on specific topics. Unlike minilessons, she posts the topic in advance and students sign up to attend either individually, with a partner, or sometimes as an entire writing club. The seminars are usually longer than minilessons, and students leave with material they can take away and use. Topics might include how to write a play or comic book, or tips about writing effectively with a partner. The seminars are sometimes taught by parents, other teachers, students from other classes, or experts in her classroom. Attendance at seminars is always optional.

This chapter synthesizes ideas from many experts and professional books about writing conferences, including writing partnerships, peer conferences, and other ways that students can learn from one another as writers. Take a minute to answer the questions in the appropriate ponder box and use the related rubric to

Book List 📖

Resources for Helping You Use Writing Partnerships and Peer Conferences

- [ ] *About the Authors: Writing Workshop with Our Youngest Writers* (Unit of Study G) by Katie Wood Ray (2004) (Grades K–2)
- [ ] *Launching the Writing Workshop* (from *Units of Study for Primary Writing*) by Lucy Calkins and Leah Mermelstein (2003) (Grades K–2)
- [ ] *Launching the Writing Workshop* (from *Units of Study for Teaching Writing, Grades 3–5*) by Lucy Calkins and Marjorie Martinelli (2006)
- [ ] *Writer to Writer* by Mary Lee Prescott-Griffin (2007) (Grades K–5)
- [ ] *Strategic Writing Conferences* by Carl Anderson (2009) (Grades 3–6)
- [ ] *How's It Going?* (pages 146–50) by Carl Anderson (2000) (Grades 2–8)
- [ ] *When Writing Workshop Isn't Working* (pages 82–84) by Mark Overmeyer (2005) (Grades 2–5)
- [ ] *Independent Writing* (Chapter 4) by Colleen Cruz (2004) (Grades 3–5)
- [ ] *Writing Circles: Kids Revolutionize Workshop* by Jim Vopat (2009) (Grades 4–12)

assess your or your school's strengths and areas for growth. If you're at the Novice or Apprentice stage on the rubric, *The Art of Teaching Writing* by Lucy Calkins will help answer questions about logistics, such as "How can I create time for conferences?" "How many conferences should I do in a day?" "How long should I spend with each student?" and "What are the other kids doing while I meet with just one student?" If you're at the Practitioner or Leader stage, the other books in the book lists address questions about what to teach, as well as more specific questions about writing partnerships and peer conferences. You can explore some of the resources listed in the chapter and on my website if you'd like to learn more about the exciting potential of writing conferences. If any of these books or DVDs sound intriguing, list them on the Professional Reading Log in Appendix A.

Ponder Box for Teachers

- How often do you confer with each student?

- How do you document your writing conferences?

- How could you hone your skills as you learn to confer effectively with students about their writing?

- What could you do to improve the quality of writing partnerships or peer conferences in your classroom?

- Which professional books or videos/DVDs about writing conferences would you like to explore further?

Ponder Box for Coaches and Principals

- Do all teachers in the school conduct writing conferences?

- Are there teachers who would be willing to have colleagues observe or videotape their writing conferences?

- How can you support your whole staff, a grade level, or a group of teachers who want to learn more about writing conferences, writing partnerships, and peer conferences?

- Which of the books and videos/DVDs listed above about writing conferences do you already have in your professional library? Which ones do you want to add to your collection?

Writing Instruction (Teacher Rubric)

	NOVICE	APPRENTICE	PRACTITIONER	LEADER
Conferences	☐ I often sit at my desk grading papers, completing administrative paperwork, or checking email while students write; I correct completed student papers and mark errors	☐ I occasionally confer with individual students; my student conferences focus primarily on editing and conventions	☐ I regularly hold individual conferences in which I often teach a new strategy; I usually direct the conversation during conferences; my conferences focus on revision and editing; my conferences are also beginning to focus on process and writer's craft; I am beginning to implement some writing partnerships (K–5) and peer conferences (3–5)	☐ I hold focused individual writing conferences using Lucy Calkins' research, decide, teach format; I use the information I gather and record to guide my individual and whole-class instruction; my conferences focus on process, writer's craft, initiative, specific writing strategies, and student self-reflection; I implement effective writing partnerships (K–5) and peer conferences (3–5)

Writing Instruction (School Rubric)

	NOVICE	APPRENTICE	PRACTITIONER	LEADER
Conferences	☐ In many classrooms, teachers often sit at their desk grading papers, completing administrative paperwork, or checking email while students write; in most classrooms, teachers correct completed student papers and mark errors	☐ Teachers in some classrooms occasionally confer with individual students; in most classrooms, student conferences focus primarily on editing and conventions	☐ In all classrooms, teachers regularly hold individual conferences in which they often teach new strategies; conferences are mostly teacher directed; in most classrooms, student conferences focus on revision and editing; in some classrooms, student conferences are also beginning to focus on process and writer's craft; in some classrooms, teachers are beginning to implement writing partnerships (K–5) and peer conferences (3–5)	☐ In all classrooms, teachers hold focused individual writing conferences using Lucy Calkins' research, decide, teach format; they use the information they gather and record to guide instruction for individual writers and the whole class; in all classrooms, student conferences focus on process, writer's craft, initiative, specific writing strategies, and student self-reflection; in most classrooms, teachers implement effective writing partnerships (K–5) and peer conferences (3–5)

Word Study and Language Conventions

Let's start with a definition. Word study is a way of analyzing the patterns of the sounds and symbols in our oral and written language through problem solving. It begins in infancy when children are first learning how to reproduce all the sounds, words, and sentences that surround them. As children grow, they continue to play with language, thus building the foundation that eventually they will connect with print. The process of writing some of those sounds leads to a beginning awareness of how to read them. In learning to read, children learn to recognize a vast number of words, which leads to an accumulation of a large bank of words they can spell. Throughout life, they accumulate an ever larger oral and written vocabulary. In late elementary school, children begin to learn the origins of words and use those patterns to continue amassing increasingly complex vocabulary with which to read, write, and understand the world around them. Our goal as teachers and parents is to support and extend this developmental progression.

First and foremost, our goal for word study should be to instill a lifetime curiosity in our students about words and how they work in our language. This fascination with words will motivate them to investigate and understand the patterns in language so they don't have to learn how to read or spell one word at a time; instead, they can extend those patterns to new words they encounter. Those same patterns will support them in acquiring new vocabulary. Years ago, spelling entailed memorizing words, letter by letter. Current research (Gentry 2004) has shown how the human brain recognizes patterns and uses patterns to learn new information. As teachers, we need to base our teaching on this research and apply the findings to our word study instruction.

The resources and ideas in this chapter are clustered around five major interwoven aspects of word study: phonological awareness, phonics, spelling, vocabulary, and other language conventions. Gay Su Pinnell and Irene Fountas authored a comprehensive *Continuum of Literacy Learning*, Second Edition (2010) in which they outline nine categories of skills, strategies, and behaviors that children need to achieve at each grade level, from kindergarten through eighth grade. The chart in Figure 5.1 shows how these five aspects relate to Fountas and Pinnell's nine categories of literacy learning. It also reinforces that we need to integrate our instruction rather than teach isolated individual skills.

Writing Curriculum

FOUNTAS AND PINNELL'S CATEGORIES OF SKILLS, STRATEGIES, AND BEHAVIORS	FRAMEWORKS FOR CHAPTER 5: WORD STUDY
Phonological awareness	Phonological awareness
Letter knowledge, letter sound relationships, high-frequency words (recognizing while reading), word meaning and vocabulary, word structures, word-solving actions	Phonics
Letter knowledge, letter sound relationships, high-frequency words (spelling), word meaning and vocabulary, word structures, word-solving actions	Spelling
Word meaning and vocabulary, word structures, word-solving actions	Vocabulary
———	Other language conventions (handwriting, punctuation, and grammar)
Early literacy concepts (often referred to in other resources as concepts of print)	

Figure 5.1

Introducing Word Study

Developing a program and articulating an approach to word study isn't easy! It's helpful to begin by creating a list of the principles of word study that could form the foundation for your program. Once you've created your list for yourself or for your school, you may want to compare it with lists in other resources.

Here is a list that curriculum consultant Bridget Doogan created based on the information from Chapter 2, "Designing a Quality Literacy Program," in *Word Matters* (Pinnell and Fountas 1998):

Word Study Principles

▶ Promote curiosity about and interest in words and the sounds of language.

▶ As an educator, build on your understanding of the reading and writing process, which includes a thorough knowledge of how letters and words work in the alphabetic system.

▶ Include instructions about self-monitoring.

▶ Incorporate individual conferences, small-group teaching, and whole-class lessons.

▶ Equip your classroom with the appropriate tools, resources, and references to support independent learning.

▶ Use systematic observation and assessment to identify children's understanding and to inform instruction.

▶ Emphasize word-solving strategies that readers and writers can apply in a generative way; help children apply techniques to many new words in different settings.

▶ Value the learners' partially correct attempts as important indicators along the way.

▶ Provide daily, active, multilevel word study opportunities.

▶ Provide specific principles and strategies that allow each learner to move forward.

▶ Make parents aware of the goals, instructional strategies, and assessment practices that document learning around word study.

Schools investigating a word study approach may want to use this chart and the information in this professional resource to evaluate what they already have in place and determine what is missing. Tanya Shahen, the literacy coach at the American School of Doha, Qatar, worked with her staff to develop agreements about best practices related to word study that are authentic, developmental, and inquiry-based:

▶ Classrooms will reflect a print-rich environment that is age and developmentally appropriate.

▶ Word study alignment and collaboration will be both vertical and horizontal.

▸ All word study activities will be differentiated (individualized, yet structured) using a variety of teaching resources.

▸ There will be a focus on an inquiry approach, explorations, and investigations about words that go beyond lists.

▸ Word study will be integrated within all aspects of the literacy program and other curricular areas.

Once you have outlined your principles and created a philosophy statement, the next step is to create a scope and sequence of skills and strategies for each of the five components of word study: phonological awareness, phonics, spelling, vocabulary, and language conventions (including handwriting, punctuation, and grammar). As you create a developmental sequence of skills in each area, you may want to refer to the *Continuum of Literacy Learning* by Gay Su Pinnell and Irene Fountas (2010) and *Spelling K–8* by Diane Snowball and Faye Bolton (1999). One word of caution is to review these lists carefully since they often have a crossover of skills from one grade to the next that tends to make each grade level's list very long. A literacy committee at your school could easily review the lists and determine which suggested skills would be more appropriate at each grade level.

As you create a developmental sequence of skills, it's important to remember that these skills should be taught in the context of authentic writing, rather than in isolation. Katie Wood Ray writes, "If you now have separate times for teaching vocabulary, spelling, handwriting, and grammar, in addition to your time for teaching writing, you might want to reconsider the necessity of this" (2006, 182). She suggests that discussions about each aspect of word study are greatly enriched when students can explore them by studying examples of well-written texts during writing workshop.

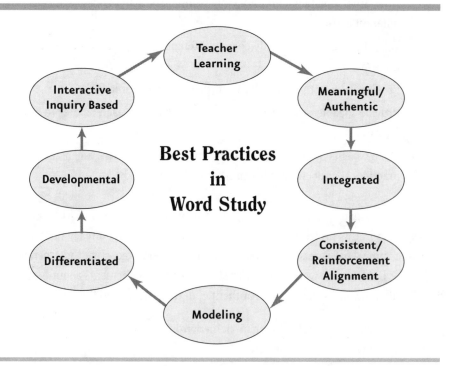

Figure 5.2 Best Practices in Word Study at the American School of Doha

It's also vital that your instruction be based on the unique needs of your students. Even if you map out your curriculum and units of study about each of these five aspects of word study, you'll need to modify your teaching based on your observations and assessments of your students. And in order to assess well, you need to have a strong understanding of the developmental nature of learning about words and learning to read and write.

Let's also take a minute to look at how word study has evolved. During the 1980s "reading wars," advocates of direct instruction and whole language argued about "part-to-whole" versus "whole-to-part" methods of teaching skills. They were seen in black-and-white terms rather than as complementary ways to teach word study, and teachers were expected to teach skills in isolation. There were extensive lists of skills that teachers taught one by one; students were expected to learn those skills and demonstrate proficiency on short tests. For instance, each week teachers sent home a list of twenty spelling words for students to memorize; students then demonstrated their proficiency on a spelling test at the end of the week. In many schools, intermediate teachers assigned a list of vocabulary words each week. Students were expected to look up the words in the dictionary, write the definitions, and then use each new word in a sentence; at the end of the week, students were given a test on which they matched the new vocabulary words to an appropriate definition. In kindergarten, teachers taught one letter and sound of the alphabet each week, often ending with *z* about nine weeks before the school year ended. Carrie remembers being required to teach seventy-five different phonetic skills to her first graders. First she had to give the class a multiple choice test on all of them at once; then she grouped the students by assessed needs, drilled them on a deficient skill (often with nonsense words) for about a week, and retested them on that one skill to check for mastery. The skills rarely connected to students' weekly reading or writing tasks.

Many teachers understood the idea that children should have authentic reading and writing experiences but were still unsure what that meant for phonics and spelling instruction. Then, *Word Matters* (1998), by Gay Su Pinnell and Irene Fountas, arrived on the professional scene and their research-based, thorough, and practical books about word study provided a general structure that could be adapted to any grade level or school community and incorporated into a workshop model of reading and writing.

According to Gay Su and Irene, "Our literacy curriculum must be designed to foster interest and joy in words and their use. Words matter because they provide us an entry into communication, humor, and pleasure. Teaching about words means recognizing—and reveling in—their meaning and their magic" (273). These remarkable educators have created a vast library of books and resources linked to these principles, in which they describe in detail how a child develops into a word solver and explorer who is curious about words and their patterns. They explain what a classroom environments needs in order to support that development within a rich literacy environment.

You may want to begin by exploring specific sections of *Word Matters* as you try out some of the strategies with your students and see the impact on their learning. The companion volume, *Voices on Word Matters* (1999), is an edited collection of contributions by many experts in the fields of emergent literacy, reading, writing, and spelling. The book begins with an overview of word study by Irene and Gay Su, followed by chapters on writing, spelling, phonics, vocabulary, and reading. Each chapter emphasizes participatory and inquiry-based word study. These two resources are invaluable as you articulate your beliefs about word study and create your curriculum for each of the components of word study.

Today, however, effective teachers no longer rely on weekly spelling tests, skill or vocabulary worksheets, or *the-letter-of-the-week* to teach word study. What we've learned from current research is that word study should be active, inquiry-based, and should be taught in the context of authentic reading and writing.

One of the biggest differences between word study today and twenty years ago is the constructivist way in which it is now approached. Rather than memorizing words or acquiring new vocabulary through passive "skill-and-drill" exercises, we now know that learning goes deeper and lasts longer when students actively construct their knowledge of how English works. They learn best by actively manipulating words and sounds through word play, engaging in word-sorting activities, discovering patterns, and by becoming "detectives" as they explore language.

In his chapter in *Voices on Word Matters*, David Booth calls attention to the investigative nature of word study: "Playing with language brings it to our conscious attention so that we can enjoy multiple aspects of language: alliteration, rhyme, and playful and intriguing uses of words. When children are invited to enjoy language by playing with it, they learn many critical early concepts effortlessly" (91). Some of our students come to school already bathed in nursery rhymes, poetry, and word games; they're familiar with the word play on TV programs like *Sesame Street*. For other students, especially those just learning English, we need to create structures that encourage this sense of exploration and experimentation. By playing with words, children construct the rules of the English language.

While *Word Matters* focuses intensely on word study instruction activities for kindergarten through second grade, if you teach third through fifth grade, Max Brand's *Word Savvy* (2004) is a helpful book for exploring ways to teach word study in an intermediate classroom. His goal is "for students to become word-savvy—to develop an understanding of how words work within the context of reading and writing, and to become excited about words as they learn to manipulate them in playful ways" (4). He accomplishes this goal by creating a specific fifteen-minute daily word study block, in addition to integrating word study throughout the rest of the day. During the first weeks of school, Max establishes routines and teaches some quick lessons about routines and strategies. He also introduces word study notebooks, with sections for spelling, vocabulary, and conventions.

How can you adapt word study to meet the needs of the English language learners in your classroom? Chapter 10 in *Balanced Literacy for English Language Learners, K–2*, by Linda Chen and Eugenia Mora-Flores (2006), contains some helpful hints and specific activities for adapting word work at each of the five stages of learning English. The authors describe how teachers can be explicit about the differences between English and other languages (for example, how the long *e* is spelled with an *i* in Spanish). They also describe how word study should incorporate aspects of morphology, so that students can grasp the patterns of word structure in English, and emphasize that second language learners need lots of opportunities to talk.

Book List

Resources for Helping You Introduce Word Study

- ☐ *Word Savvy* by Max Brand (2004) (Grades 3–6)
- ☐ *Word Matters* by Gay Su Pinnell and Irene Fountas (1998) (Grades K–3)
- ☐ *Voices on Word Matters* edited by Gay Su Pinnell and Irene Fountas (1999) (Grades K–5)
- ☐ *The Wonder of Word Study* by Lauren Berman Lucht (2006) (Grades K–2)
- ☐ *Word Study* (DVD) by Irene Fountas and Gay Su Pinnell (2005) (Grades K–3)
- ☐ *Word Journeys* by Kathy Ganske (2000) (Grades K–6)
- ☐ *Words Their Way with English Learners: Word Study for Phonics, Vocabulary, and Spelling Instruction* by Donald R. Bear et al. (2007) (Grades K–8)
- ☐ *A Day of Words* by Max Brand (2005) (Grades 4–6)

Now that we've explored word study in general terms, let's take a closer look at each of the five components of word study: phonemic awareness, phonics, spelling, vocabulary, and other language conventions (handwriting, punctuation, and grammar).

Phonological Awareness

Phonological awareness involves hearing and manipulating the sounds of words without a connection to print. Anna Lyon and Paula Moore (2003) state, "Note that phonological awareness has nothing to do with letters; it is all about sounds" (3). Prekindergarten and kindergarten teachers often engage children in playing with language in the classroom. Through word play with songs, chants, nursery rhymes, and poetry, young children usually learn how to replicate and manipulate sounds. By singing a song like "There Was an Old Lady Who Swallowed a Fly," which has the rhyming words *fly–why–die, spider–beside her,* and *bird–absurd,* children are building foundational oral language skills that they can build on in their future work in reading and writing. If you already incorporate songs, rhymes, and poems, you should feel affirmed that you are addressing phonological awareness in a playful, authentic context.

There are many components of phonological awareness, including gross differences, segmenting words, rhyming, alliteration, and phonemic awareness. In *Balanced Literacy* (2006), Linda Chen and Eugenia Mora-Flores define *phonemic awareness* as "the ability of children to isolate, identify, and manipulate [the smallest units of] spoken sounds, called phonemes" (161). Phonemic awareness can then be broken down further into initial consonant segmentation, segmentation of onset and rime, phoneme segmentation, blending phonemes, and phoneme manipulation. People often equate phonological awareness with phonemic awareness, but *phonemic awareness is just one component of phonological awareness*. Pulling information from a variety of resources, Carrie developed a prekindergarten through grade 1 phonological awareness continuum, which we've included in Appendix E.

Research clearly shows that phonological awareness is built through natural word play. *Direct explicit instruction is not necessary for most children.* Through consistent play with language at home and in their preschool and kindergarten classroom experiences, most children assimilate this awareness of oral language concepts naturally. However, it is important for teachers to monitor each child's development of these concepts and provide explicit instruction to students who are lagging behind. A lack of proficiency in recognizing and producing rhyming words, one of the components of phonological awareness, is a red flag that a student is probably going to struggle during beginning reading instruction.

One new assessment tool on the market for determining student proficiency is *Developmental Reading Assessment 2: Word Analysis* (Beaver and Clark 2004), which assesses phonological awareness, phonics, and spelling. There are six assessment items that can be administered to all kindergarten students by the end of their first semester (a total of eleven by the end of the school year) to determine which students are proficient and which students still need support. Once a teacher has administered the assessment to his kindergartners, he can then provide small-group instruction focused on helping students who need an extra boost. For the small percentage of students who still need further support after this classroom intervention, the classroom teacher should collaborate with the reading specialist or resource teacher to determine appropriate follow-up intervention. For the minority of children who need direct explicit instruction, twenty minutes two or three times a week over an eight- or nine-week period is usually plenty. Five additional assessment tasks are administered to all students throughout the second semester. Teachers in grades 1–5 can use other tasks of this same assessment to determine the phonological, phonetic, and spelling needs of their struggling readers to determine specific next steps for instruction.

What would developmentally appropriate instruction in *phonological awareness* look like in a classroom? Those of you who are preschool or kindergarten teachers are already supporting children with phonological awareness but you may not realize it. As you have children sing, chant, and recite rhymes and poetry with you, they are developing an "ear" for language and its various sounds and combinations. You stop and point out which words rhyme. You have children help you manipulate the words in those songs, chants, and poems to create new versions with new words. The focus may be on creating rhyming words or on filling in other words with the same first sound (alliteration).

Sometimes you may use the students' names for your word play, such as saying *Marilyn* and then helping the children clap on each of the three parts (syllables). You won't use the word *syllable*, but you are helping them segment words and you are doing it with the most important words to five-year-olds—their own names! Another way you can use their names is to have the children group the names by common first sounds—Alyse, Alfonso, Alfred, and Anna—in order to support initial sound segmentation. And once in a while you may help them make up silly names by manipulating phonemes: "What if we take *Justin* and take off the ending part *-tin* and add the end sound of *Jake,* which is *-ake* and make a new name, *Jusake*?" Lots of giggles will erupt as children all over the room try the same thing with their own names. This type of natural word play should occur daily in the classroom but in short playful bursts. (For further ideas about instruction for phonological awareness, see the book list in the phonics section on page 163.)

Teaching Phonics

Phonics is the ability to match spoken sounds (phonemes) with their corresponding letters and letter combinations, called graphemes. *Phonics* has to do with the connection between sounds and printed symbols. Once children have a solid initial foundation of phonological awareness and are becoming fascinated with print, you can begin helping students develop an awareness of how oral language is related to written language. You can build this awareness by teaching letters and sounds in context through authentic interactive, shared, and guided reading and writing activities during reading and writing workshop, rather than teaching "the letter of the week" or skills in isolation.

We know after decades of research that phonics drills and worksheets do *not* improve literacy. We also know that phonics instruction should mostly be completed by the end of third grade, with other aspects of word study continuing through the intermediate grades. If you're interested in exploring this topic further, Margaret Moustafa's book *Beyond Traditional Phonics* (1997) critiques research in this area and provides support for effective whole-to-part, research-based, intentional instruction. Word walls and charts, word sorts, and word study notebooks (which we'll explore in the next section), in addition to authentic reading and writing activities, are all ways to explore letter sounds, names, and words—which is phonics. Many primary teachers use individual whiteboards to engage students in actively exploring letter sounds and word patterns.

In her section in *Smart Answers to Tough Questions* (2007, 67–88), Elaine Garan discusses the role of phonics and phonemic awareness in teaching children to read:

❶ Teach the skills in context.

❷ Expose students to lots of texts through reading and writing.

❸ Keep phonics instruction and phonemic awareness in perspective as a small part of teaching reading.

❹ Teach consonants first since they're more common and regular.

❺ Focus on a few consistent rules/patterns and always teach them in context.

❻ Use big books and enlarged texts.

When Carrie was teaching in Denver she taught phonics this way:

Every day in my first-grade classroom, we focused on phonics throughout the day. There was always a morning message that I wrote and had the children read with me. I incorporated a few high-frequency words in a color different from the rest of the sentence that helped my students use these anchor words to read the rest of the text. I focused on a few different phonetic elements each week and blended those into the text of the message. For example, when we were focusing on the *sh* and *ch* digraphs, I used words like *shoes* and *chair* and wrote the blends in those words in a different color to alert the children to the new learning. Sometimes I would even leave out a word or two in the sentence, and as a group we would determine what the word should be, figure out together how to spell the word, then fill in the word. This took less than ten minutes a day and helped the children integrate the phonics we had focused on.

But that didn't end my daily phonics instruction. At the beginning of writing workshop, I often incorporated modeled or interactive writing in which I also integrated phonics. The children would help me to puzzle out the spelling of various words I was using in my own writing.

Because phonics is a strong factor in learning to read, my reading instruction overflowed with integrated phonics work. Michael Opitz (2000) defines a phonics task as "decoding a word with a given number of sounds." This decoding skill is a big part of first-grade reading instruction. Often I would focus my students on this skill as we read a large-print book together. For example, as we read the word *looking* in the responses to the phrase "Brown bear, brown bear, what do you see?" in *Brown Bear, Brown Bear* (by Bill Martin 1992), I would point out the phonetic element *ing* and stress the blended sounds in this combination of letters. Then we would brainstorm other words that ended in *ing* and write them on a chart. Children looked for words that end in *ing* in their independent and guided reading and added them to the chart as well.

Many teachers (and schools and districts) have been searching for an instructional approach to phonics that fits within a workshop model. Once they have assessed their students, many teachers rely on ideas from *Words Their Way* by Donald Bear and his colleagues (2008) and *Word Matters* by Gay Su Pinnell and Irene Fountas (1998) for *individual and small-group instruction* in order to integrate word-solving strategies into writing workshop, interactive writing, and reading instruction, including guided reading.

Many schools also find that *Phonics Lessons (Grades K, 1, and 2)*, by Gay Su Pinnell and Irene Fountas (2006) and *Word Study Lessons* (Grade 3) by Irene Fountas and Gay Su Pinnell (2006), provide the scope and sequence they need for *large- and small-group instruction* in phonics and spelling. You can easily download the teaching resources included on the accompanying CD-ROMs. In addition, the hundreds of poems and rhymes in Gay Su and Irene's ancillary *Sing a Song of Poetry* volumes (2003) eliminate the need to go searching for a specific poem to match a specific phonetic element.

Book List

Resources for Helping You Teach Phonological Awareness, Phonemic Awareness, and Phonics

☐ *Beyond Traditional Phonics* by Margaret Moustafa (1997) (Grades K–2)

☐ *Rhymes and Reasons: Literature and Language Play for Phonological Awareness* by Michael Opitz (2000) (Grades PreK–2)

☐ *The Phonological Awareness Handbook for Kindergarten and Primary Teachers* by Lita Ericson and Moira Fraser Juliebo (1998) (Grades K–2)

☐ *Words Their Way* (and related books by stages) by Donald Bear et al. (2008) (Grades PreK–8)

☐ *Word Matters* by Gay Su Pinnell and Irene Fountas (1998) (Grades K–3)

☐ *Making Words* by Dorothy Hall and Patricia Cunningham (2009) (separate books for kindergarten and grades 1–5)

☐ *Word Solvers* (Chapters 4 and 5) by Michèle Dufresne (2002) (Grades K–3)

☐ *Phonics Lessons* (with CD-ROMs) by Gay Su Pinnell and Irene Fountas (2006) (separate books for K, 1, 2)

☐ *Word Study Lessons* by Irene Fountas and Gay Su Pinnell (2006) (Grade 3)

☐ *Sing a Song of Poetry* by Gay Su Pinnell and Irene Fountas (2003) (separate books for K, 1, 2)

☐ *The Continuum of Literacy Learning: A Guide to Teaching,* 2nd ed. by Gay Su Pinnell and Irene Fountas (2010) (Grades K–2, 3–5, and K–8 versions)

☐ *Phonics, Naturally* by Robin Campbell (2004) (Grades K–1)

☐ *Sound Systems: Explicit, Systematic Phonics in Early Literacy Contexts* by Anna Lyon and Paula Moore (2003) (Grades K–3)

☐ *The Reading Edge* by Kaz Miyata and Cathy Miyata (2006) (Grades K–3)

☐ *Phonics They Use* by Patricia Cunningham (2009) (Grades K–5)

☐ *Phonics from A–Z* by Wiley Blevins (2006) (Grades K–3)

☐ *Word Journeys* by Kathy Ganske (2000) (Grades K–6)

☐ *Smart Answers to Tough Questions* by Elaine Garan (2007) (Grades K–5)

☐ *Developmental Reading Assessment 2: Word Analysis* by Joetta Beaver and Mark Clark (2004) (Grades K–5)

Ponder Box for Teachers

- As a preschool and kindergarten teacher, how do you support your students' phonological awareness? As a first- or second-grade teacher, how do you continue to support students' phonological awareness?

- What type of phonological awareness assessment are you currently using?

- What are some intervention strategies you have provided for students who are struggling with phonological awareness?

- As a kindergarten through grade 3 teacher, how do you teach phonics?

- What needs do your students have in phonics and how are you addressing those needs?

Ponder Box for Coaches and Principals

- Do you have a consistent approach to providing support to students in developing phonological awareness?

- Do you have a common phonological awareness assessment currently in place?

- What system do you have in place for intervention when students are struggling with phonological awareness?

- How is phonics taught at your school?

- What weaknesses do you notice in your school's phonics instruction? How are you addressing them?

- Is there consistency within and between grade levels?

- How could you share ideas and develop schoolwide agreements about teaching phonics and phonological awareness?

Teaching Spelling and Word-Solving Strategies

As a parent, I tacked my kids' weekly spelling lists to our refrigerator door with magnets. I dutifully quizzed them through the week with the hope they'd get a gold star on their Friday spelling test. As a beginning teacher, I divided my class into three groups based on their spelling proficiency. On Mondays I met with each group and read off the appropriate spelling list, then corrected the tests each Friday at lunch. It was easy and concrete. Most of my kids obligingly memorized the words. But all too often I would see those same words misspelled in their journals on Friday afternoon. The problem with this traditional model is that I was *assigning* and *testing* spelling words but not really *teaching spelling*.

So what's the alternative? How *do* you teach spelling? Very few schools I visit have effective spelling instruction solidly in place. In schools where teachers *do* feel good about their spelling approach, the names that pop up most frequently as authors of helpful professional books are Cindy Marten, Richard Gentry, Sandra Wilde, Max Brand, Diane Snowball/Faye Bolton, and Donald Bear and his colleagues.

Cindy Marten writes, "When our word-study instruction includes helping our students discover and then generalize key spelling rules and patterns, the amount of correct spelling in student writing increases exponentially" (2003, 68). Her book *Word Crafting* (2003) is a perfect resource for investigating spelling—by yourself, as a grade-level team, or as an entire elementary school faculty. Spelling *is* important. In his introduction to *Word Crafting*, Donald Graves writes, "In a survey of American parents on the importance of major areas of the curriculum, reading was first, mathematics second, and spelling third. Principals and teachers know that if spelling is neglected, parents will be critical. Cindy Marten's book fills an important void in providing lasting spelling power for students" (vii). That's high praise from the father of writing workshop!

Cindy claims that we don't have to write our own spelling curriculum or purchase a spelling program; we just need to learn more about how spelling develops and then teach spelling as a craft in the context of authentic writing. Cindy's synthesis of six key research articles on spelling (27–31) is a helpful starting point for discussions about spelling. Cindy explains that we need to help our students develop a spelling consciousness. They must care about their writing enough to recognize that spelling errors interfere with the reader's ability to concentrate on meaning. By using conventional spelling, they are being considerate of their readers and making a good impression. You might want to weave her research and tips into your newsletters.

It's also important to understand the developmental nature of spelling. Just as babies make approximations as they learn to speak, children's spelling takes a predictable path as they journey toward conventional spelling. As Elaine Garan (2007) says, "Invented spelling is a necessary and temporary developmental stop on the path to conventional spelling" (116). Children's invented spelling has two additional benefits. First, it provides a context for teaching letter names and sounds during writing workshop. In addition, these approximations are a window into our students' thinking about language and help us identify the next teaching point within their "zone of proximal development." We can explore spelling rules and patterns through the use of word sorts and word walls, we can point out spelling through modeled and shared writing, but the most important thing we can do to help young writers is to immerse them in authentic reading and writing.

Once we foster a spelling consciousness in our students and understand the developmental stages, our next step is to learn how to assess spelling development and diagnose difficulties. Cindy includes a series of simple, teacher-friendly inventories in her appendix based on *Words Their Way* inventories: "The inventory is designed to tell us the stage at which the student's linguistic knowledge begins to break down" (40).

That gap becomes our teaching point and enables us to create flexible groups of students with similar needs for instruction as we teach spelling patterns, help our students memorize frequently misspelled words, and, most important, immerse our students in lots and lots of reading and writing. The appendix also contains helpful websites, and lists of poems and children's books that support word study.

Cindy also describes in detail the five components of a solid, research-based word study program (65–82):

❶ Teaching students spelling strategies

❷ Helping students memorize high-frequency words

❸ Teaching students to generalize spelling patterns

❹ Creating conditions that develop spelling consciousness

❺ Communicating with parents about your methods

One of the unique aspects of her book is her notion of approaching spelling with an inquisitive, exploratory stance and a sense of play: "One of the key elements of word crafting is that we work to create meaningful contexts in our classrooms that help our students become intrigued by words. Yes, we are looking at individual letter sounds and word patterns, but we are doing it in a spirit of engagement and inquiry" (23).

Are you a good speller? Or do you find spelling a challenge? In most workshops and schools, I find that about a fourth of the teachers in the room are in the first group; another fourth sheepishly admit that spelling is not their strong suit; the rest fall somewhere in between. Research shows that no matter how spelling is taught, 20 percent of the population will remain poor spellers (Garan 2007, 122). But teachers who aren't strong spellers still work effectively with students, communicate with parents, and have a good life! What have they learned to do? They use the spell-check program on their computer, spell by analogy (I think of *nose* when I'm deciding between *choose* and *chose*), or write down several different spellings to see which one looks right. Max Brand (2004) often writes a common misspelling on the board; he and his students then talk about all the strategies that might help them figure out the correct spelling of that word. Spelling then becomes part of a conversation and an inquiry into how English works.

I grew up in Turkey and quickly learned that the great thing about the Turkish language is that it's totally phonetic. Anyone can pick up a book and the words sound like they are written. If only English were that easy! We've assimilated words from many other countries, and many of the rules we teach kids have exceptions. So what rules do you think hold up best? (This would be a great question to pose at a staff meeting.) In the appendix of *My Kid Can't Spell!* (1997, 83–84), Richard Gentry recommends five easily taught rules:

❶ The *qu* rule (*q* is always followed by *u*)

❷ The syllable rule (every syllable has a vowel or *y*)

❸ The silent *e* rule (when words end in silent *e*, drop the *e* when adding endings beginning with a vowel and keep the *e* when adding endings beginning with a consonant)

❹ Changing *y* to *i* (when the singular form ends with a consonant plus *y*, change the *y* to *i* and add *es*; when the singular form ends with a vowel plus *y*, add *s*)

❺ The *ie* or *ei* rule:

> Write *i* before *e*
> Except after *c*
> Or when sounded like *a*
> As in *neighbor* and *weigh*.
> *Weird* and *neither*
> Aren't the same *either*.

He goes on to list eighteen exceptions.

After reading Richard's book, I decided to investigate the *ie/ei* rule. My oldest son's name is Keith, so we already had one exception. I put a sticky note on the refrigerator and for a year my whole family wrote down as many exceptions as we could. Anne Klein tried the same idea in her classroom (the accompanying photo shows the chart they made). Rather than giving students a list of rules and exceptions, we can make spelling active and engaging if we approach word study with a spirit of inquiry. Students become actively engaged as they help Anne create charts about spelling strategies that they can then use for discussions and as references.

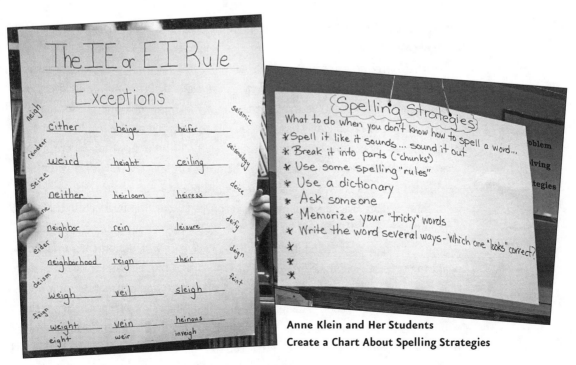

**Anne Klein and Her Students Create a List of
Exceptions to the IE/EI Rule**

**Anne Klein and Her Students
Create a Chart About Spelling Strategies**

Students can also rely on friends and colleagues to proofread anything that they send out into the world. Colleen Cruz (2008) states that "perhaps the most handy tool we have and yet probably the one we teach students to use the least is spelling experts" (40). Who are the spelling experts in your classroom? (When my son's kindergarten teacher wrote "punctuation expert" on his hand, he wouldn't take a bath for three days!) Just as you sometimes ask your spouse or the teacher next door to spell a word for you or edit something you've written, students can learn when and how to ask the spelling experts in their classroom for assistance. When editing, students can "have a go" at writing a word or ask a friend for help before coming to you for the correct spelling of a word. When you just "give them the word," you're doing all the work. Approximating, scrutinizing the word, and talking about spelling with their peers all promote *active* engagement with language.

How do your kids feel about spelling? In answer to his survey at the beginning of the year, one of Max Brand's students wrote, "I absolutely hate spelling tests. They pour stress all over me" (2004, 16). Anne Klein has her students complete the following spelling survey at the beginning of the year:

❶ Are you a good speller? Why do you think so?

❷ What do you do when you don't know how to spell a word?

❸ What are other ways to figure out how to spell a word?

❹ What kinds of words are hard for you to spell?

❺ How do people get to be good spellers?

❻ When is correct spelling important?

Instead of just mulling over the answers, Anne leads classroom discussions about each of these topics and creates anchor charts based on their responses.

What words do you have trouble spelling? I still get confused by *embarrassed, millennium, accommodation, occurrence, ecstasy,* and *occasional,* no matter how many times I use them. (I've written them in my address book under *S* for handy reference!) Max Brand (2004) has his students draw a grid on the inside cover of their word study notebook (a square for each letter) where they then record high-frequency words they often misspell. It's helpful to develop awareness of your spelling challenges and a strategy for spelling those words correctly.

Intermediate teachers looking for a resource for spelling instruction that is straightforward, easy to understand without extensive training, sensible (two fifteen-minute lessons a week!), and includes all the necessary instructional materials may want to purchase *Spelling Strategies and Patterns* (2008), by Sandra Wilde. Sandra has researched and written about spelling development and instruction for a number of years and this book is delightfully practical. She acknowledges up front that "most of the words that we know how to spell are acquired through reading, not intentional memorization" (vi) and that the two most important activities to support spelling growth and proficiency are reading and writing. Nevertheless, as students are building their knowledge of spelling, they still deserve a small amount of explicit spelling instruction. No other professional resource is as realistic and sensible about spelling instruction!

Sandra's book includes sixty-five spelling lessons (thirty-two on strategies and thirty-three on patterns). The strategy lessons help students develop spelling techniques they can use over and over, while the pattern lessons help them notice recurring letter combinations. Sandra doesn't suggest that students *memorize* numerous rules; she recommends that they *explore* and *understand* strategies and patterns. She recommends presenting one fifteen-minute strategy lesson and one fifteen-minute pattern lesson each week. Students also keep track of their personal word lists, strategies, and insights in a spelling or word study journal. A highlight of the appendix is the listing in increments of the 500 high-frequency words that a school could use to create grade-level lists of "no excuse" words. The accompanying CD-ROM includes video clips of Sandra teaching spelling lessons and interacting with students, as well as her comments about the spelling in student samples. Any intermediate grade teacher can pick up *Spelling Strategies and Patterns* and within half an hour have a handle on the overall picture of a do-able spelling approach.

After you've read some books about teaching spelling, you may want to include a paragraph or two about how you teach spelling in your classroom newsletter or in a handout for back-to-school night. You and your colleagues could also create a common philosophy statement similar to this one from the American School in London:

> As a Lower School faculty, we are committed to being conversant with the latest research on the teaching of spelling and to employing this knowledge in our work with students.
>
> As research demonstrates, we believe that spelling is interrelated and interconnected with all academic subjects and should not be taught in isolation. An effective spelling program helps children recognize and develop the strategies and habits of competent spellers, while always keeping in mind that the purpose of spelling is to improve the quality of writing by making it easier for others to read their writing.
>
> We believe spelling matters. Children should do their best in spelling, since it is an important component in the writing process. At the same time, we believe it is important for children to be encouraged to take risks with their writing, such as using invented spelling, especially in the early stages of writing development. It is also important for them to discover spelling strategies, patterns and monitoring systems that are effective.

You'll also want to articulate some guiding principles related to spelling, perhaps using Regie Routman's list from *Conversations* (2000, 118–19) as a starting point:

▶ Look for what students use but confuse.

▶ A step backward is a step forward.

▶ Use words students can read.

- Compare words "that do" with words "that don't."
- Sort by sound and sight.
- Begin with obvious contrasts.
- Don't hide exceptions.
- Avoid rules.
- Work for automaticity.
- Return to meaningful texts.

Under the leadership of their principal, Julie Ryan, the staff of the American School in London (ASL) created a list of spelling goals for students, followed by the instructional components that help students meet these goals:

Spelling Goals

- Students will be able to take risks in spelling appropriate to their developmental stage.
- The ASL community (teachers, students, administrators, and parents) will develop an awareness of the importance of strategic word study in and out of the classroom.
- Students will understand that accurate spelling makes them better writers, readers, and communicators.
- Students will see themselves as confident spellers who are developing spelling consciousness and care about words being spelled correctly.
- Students will be able to understand the orthography of spelling—how words are formed and related based on sounds, patterns, and meaning.
- Students will learn words that they spell frequently and try to apply them consistently within their writing.
- Students will be able to purposefully implement spelling strategies in written work.
- Students will use a variety of resources to help with spelling.

Spelling Instruction Components to Meet Goals

- The ASL community will encourage risk taking and will value writing and ideas appropriate to the stage of development of student spelling.
- Teachers will communicate tips for spelling work at home through reports, conferences, coffees, home word games, and newsletters.
- Teachers will provide opportunities to share work in progress, to build editing skills, and to share completed work.
- Teachers and students will monitor progress through a variety of ongoing formal and informal assessments to determine each student's developmental level.

- Teachers will explicitly teach various methods for memorizing high-frequency words identified by the school as appropriate for students' developmental level.

- Teachers will model spelling strategies through authentic reading and writing and instructional word work to support students in generalizing spelling sounds, patterns, meanings, and rules.

- Teachers will show students how to use a variety of spelling tools (such as dictionaries, Franklin Spelling Ace electronics, word study books, word walls) and provide regular opportunities to use them.

Let's now take a closer look at how word sorts, making words, and word walls can become integral parts of your spelling and word study program.

Word Sorts and Making Words

In a word sort, children place words into categories that either they or the teacher develop in order to discover patterns and generalizations about words and spelling. In *Voices on Word Matters* (Pinnell and Fountas 1999) Jerry Zutell presents a brief history of word study, then explains the main types of word sorting: picture sorts, concept sorts, spelling sorts, closed sorts (when the teacher determines the categories), or open sorts (when students choose the categories).

One of the most helpful books about word sorting is *Words Their Way* (2008), by Donald Bear and his colleagues. This comprehensive research-based book has revolutionized word study in schools worldwide. The basic premise is that word study should be differentiated according to five developmental stages of student proficiency (emergent, letter name–alphabetic, word patterns, syllables and affixes, and derivations). The authors include an extensive (but easy-to-use) assessment for determining a student's stage, as well as a scope-and-sequence outline of next steps. They also offer ways to organize your word study and include some sample schedules. An accompanying CD-ROM includes word sorts for each developmental stage, along with supporting instructional materials. Individual professional resources about specific developmental stages are also available (such as *Words Their Way: Word Sorts for Letter Name–Alphabetic Spellers* by Francine Johnston and colleagues, 2009). The companion website is updated continually. (The necessary professional development is best provided by an outside consultant or by teachers who have already used this program in their own classrooms.)

First-grade teacher Michelle Morten says, "*Words Their Way* is my favorite resource for teaching spelling. I love how it gets the kids into patterning, and it's easy to tie into shared reading because there is a poem for almost every word sort." Michelle provides many different ways for her primary students to manipulate letters and words. Students use letter cubes for sight words and replicate their spelling words using letter tiles, Lego cubes, and colored markers. She finds that once the routines of sorting and follow-up activities have been established, the students are able and eager to notice word patterns, create new words, apply the patterns in their writing, and discuss patterns with ease. By differentiating the word sorts and working with small groups, she can attend to what the students are "using but confusing" in their spelling.

Word-sorting activities are not just for primary students. Kate Morris and Sherri Ballew also use *Words Their Way* word sorts in their fourth-grade classrooms. This year, Sherri connected the words to the students' reading: "I started meeting with groups about their sorts and helping them come up with a spelling 'rule' that showed what they were studying that week. Something like, 'When making a word that ends with *y* plural, you drop the *y* and add *ies*.' Then, instead of testing them on a list of words from their sort, I asked them to write what spelling rule they studied and show examples of how to use it. I also asked them to look for their spelling words in their 'just right' chapter books during the week."

Word Sorting Activities in Michelle Morton's Primary Classroom

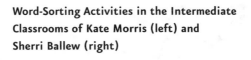

Word Walls

Students also need to learn how to spell high-frequency words. One way to ensure this is to create a "word wall." In kindergarten classrooms, children often begin to read by learning the letters and sounds in their own name and the names of their friends, so you may want to place students' photographs beside their names. Later in the year in kindergarten and in first grade, teachers often begin a more intentional focus on letter sounds and blends using their word walls. Kendra Daly taught her students short vowel sounds by linking them to hand signals. She then took pictures of the kids saying the sound and making the action and added those to her word wall. The visual reminder of the kinesthetic movement was particularly helpful for her many English language learners. As the year progresses in first grade, teachers can up the ante with discussions about vowel combinations and word families.

By second grade, word wall words include high-frequency words and more irregular spellings, as well as contractions. Megan Sloan has students collect "interesting words" for a word wall. Word walls in intermediate grades contain high-frequency words for the appropriate grade level, contractions, homophones, compound words, and words with common prefixes and suffixes. You can also create word walls with content area vocabulary connected to your units of study.

Students are more likely to refer to a word wall they have helped create. When I taught second grade, so many children struggled with words beginning with *w* that we created a "tricky w" word chart that included *when, where, who, why, what,* and *which*; the children were invested in using those words when they wrote. This worked so well that we created another chart for *their, there,* and *they're,* this time including a sentence using (and highlighting) each of the words. Janet Allen writes, "I have found few word walls that are successful if they are prepared in the absence of teaching and learning. You will want your word wall to be a living part of the classroom with new words being added each day as they are encountered and taught" (2007, 20). You might consider using Velcro, magnetic tape, or even sticky notes so that students can use the words or re-sort them. Donna Koehneke intentionally places her wall low to the ground so that her first graders can manipulate the words.

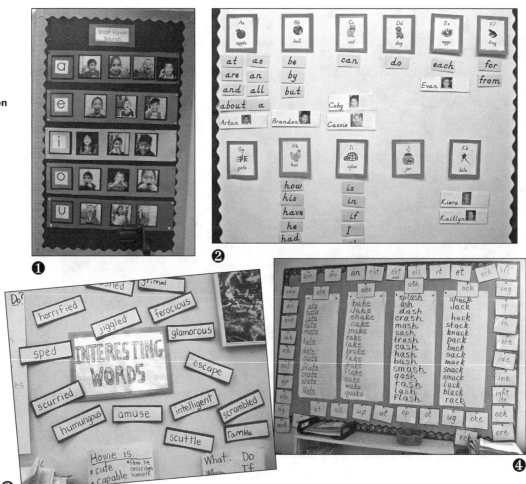

Word Walls in the Primary Classrooms of Kendra Daly (1), Deb Woodfield (2), Megan Sloan (3), and Cheryl Perkins (4)

Eliza Lewis says her first graders really use their word wall. They update the collection of words over the year, adding one or two words at a time and removing words that are no longer needed. One hundred high-frequency words appear on the wall at some point but never all at the same time. Eliza also adds common words that her students ask to include. Eliza writes, "The only thing better than adding new words to the word wall is taking off the words that we no longer need!"

Janet Allen (2007) recommends that each intermediate student keep a personal word wall in their writing folder or word study notebook for each new unit of study. They can note word origins and meanings and use sketches to help them remember the meaning of the new words they're learning.

Max Brand (2004, 140) states that word walls in intermediate grades:

▶ Support students' learning of high-frequency words.

▶ Provide example words highlighting difficult concepts as a help to students when spelling unfamiliar words.

▶ Support students' vocabulary development.

▶ Demonstrate how to collect words found in reading.

- Provide a space for students to display words that are important to them.
- Provide a space for students to sort and categorize words and phrases.

The type of word wall Max creates depends on the grade level he's teaching and the needs of his particular students. He usually begins with a display of high-frequency words and content area vocabulary. As he confers with students and sees misspellings of those words, he can refer them to the chart. Here were a few of the other charts Max creates during the year:

- Interesting words
- Homophones
- Unfamiliar words
- Cool words
- Words with unusual spellings
- Long words
- Words from other languages
- Made-up words

However, you don't have to limit yourself to *word* walls. Max's kids also find "golden lines" (a memorable quote from a book) and "lines that make you stop and think" and record the book title, author, and page number. Collecting delicious and interesting words and lines helps students both as readers and as writers. Max says, "Through the variety of words and writing on the wall, the students had developed into a community of learners who were interested in words" (150).

Andrea Smith (2009) has her students take or find digital pictures to accompany content area vocabulary. Students could also cut out pictures from magazines to illustrate the words. Adding photographs and illustrations provides additional visual support for your English language learners.

One other cautionary note about spelling instruction: it's important that students memorize some high-frequency words and be held accountable for accurate spelling in their independent writing. In my own second-grade classroom, I implemented the following accountability system. Each week I reviewed one of their recent pieces of writing in their writing folders for accurate spelling of high-frequency words. I returned them with notes asking them to find and correct the high-frequency words they had misspelled. After a few weeks, there was a dramatic increase in correct spelling of high-frequency words. It's important to make your expectations clear, to be consistent, and to monitor their work to make sure that they are following through!

Word sorts, word walls, word charts, and word study notebooks can help *all* students actively discover how English works. Since you probably have spellers at three or even four grade levels or stages in your classroom, using a combination of these activities, along with spelling minilessons, can help students improve far more effectively than a traditional spelling program.

Book List

Resources for Helping You Teach Spelling

☐ *My Kid Can't Spell* by Richard Gentry (1997) (Grades K–5)

☐ *Word Crafting* by Cindy Marten (2003) (Grades K–5)

☐ *Word Savvy* by Max Brand (2004) (Grades 3–6)

☐ *Spelling Strategies* (with CD-ROM) by Sandra Wilde (2008) (Grades 3–5)

☐ *Spelling K–8: Planning and Teaching* by Diane Snowball and Faye Bolton (1999) (Grades K–8)

☐ *The Science of Spelling* by Richard Gentry (2004) (Grades K–5)

☐ *Teaching Kids to Spell* by Richard Gentry and Jean Wallace Gillet (1993) (Grades K–5)

☐ *Focus on Spelling* (DVD) by Diane Snowball (2006) (Grades K–8)

☐ *Smart Answers to Tough Questions* by Elaine Garan (2007) (Grades K–5)

☐ *Voices on Word Matters* (Chapter 10) edited by Gay Su Pinnell and Irene Fountas (1999) (Grades K–5)

☐ *Words Their Way: Word Study for Phonics, Vocabulary, and Spelling Instruction* by Donald Bear et al. (2008) (Grades K–8)

☐ *Words Their Way: Letter and Picture Sorts for Emergent Spellers* by Donald Bear et al. (2010) (Grades K–1)

☐ *Words Their Way: Word Sorts for Within Word Pattern Spellers* by Marcia Invernizzi et al. (2009) (Grades 1–4)

☐ *Words Their Way: Word Sorts for Letter Name–Alphabetic Spellers* by Francine Johnston et al. (2009) (Grades K–3)

☐ *Words Their Way: Word Sorts for Syllables and Affixes Spellers* by Francine Johnston et al. (2009) (Grades 3–5)

☐ *Words Their Way: Word Sorts for Derivational Relations Spellers* by Shane Templeton et al. (2009) (Grades 4–8)

☐ *Words Their Way with English Learners: Word Study for Phonics, Vocabulary, and Spelling Instruction* by Lori Helman et al. (2008) (Grades K–8)

☐ *Words Their Way: Letter-Name Alphabetic Sorts for Spanish-Speaking English Learners* by Lori Helman et al. (2009) (Grades K–3)

☐ *Words Their Way: Emergent Sorts for Spanish-Speaking English Learners* by Lori Helman et al. (2009) (Grades K–2)

☐ *Making Words* by Patricia Cunningham and Dorothy Hall (2009) (separate books for K, 1, 2, 2, 4, 5)

☐ *Word Journeys* by Kathy Ganske (2000) (Grades K–6)

☐ *The Continuum of Literacy Learning* by Gay Su Pinnell and Irene Fountas (2007) (Grades K–2, 3–8, K–8)

Ponder Box for Teachers

- How do you teach spelling?

- What aspects of spelling do your students find most challenging?

- How do you use word sort and word walls to teach spelling?

- How do you support your students with learning the spelling of high-frequency words?

Ponder Box for Coaches and Principals

- How is spelling taught at your school?

- Is there consistency within and between grade levels?

- How could you develop schoolwide agreements about teaching spelling?

- How could you support professional conversations about word sorts and word walls in your school?

- Have you developed schoolwide grade-level lists of high-frequency words?

- What resources about spelling would be helpful to read in grade-level teams or as a staff?

Teaching Vocabulary

When I travel, I prepare an index card with ten or twenty key phrases that I'll need in that country. I read the pronunciations in the travel guide book and practice "good morning" in the elevator on the way down to breakfast, but it's not until I've heard the words spoken and used them correctly myself a dozen times or more in real situations that they actually stick. Similarly, Nancy Akhavan states, "Some researchers estimate that it takes at least twelve purposeful encounters with a word for children to *own* it" (2007, 72). Research tells us that drilling and memorization often doesn't stick or transfer. What students need are many opportunities to play with new words, explore their meanings and origins, and use them in authentic ways. In addition, vocabulary instruction should be intertwined with reading and writing instruction.

Do you like to do crossword puzzles? Do you play Scrabble or Boggle? It's important to share how *you* discover and savor new words as an adult reader and writer. *Word Nerd* (2008) by Susin Nielsen is a story about a dorky boy (with an overprotective mother) who blossoms when he secretly joins a Scrabble club. If you teach fifth grade, you might consider reading this book aloud and putting out a Scrabble board and Scrabble dictionary for your students. There are also armloads of great literature you could incorporate into vocabulary lessons. For instance, if you teach fourth or fifth grade, you could read aloud *The Disreputable History of Frankie Landau-Banks*, by E. Lockhart (2008), highlighting Frankie's facility with inventing words, or you could savor the memorable language and descriptions in *Savvy*, by Ingrid Law (2008). There's a whole series of books by Brian Clearly about parts of speech, such as *Hairy, Scary, Ordinary: What Is an Adjective?* (2001). Teachers of any grade might want to read Heather Henson's picture book *That Book Woman* (2008), which overflows with alliteration, similes, metaphors, and colloquial language.

Some teachers read aloud *Miss Alaineus*, by Debra Frasier (2000), and then have students come to school dressed as vocabulary words (*precipitation* or *mysterious*, for example). Debra provides a guide and photographs of vocabulary parades on her website (www.frasierbooks.com). Vocabulary study can become engaging and active if you incorporate games and word sorts and weave discussions about word origins and lovely language into reading and writing workshop.

Sherri Ballew's fourth graders use their word wall to learn about prefixes, suffixes, and root words. After her students learn the meaning of a prefix, they find examples in books they're read together as a class or on their own. Megan Sloan creates a word wall for discussions about vocabulary and word choice (see Sloan 2005). When she reads aloud, she calls attention to interesting words. Megan and her students discuss the meaning of the words, then decide which ones to add to their chart of interesting words.

I always pick up new ideas when I visit Megan Sloan's classroom and I can always see the footprints of the professional books she has read. For instance, when she read Linda Hoyt's book, *Revisit, Reflect, Retell* (2008), Megan was intrigued by the idea of an "Alphabox chart" (16). When she read *Moxy Maxwell Does Not Love Stuart Little* by Peggy Gifford (2008) aloud, she and her students kept track of interesting words on an "Alphabox chart." The chart has twenty boxes, each with a letter or two from the alphabet. Megan and her students record some of the interesting words that the author uses.

In *The Vocabulary-Enriched Classroom* (2006), Cathy Collins Block and John Mangieri articulate five "word-learning beliefs" that support students' vocabulary acquisition:

Belief 1: All words are not of equal importance.

Belief 2: Students retain words they truly understand and can use when they speak, listen, read, and write.

Megan Sloan Teaches Vocabulary Using an Interesting Word Wall and an Alphabox Chart

Belief 3: Students increase their vocabulary more rapidly when they learn how to use a one word-meaning clue with one vocabulary-building strategy each week.

Belief 4: When students understand words frequently used in texts, they develop a positive attitude toward reading.

Belief 5: Expert readers know a large number of important words that encompass all parts of speech.

Nancy Akhavan's very practical book *Accelerated Vocabulary Instruction* (2007) recommends carving out fifteen or twenty minutes a day for vocabulary units of study. Each unit begins with a connection, teaching for ten minutes, then five minutes of guided practice and a quick wrap-up. As the principal, Nancy describes how intentional instruction and "classrooms dripping with words" helped her poverty-impacted school in California school dramatically improve its test scores. At Nancy's school, second-through fifth-grade teachers presented eight new words each week to their students. "You can break word learning into four days of instruction, teaching two words each day, and keeping one day for conferring and assessment" (74).

Nancy presents a convincing case that knowing vocabulary helps children succeed in school. You can give struggling students and English language learners an extra boost and close the achievement gap by teaching these kids the vocabulary they need. Her book includes six units of study, mapped out by month, with examples of five or more specific, well-paced minilessons. Each minilesson includes the teaching point, tips for preparation, and a description of the lesson, often with photographs from a classroom. The minilessons are very engaging. For instance, in the activity on page 98, students brainstorm nonsense words using prefixes and suffixes. Nancy outlines the prefixes most often used in school texts and even includes overhead transparencies for you to use. She recognizes the challenges of busy teachers and has laid it all out for you.

Sara Holbrook also has some lively and engaging ways to teach vocabulary through poetry in her book *High Definition* (2010). After all, poetry is about knowing and choosing the right words. You might also want to read Sara's new poetry books for kids, *Normally Weird* (2010) and *Zombies! Evacuate the School!* (2010), or Michael Salinger's book *Well Defined: Vocabulary in Rhyme* (2009) and have your students create similar tickle-your-funny-bone poems about baffling vocabulary words.

Vocabulary instruction is closely linked to learning in content areas (math, language arts, science, and social studies), as Sara demonstrates in her lively professional book *Practical Poetry* (2005). She describes how poetry demands keen observation, requires precise language, encourages good organization and reading fluency, and helps student learn about themselves and the world using powerful language. Poetry can help students

Content Area Vocabulary Activities in Susan Winter's Classroom

make powerful connections that linger as they delve into content area exploration and learning.

In the last few years, the teachers at the American International School of Muscat (TAISM) have read several books, including *Word Savvy* (2004) by Max Brand and *Accelerated Vocabulary Instruction* (2007) by Nancy Akhavan. This spring, they're planning a professional book study of *Learning Words Inside and Out* (2009) by Nancy Frey and Douglas Fisher, which includes tons of online resources for book study groups, including podcasts, study guides, and PowerPoint slides. The authors explain how to immerse students in subject-area/content-area vocabulary in order to increase students' understanding and motivation. They suggest many ways to help students fall in love with words. The first chapter, "Why Teaching Subject Area Words Can Make or Break Achievement," is powerful enough to justify the cost of the book. The remaining chapters center around five tenets:

▶ Make it intentional—select words for instruction that are worth precious classroom time.

▶ Make it transparent—give students word-solving strategies by modeling your thinking when reading aloud.

▶ Make it useable—provide oral and written practice through authentic partner activities.

▶ Make it personal—help words stick by using well-designed independent activities.

▶ Make it a priority—create a schoolwide focus on word learning.

At TAISM, some vocabulary work at the school takes place during interactive read-alouds or guided reading. Students generally record and sketch new vocabulary words on whiteboards and vocabulary bookmarks or in word study notebooks. Teachers sometimes use word webs, cloze activities, or quick student dictations with a partner to learn new

**Word Study in Kenneth Ingram's and Linda
Brubaker's Classrooms**

vocabulary. Or they may use a strategy called "mindsketching," on which students write the word, draw a quick sketch, write the word in a sentence, and add a definition in their own words. When students sketch what a word means, they tap into their background knowledge and think analytically. The drawing helps them retain the word and makes vocabulary study fun. The ESL/ELL teachers at the school also use pictures and artwork as students work with word families and spelling patterns.

In Chapter 6 of *Word Savvy* (2004), Max Brand describes how he teaches math, science, and social studies vocabulary in fun and engaging ways in his intermediate classroom. He often begins with discovery. His students record words they don't know in their word study notebooks. Conversations about vocabulary are interwoven

Book List

Resources for Helping You Teach Vocabulary

- [ ] *The Vocabulary-Enriched Classroom* by Cathy Collins Block and John Mangieri (2006) (Grades 3–8)
- [ ] *Accelerated Vocabulary Instruction* by Nancy Akhavan (2007) Grades 2–6)
- [ ] *Learning Words Inside and Out* by Nancy Frey and Douglas Fisher (2009) (Grades 1–6)
- [ ] *Word Savvy* (Chapters 6 and 7) by Max Brand (2004) (Grades 3–6)
- [ ] *A Day of Words* (DVD) by Max Brand (2005) (Grades 3–6)
- [ ] *What Really Matters in Vocabulary* by Patricia Cunningham (2009) (Grades K–5)
- [ ] *Inside Words* (with CD-ROM) by Janet Allen (2007) (Grades 4–12)
- [ ] *Words, Words, Words* by Janet Allen (1999) (Grades 4–12)
- [ ] *Words Their Way with English Learners: Word Study for Phonics, Vocabulary, and Spelling Instruction* by Donald Bear et al. (2007) (and other resources in this series)
- [ ] *Words Their Way: Word Study for Phonics, Vocabulary, and Spelling Instruction* by Donald Bear et al. (2008)
- [ ] *The Vocabulary Book* by Michael Graves (2005) (Grades K–12)
- [ ] *Creating Robust Vocabulary* by Isabel Beck et al. (2008) (Grades K–12)
- [ ] *Bringing Words to Life* by Isabel Beck et al. (2002) (Grades K–12)
- [ ] *Teaching Individual Words* by Michael Graves (2008) (Grades K–8)
- [ ] *Word Journeys* by Kathy Ganske (2000) (Grades K–6)
- [ ] *Making Words Stick* by Kellie Buis (2004) (Grades K–8)
- [ ] *The Word-Conscious Classroom* by Judith Scott, Bonnie Skobel, and Jan Wells (2008) (Grades 4–8)
- [ ] *Instructional Strategies for Teaching Content Vocabulary* by Janis Harmon, Karen Wood, and Wanda Hedrick (2006) (Grades 4–12)
- [ ] *High Definition* by Sara Holbrook (2010) (Grades 2–8)
- [ ] *Practical Poetry* by Sara Holbrook (2005) (Grades 4–8)

with content-area discussions and discoveries. Max's students *use* their new vocabulary in meaningful contexts: read-alouds, graphic organizers, and conversation. He also builds students' interest in words by using word walls and anchor charts.

When I was a student, I was incredibly bored when I had to look up words in a dictionary, write down the definitions, and then use the words in sentences. Research shows this is probably the least effective way to learn vocabulary; there is very little long-term benefit. Thank heavens we now know more effective ways to incorporate vocabulary study into our reading and writing workshops. You may want to have your intermediate students keep track of your vocabulary minilessons in their word-study notebooks and designate sections for challenging words, interesting words, and the new words they encounter as they read independently and in literature circles.

Ponder Box for Teachers

- How do you teach vocabulary?

- How can you make vocabulary instruction more participatory and active for students?

Ponder Box for Coaches and Principals

- How is vocabulary taught at your school?

- Is there consistency within and between grade levels?

- How can you share ideas and develop schoolwide agreements about teaching vocabulary?

- What resources about vocabulary would be helpful to read in grade-level teams or as a staff?

Teaching Other Language Conventions: Handwriting, Punctuation, and Grammar

In *Writing for Readers: Teaching Skills and Strategies*, from *Units of Study for Primary Writing* (2003), Lucy Calkins and Natalie Louis present initial lessons about the conventions of language. The fact that readers may struggle to read their writing is a new concept for children whose prior writing instruction has emphasized believing in themselves as writers and building fluency. However, part of the purpose of writing is for others to be able to read and enjoy it; in order to make their writing readable, students have to pay attention to conventions like spelling, punctuation, grammar, and handwriting. In this unit, students learn conventions in the context of their own writing. Lucy and Natalie point out that this unit can't stand alone: "It relies upon teachers explicitly teaching phonics and high-frequency words during word-study time and through interactive writing and shared reading" (iv). It's worth a quick reminder here that, like phonics, spelling, and vocabulary, these additional conventions of language should be taught within the context of real reading and writing, rather than in isolation. Your challenge as teachers is to figure out how to weave an exploration of handwriting, punctuation, and grammar into writing (and reading) workshop and your units of study.

Teaching Handwriting

Handwriting (or penmanship) is closely associated with teaching letters and letter sounds. Rather than spending time on isolated drills or copying sentences, it makes more sense to embed handwriting instruction within writing workshop so that the focus remains on legibility in order to communicate. Regie Routman has a short section on handwriting in *Writing Essentials* (2005, 66–69) in which she discusses how legible handwriting is political since writing is often judged on clarity and legibility. She suggests that teachers need to have high expectations: "When we raise our expectations and refuse to accept poor handwriting, kids' writing improves" (66). But that means we have to teach students how to write legibly, demonstrate good handwriting, and give writers an audience for their work so that they care enough to become invested in writing neatly. We raise the bar when we expect quality from our students.

For a review of research and a succinct description of how to teach handwriting, you might want to refer to Chapter 16 (pages 227–40) in *Guiding K–3 Writers to Independence* (2008), by Patricia Scharer and Gay Su Pinnell. They recommend that teachers:

❶ Provide brief lessons (five minutes) twice a week.

❷ Begin with children's names.

❸ Use specific and consistent language.

❹ Provide opportunities for guided and independent practice.

❺ Ask children to notice the specific features of letters as linked to letter sounds.

❻ Look for improvement.

The authors advocate using a gradual release instructional model when teaching letter formation. They emphasize that handwriting lessons should be focused and very short so that students can concentrate their energy on the content. You'll need to observe each of your students closely in order to determine who needs further support with penmanship so you can group students and tailor your instruction according to their specific needs.

Ralph Fletcher's admonitions in *Boy Writers* (2006) are helpful to keep in mind so that we don't get hung up on neatness. Chapter 8 addresses the challenge that many boys face with handwriting. Ralph mentions that many young writers talk about how they get "handaches" from the physical act of writing. He quotes researchers who have found that the fine motor skills of boys can lag several years behind that of girls. Ralph urges teachers to focus on content first and to provide alternatives for boys, such as allowing them to compose on the computer. My son pleaded with his fourth-grade teacher to let him compose his writer's notebook entries on the computer instead of by hand. I can't imagine how I would have written this book if I had been required to write it out by hand instead of drafting and revising (and revising and revising) on the computer! Ralph urges teachers to keep the big picture in mind: "Sure, handwriting matters, but it is really just a minor duke in the mighty kingdom of writing" (77).

As with all aspects of learning, children come into a classroom with different levels of proficiency in handwriting and therefore need differentiated instruction. Jen Munnerlyn's students focus less on learning how to write cursive letters in isolation and more on writing words and sentences within a writing workshop. During the first month of school, Jen asks her students to copy the following sentence in cursive onto a half sheet of lined paper: *I am excited to learn to write in cursive!* These samples are dated and kept in each student's section of her teacher's notebook. After reviewing each child's sample, Jen groups students by their levels of proficiency. The early cursive writers are given the school-purchased handwriting book to begin working on individual letter formation. The writers who have some control of cursive but need work on specific letters are given both the handwriting book and several sheets of large-lined paper. The group that has a strong mastery of cursive are given only lined paper.

For the rest of the year Jen holds twice-weekly handwriting practice sessions. While classical music plays, children work at their own pace on either practicing letter formation or copying poems in cursive. When students find letters they need to review, they use the individual letter practice pages or the alphabet guide in the back of the handwriting book. Jen or another student demonstrates letter formation when requested. By the end of the year everyone has a "poetry pad" of large construction paper pages, each with a photocopied poem and the student's handwritten copy next to it. Some students have only two or three poems; others have as many as twenty.

Right before her spring parent-teacher conference, Jen asks her students to write *I am excited to learn to write in cursive!* again on a lined sheet of paper and they compare this with the sample from earlier in the year. Students reflect on their improvement and on how their handwriting has changed and become more personalized. Many students have trouble believing the initial sample is theirs! Parents enjoy seeing the growth their children have made in handwriting over the year, and each student has a beautiful collection of their favorite poems.

Teaching Punctuation

The study of punctuation in a writing workshop context should also begin with a spirit of inquiry and be developmentally appropriate. Katie Wood Ray's first chapter in *Study Driven* (2006) captures this exploratory stance in Lisa Cleaveland's first-grade classroom. Katie and Lisa have another helpful example of a punctuation study in the primary grades on pages 205–13 in *About the Authors* (2004), along with a list of ten helpful picture books about punctuation to use with developing writers.

Punctuation enables authors to convey emotion, pacing, and voice, which impacts the way readers will "hear" the words on the page. Carrie has a far better grasp of semicolons that I do; inevitably, she would find one or two to insert whenever I sent her drafts of chapters. Suddenly I started noticing semicolons everywhere; I also began to overuse them! Mary Ehrenworth and Vicki Vinton explain, "The semicolon and the colon bring a grin to the face of a writer who has studied usage. Few understand them, fewer still use them artfully, which means that the writer who feels confident wielding semicolons and colons feels particularly powerful" (2005, 79). Just as I began to overuse semicolons, kindergartners, when they first learn about exclamation marks, experiment with this fun way to show emotion through punctuation, often going overboard.

Do you have a student who overuses a punctuation mark? Do you have students who seem to know the rules but don't always apply them? Do you have other students who ignore punctuation until the editing stage, then become overwhelmed with trying to "fix" everything? Dan Feigelson's book *Practical Punctuation* (2008) is guaranteed to inspire you with a new vision of how to teach punctuation effectively. His strongest advice is to "put the *why* before the *what* (the purpose before the particulars)" (4). As with any learning, if we engage children in authentic inquiry into a topic, their curiosity will motivate them to discover more on their own. Dan builds on students' wondering as he outlines grade-level units of study around punctuation: ending punctuation in K–2; comma exploration in grades 3–5; and internal punctuation and cadence in grades 5–7. In this last unit, you learn how to guide your students to focus on the prosody (rhythm) of their writing and specific strategies to make the rhythm match the mood of the text. This unit zeroes in on how dashes, colons, other internal punctuation, and even sentence length can be used intentionally to create mood or tone.

Dan reminds us that these units are only guides and encourages us to adapt the unit to fit the needs of our classroom or even develop our own unit of study, modeled after one of these examples. He shows how published authors do not see punctuation as a set of rules but rather as a crafting tool. This notion of punctuation as an instrument of craft comes alive in his transcripts of interviews with the authors Frank McCourt and Natalie Babbitt, among others. This book is a "must" for all elementary and middle school teachers who want to help their students to become the "punctuation zealots" Dan strives to create in his teaching. Jodi Bonnette, the primary school literacy coach at the Singapore American School, says enthusiastically:

This wonderful resource has changed the way I think about teaching punctuation. As a literacy coach, I have been facilitating conversations about how and what we teach about punctuation, grammar, and capitalization. As I met with each grade level to discuss conventions, I used the first chapter of *Practical Punctuation*, "Purpose Before Particulars." We jigsaw-read this chapter; each group read and discussed a section, then shared the ideas with the group. Teachers then applied the ideas in their classrooms.

Dan stresses the importance of teaching students the purpose of punctuation before teaching them a set of rules. It helps to see the connection between punctuation in reading and using punctuation in writing and to see punctuation as a craft rather than just a set of rules. We've begun whole-school discussions about how punctuation helps readers understand texts.

I found this resource so helpful that I bought one as a gift for all my grade-level language arts representatives as a thank-you for all their hard work in our curriculum development this year!

Stephanie Zarikow is a fifth-grade teacher at Jodi's school. She introduced a punctuation lesson centered on striving for accuracy by sharing the following quotes:

Whenever you do a thing, act as if all the world were watching.

—Thomas Jefferson

A man who has committed a mistake and does not correct it is committing another mistake.

—Confucius

Stephanie and her students then talked about punctuation and its importance in relation to accuracy. She read the picture book *Punctuation Takes a Vacation* by Robin Pulver (2004); then her students began a class list of the punctuation and capitalization conventions they would strive to follow in their writing:

Strive for Accuracy

We all agree to strive for accuracy in punctuation and capitalization by:

- capitalizing the beginning of
  - sentences
  - days of the week
  - places
  - dates
- adding either a period, exclamation, or other punctuation mark to the end of sentences
- adding colons to times (e.g., 11:00)
- indenting the beginning of paragraphs
- adding commas when listing things or when adding a date

This list grew as the year progressed. Stephanie has found the lessons from *Practical Punctuation* really enhance her teaching of punctuation within a writing workshop framework.

Sherri Ballew's punctuation minilessons arise from the needs of her fourth graders. She approaches the topic through inquiry. For example, when her students were writing personal narratives, she realized that they needed help punctuating dialogue. Sherry displayed an example from a shared reading lesson, and together she and her students discussed where the author used quotation marks and what other punctuation occurred around it. They also explored various ways authors use paragraphing and punctuation to provide clues about who is talking. Sherri then held students accountable for punctuating dialogue correctly as they edited their personal narratives. She did the same thing with starting new paragraphs. She projected a section from the novel *Masterpiece* (2008) by Elise Broach and the class created a chart about what paragraphs look like and when writers start new paragraphs. Sherri then held her students accountable for using paragraphs correctly, encouraging them to refer back to the chart and her minilesson.

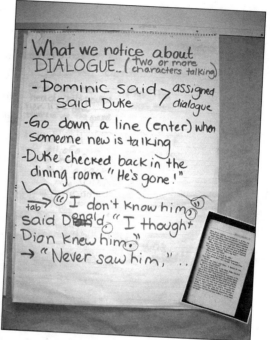

A Dialogue Minilesson in Sherri Ballew's Classroom

Max Brand (2004) also takes an investigative stance with regard to conventions. Max asks his students to list proper nouns that are capitalized and note what they are learning about this specific convention in their word study notebooks. He writes, "The searching, recording, dialogue about, and use of these proper nouns has helped my students develop an eye for capitalization while writing" (96).

I picked up so many ideas from Janet Angelillo's book *A Fresh Approach to Teaching Punctuation* (2002) that I can only echo Lucy Calkins' comment on the back cover: "Janet knows that punctuation is the key to complex sentence structure and complex thinking, and that it can be taught using the very methods that serve us so well in the writing workshop." Janet outlines how to teach punctuation by exploring the work of published authors and providing instruction about written conventions as part of larger units of inquiry. "I realized how much fun punctuation could be, because I read widely and began to think deeply about the punctuation in the books I was reading. This kind of reading and thinking is important in making sure your knowledge is current and clear. It can also help you see the possibilities for fun in punctuation" (33). Janet has created four units of study, each lasting two or three weeks, built around an author or a genre and including read-alouds and other oral reading activities.

Janet also has several great tips for teaching punctuation during individual conferences:

▶ Teach only one point per conference.

▶ Show the student what needs to be done using literature or your writing.

▶ Do not make the changes for the student.

▶ Teach the writer, not the writing (something they can apply to all their work).

▶ Keep notes of what you teach and how you plan to follow up.

▶ Hold the student accountable for what you taught.

Rather than mark punctuation errors with a red pen, we can approach them as windows into what students know in order to ascertain where they need additional information or guidance. We have to celebrate approximations and allow students room to "play." All of us, teachers and students alike, can begin to read with an appreciation of how writers use punctuation to capture voice and convey ideas as we hunt for different uses of punctuation in the books we read.

Like Janet Angelillo and Max Brand, Jeff Anderson tackles the challenge of how to make grammar and mechanics compelling and meaningful to students in his book *Mechanically Inclined* (2005). Rather than seeing grammar/mechanics and writing workshop as either/ors, he advocates teaching grammar and mechanics *in context*. His writing workshops incorporate lessons about process, product, skills, and conventions so that students can learn how to write with vitality and clarity. Jeff models and encourages students with short bursts of daily instructional practice. He recommends that you help your students "try on" lessons about mechanics in their writer's notebook, analyze mentor texts to determine how authors use conventions to convey their messages, and experiment with "express-lane edits," all of

Book List 📖

Resources for Helping You Teach Punctuation

☐ *Study Driven* (Chapter 1) by Katie Wood Ray (2006) (Grades K–6)

☐ *About the Authors* (pages 205–13) by Katie Wood Ray with Lisa Cleaveland (2004) (Grades K–2)

☐ *Practical Punctuation* by Dan Feigelson (2008) (Grades K–7)

☐ *Writing for Readers: Teaching Skills and Strategies* (from *Units of Study for Primary Writing*) by Lucy Calkins and Natalie Louis (2003) (Grades K–2)

☐ *A Fresh Approach to Teaching Punctuation* by Janet Angelillo (2002) (Grades 2–5)

☐ *Mechanically Inclined* by Jeff Anderson (2005) (Grades 4–8)

☐ *Teaching Apostrophes* (DVD) by Jeff Anderson (2008) (Grades K–8)

☐ *The Power of Grammar* (Chapter 3) by Mary Ehrenworth and Vicki Vinton (2005) (Grades 4–9)

☐ *The Continuum of Literacy Learning* by Gay Su Pinnell and Irene Fountas (2007) (Grades K–2, 3–8, K–8)

which take the pressure off students to be "right" while still providing meaningful laboratories for learning about grammar and mechanics.

Mary Enhrenworth and Vicki Vinton write, "We need to release punctuation from the muck of worksheets. We need to know and have words for how punctuation enlivens writing, how it shapes meaning, how it matters to us as people who write and teach writing. We need to say what punctuation does for us and what it can do for the students we teach" (2005, 53).

Ponder Box for Teachers

- How do you teach punctuation?

- In what areas of punctuation do your students need more support?

Ponder Box for Coaches and Principals

- How is punctuation taught at your school?

- How can you foster consistency within and between grade levels?

- How can you help teachers share ideas and develop schoolwide agreements about teaching punctuation?

- What resources about punctuation would be helpful to read in grade-level teams or as a staff?

Teaching Grammar

My mother-in-law constantly bemoans the fact that people use *I* and *me* incorrectly and end sentences with prepositions. While these errors slip by most people, to Mary Fran, grammatical errors are like fingernails on a blackboard. She grew up in an era when students diligently memorized grammar rules. However, they didn't automatically use these conventions correctly in their daily conversations and written work.

In *Grammar Study* (2008), Janet Angelillo describes some of her former teachers as people who were "impatient, expected instant perfection, or were grammar snobs" (31). Janet has a totally different and more inviting way to approach grammar in the intermediate grades and middle school—through units of study and mentor texts. She demonstrates how to map out a path for grammar instruction for the entire school year, beginning by evaluating students' strengths and needs from an early writing sample and following up with individual writing conferences. After writing workshop is launched, she and her students embark on a unit of study designed to create a curiosity and a love of studying language as they search for words and sentences in literature. Rather than teaching grammar in isolation, Janet infuses grammar study into every unit, genre study, and discussion about writing traits. "Grammar is the skeleton onto which we build voice, sentence fluency, and other qualities of good writing" (47). We can weave tips about grammar into individual conferences and shared writing and have students record their discoveries in their word study notebooks.

Many of us believe grammar is governed by very strict rules, but Janet's book definitely changes that impression and may even surprise us. Janet says, "Grammar does not constrain. It's not a leftover girdle from the 1950s" (123). She demonstrates that if students "write with strict adherence to 'the rules' of formal grammar," the result is writing that is "institutional gray" (44). In Chapter 7, Janet shares a "continuum of proposed grammar teaching" that one school crafted to guide schoolwide expectations, second through sixth grade.

We know that learning all the parts of speech doesn't mean that students will become good writers. Rules aren't the best way to engage young students. Labeling allows us to *analyze* writing, but we become proficient only with practice in applying our new skills. As teachers, we need to think aloud about tense and grammar, just as we do when we choose topics or revise. It's important to demonstrate how considerations about grammar occur *as we compose* and not just as part of editing. Just as I've suggested we do for studies of words, punctuation, and vocabulary, we can explore grammar through inquiry. We can also read some of the delightful children's books about grammar, such as *Nouns and Verbs Have a Field Day* (2001) by Robin Pulver. Above all, we can teach grammar by rolling around in the well-crafted words and sentences we find in exemplary texts and exquisite writing.

Anne Klein looks at her fifth graders' work and plans her focus lessons around the specific needs she notices. For instance, she might do a minilesson about when to use *a* or *an* or how to use correct capitalization, or just the right punctuation mark. Anne presents a quick minilesson using her own writing or a page from a book, then asks her students to select a piece of writing they are working on and check for that rule. She also comments informally throughout the year when she notices someone using punctuation or grammar correctly as she walks around the room and confers with students.

In *The Power of Grammar* (2005), Mary Ehrenworth and Vicki Vinton argue convincingly that grammar instruction cannot be ignored: "We have come to understand that grammar is intimately linked with power. . . . Teaching students the language of power does not necessarily mean asking them to conform to it. It means giving them the knowledge they will need to make informed and meaningful language choices" (4–6). They demonstrate how we can embed grammar study in writing workshop in upper elementary and middle school classrooms as part of discussions about voice and strong writing. Rather than viewing grammar as something students have to *fix* as part of editing, we can talk about word choice and grammar as part of writing well. Mary and Vicki embed grammar into units of study through *direct instruction, inquiry,* and *apprenticeship,* each of which they describe in detail. Grammar instruction becomes a way to linger in texts and to read as writers: "To get students engaged in grammar this way, we need to make it seductive, something they can't resist. We need to make them want to play with it, to dig in and get their hands dirty. We need to stop imposing it on them and invite them to explore it with us, discovering for themselves why the rules are there and what meaningful purpose they serve" (89).

Modifying Word Study for English Language Learners

Sandy Figueroa is a principal in a school where most of the students are English language learners. She and her staff read and discussed *Essential Linguistics: What You Need to Know to Teach Reading, ESL, Spelling, Phonics, and Grammar* (2004) by David and Yvonne Freeman in order to sort out their beliefs and practices about word study. David and Yvonne are much-needed voices in the educational wilderness about working with English language learners, keeping educators grounded in solid theory and practice. Their book includes many practical examples and classroom applications, with specific chapters on oral language acquisition, phonics, spelling, and grammar.

The second chapter in *Words Their Way with English Learners* (2007), by Donald Bear and his colleagues, is about assessing spelling development in order to analyze and assess students' word knowledge and plan for instruction. The authors provide information about how to score and analyze spelling to determine each student's developmental stage. This information allows teachers to differentiate instruction and form instructional groups based on students' spelling development.

In *Getting Grammar* (2006), Donna Topping and Sandra Hoffman present a smorgasbord of minilessons for teaching grammar and parts of speech in inviting ways in intermediate classrooms by incorporating writing, discussions, drama, games, art, and music. They include lists of children's books to weave into minilessons on each topic. One of the most valuable aspects of the book is the list at the end of each chapter explaining the difficulties that children who speak other languages (such as Spanish, Vietnamese, Japanese, Mandarin, Korean, Swahili, or Farsi) have with different aspects of grammar. The authors write, "Young speakers of these languages enter American classrooms and, all too often, are labeled as *deficient* or *disabled* when they are not. They simply bring their first-language grammar to the study of English, grammar that may or may not be a match for the way English works" (10).

Ponder Box for Teachers

- How do you teach grammar?
- In what areas of grammatical usage do your students need support?

Ponder Box for Coaches and Principals

- How is grammar taught at your school?

- Is there consistency within and between grade levels?

- How can you open up discussions about this topic and develop schoolwide agreements about teaching grammar?

- What resources about grammar would be helpful to read in grade-level teams or as a staff?

Book List

Resources for Helping You Teach Grammar

- ☐ *The Power of Grammar* by Mary Ehrenworth and Vicki Vinton (2005) (Grades 4–9)
- ☐ *Essential Linguistics: What You Need to Know to Teach Reading, ESL, Spelling, Phonics, and Grammar* by David and Yvonne Freeman (2004) (Grades K–12)
- ☐ *Getting Grammar* by Donna Topping and Sandra Josephs Hoffman (2006) (Grades 3–6)
- ☐ *Grammar Study* by Janet Angelillo (2008) (Grades 3–7)
- ☐ *The Craft of Grammar* (DVD) by Carl Anderson (2007) (Grades 4–8)
- ☐ *Getting It Right* by Michael Smith and Jeffrey Wilhelm (2007) (Grades 4–12)

Communicating with Parents About Word Study

As we mentioned earlier in this chapter, parents rank spelling right after reading and math in importance in their children's education. We need to help our parents understand *why* we are teaching word study differently, *what* that looks and sounds like in our classrooms, and *how* spelling fits into the bigger picture of word study. I share below a number of resources about communicating with parents about spelling. Each of these examples could also be expanded to include other areas of word study—phonological awareness, phonics, vocabulary, and other conventions of language. The important thing is that whatever you are doing in your classroom that *you* have recently learned about and are exploring should also be explained to parents. They deserve to be educated right alongside you as you learn and grow as word study experts.

In *Literacy at the Crossroads* (1996), Regie Routman writes that we need to get political about spelling: "Many parents fear that their kids will never learn to spell correctly and that they will keep their 'bad habits.' Unless we inform parents of the developmental nature of learning to spell—along with the strategies and activities we are employing to teach spelling—parents are unsupportive of what they view as a nontraditional, questionable practice" (109). Regie goes on to list a dozen things we can do to communicate how we teach spelling (117–19):

- Be sure something goes home in final copy on a regular basis.

- When a piece of writing goes public, be sure it's correct.

- Stamp or label writing that has not been teacher-edited as "unedited" or "student edited."

- Include the *what* and *how* of your spelling program in parent newsletters.

- Share the research on how children learn to spell.

- Share the developmental stages of spelling that all children go through.

- Have expectations for editing and spelling visible and accessible in the classroom.

- Have students document their individual spelling work.

- Have students save examples of editing work.

- Keep track of the spelling lessons you teach.

- Speak openly and knowledgeably about the importance of being a competent speller.

- Help students develop spelling strategies, "spelling sense," and spelling resources.

What are some ways that you can communicate with families about words study? Melissa Clark uses the assessment materials in *Words Their Way* (2007) by Donald Bear and his colleagues to differentiate her spelling instruction. Hands-on homework assignments support the developmentally appropriate, research-based, enjoyable activities students are doing in her classroom. Melissa writes:

Each night the children sort their individual words, read their words to a parent, and use six of the words in a fun way. They may write them with rainbow colors, write them on the computer, or look for them in magazines. They are not just learning a list of spelling words but are learning about word patterns and spelling rules. I administer the Primary School Spelling Inventory three times throughout the year and track each child's progress. I am able to see individual growth and readjust my word work groups as needed.

To help bridge the gap between home and school, Susan Hahn, the literacy coach at Saigon South International School in Vietnam, developed a formal statement about how spelling is taught at their school, which is shared at open house and posted on the school's website (Figure 5.3):

Introduction to Spelling: Grades K–5

At SSIS we value and encourage parent participation and would like to make sure you are aware of current research and approaches to the curriculum.

English is an integral part of all subject areas, either as a tool for speech and discussion or for reading, writing, and recording. Spelling is very important and confidence in this area gives students freedom to explore and develop what they are able to write. We hope this introduction will give you some understanding of what and how we teach, and how you can help your child at home. Teachers are willing to answer any questions you may have.

Spelling in the Curriculum

Spelling is taught as part of daily literacy lessons. In kindergarten and grade 1 children use a systematic, sequential phonics scheme to learn phonic patterns, which helps them build words when writing and decode words when reading. Word study includes making words, a focus on weekly word wall words, and hands-on activities to reinforce spelling patterns.

In grades 2–3, we develop the children's awareness of spelling patterns and rules by supporting them in the study and exploration of more complex words. The children learn how to use suffixes and prefixes. In grades 3–5, children develop knowledge of word origins and the more unusual and exceptional word patterns.

Weekly word study lessons emphasize spelling patterns, explorations, and word sorts. Each week children choose words from a list of words that exemplify the spelling pattern for the week. On Friday they take an individual practice assessment on their personal words. Words of varying difficulty are offered and we differentiate instruction to meet the needs of the varying levels of spelling development. Though students in grades 3–5 will be studying personal lists of words chosen from a grade-level menu, all students will be instructed in the weekly focus or spelling feature.

In addition, every six weeks students in grades 1–5 take common spelling assessments. These assessments focus on high-frequency words and words with spelling patterns to which the students have been introduced. A developmental spelling assessment is administered twice a year, to help teachers differentiate instruction according to individual needs.

Figure 5.3 Spelling Instruction at Saigon South International School

If some of your students have parents who are overly concerned about spelling (and I suspect you have encountered several over the years), you might want to have a copy of *My Kid Can't Spell!* (1997) by Richard Gentry handy, either to pull out pertinent examples or to lend to parents. He wrote this book specifically to help parents understand the developmental nature of spelling and how families can provide appropriate help for spelling at home. We need to tell parents that we *do* care about correct spelling and then explain our spelling program and rationale, as supported by research. Every principal and teacher should have a copy of this book on their shelves and three or four copies in the library. Richard uses his nephew, Blake, as an example as he explains the five stages of spelling development and what typical spelling should look like at each grade level. He points out when to be concerned and what parents can do to support spelling at home in appropriate ways.

At the Shekou International School, teachers hold regular parent meetings to let parents know how they can support literacy at home. Treena Casey, the curriculum director, created a handout for a parent workshop with suggestions about how families can help their children with spelling.

These are strategies you might have your child try to help them spell grade-level words correctly:

❶ Look at the letters, say the word, cover the word, write each word five times.

❷ Create a spelling song. Say the letters out loud and then sing the word to a rhythm or a song pattern (e.g., "Old McDonald," "Bingo," any nonsense song).

❸ Write each word on your hand, in the air, or on someone's back using your finger and saying the word first then each letter as you write it. Maybe you can even try to have the person guess the letters as you write it and then the word.

❹ Have a family member choose a word. They will tell you the word and you will spell it aloud to them.

❺ Make a silly sentence using the spelling word.

❻ Type the spelling words three times on the computer, using a different font each time.

❼ Write the words three times using crayons or markers, using a different color for each letter.

In *Word Crafting* (2003), Cindy Marten writes, "It is very important to let parents know about your spelling program so that they can understand, feel included in, and reinforce the excitement that the children are experiencing" (80). She has a sample parent letter on page 82 and a helpful list in the appendix with ways families can support spelling at home for each of the three stages of spelling development

(140–42). Parents need to understand each of these stages and what they can do to help. There's also a helpful parent letter in *The Spelling Book: Teaching Children How to Spell, Not What to Spell* (1998) by Gladys Rosencrans.

If parents make kids correct every spelling error at home, students soon start writing really short pieces! It's more effective to talk to them about spelling rules and patterns and to edit for just a few words. In *Spelling Strategies and Patterns* (2008), Sandra Wilde states that the most important thing parents can do is to encourage their child to read, since that's how we learn to spell most words. When we approach word study through inquiry, we need to share what we've learned with parents. Our word study approaches will be much more successful if we can involve families as partners.

Using the word study rubrics and ponder boxes below, take a minute to assess which of the aspects of word study, phonological awareness, phonics, spelling, vocabulary, and the other conventions of language (handwriting, punctuation, and grammar) you or your school already have in place in your classroom or your school, as well as your *next steps* in strengthening these aspects of literacy.

Book List

Resources for Helping You Communicate with Parents About Spelling and Word Study

- ☐ *My Kid Can't Spell!* by Richard Gentry (1997) (Grades K–5)
- ☐ *Word Crafting* by Cindy Marten (2003) (Grades K–5)
- ☐ *Spelling Strategies and Patterns* (with CD-ROM) by Sandra Wilde (2008) (Grades 3–5)
- ☐ *The Spelling Book* (Chapter 8) by Gladys Rosencrans (1998) (Grades K–5)

Ponder Box for Teachers

- How can you refine how you teach the various aspects of word study (phonological awareness, phonics, spelling, vocabulary), and the other conventions of language (handwriting, punctuation, and grammar)?

- In what areas do your students need additional support?

- How do you modify word study for your English language learners?

- How can you provide information for parents about how you teach word study and what can parents do to provide support at home?

Ponder Box for Coaches and Principals

- How can you refine how the teachers in your school teach the various aspects of word study (phonological awareness, phonics, spelling, vocabulary), and the other conventions of language (handwriting, punctuation, and grammar) at your school?

- Across your school, in what areas do your students need additional support?

- How do teachers in the school modify word study for their English language learners?

- Which professional books or videos/DVDs about aspects of word study do you already have in your professional library?

- Which would you like to add?

- How can you provide information for parents about how word study is taught at each grade level and what can parents do to provide support at home?

Writing Instruction (Teacher Rubric)

NOVICE	APPRENTICE	PRACTITIONER	LEADER
☐ I rely on a published program and teacher's manual or a designated spelling list for spelling instruction; I give weekly spelling tests with little instruction; I rely on worksheets and memorization to teach vocabulary, grammar, and punctuation	☐ I use a published program and teacher's manual flexibly to determine which spelling skills and strategies to teach; I group students for spelling instruction and give weekly spelling tests; I rely on memorization and student activities to teach vocabulary, grammar, and punctuation; I introduce our word wall all at once and students occasionally refer to it	☐ I use a variety of resources to teach spelling skills and strategies; I am beginning to replace weekly spelling tests with individualized and small-group spelling instruction and assessment; I use mini-lessons, exemplars, word sorts, and activities to teach vocabulary, grammar, and punctuation; I am beginning to use our word wall effectively to teach spelling and vocabulary; students are beginning to use the word wall during independent work time; the students and I develop and add to our word wall throughout the year; I provide information about how I teach word study, spelling, and vocabulary to parents at Open House and in newsletters	☐ I use a variety of resources as part of a schoolwide approach to intentionally teach spelling skills and strategies based on students' needs and to facilitate student inquiry; I teach spelling as a part of word study, and group students or individualize instruction based on students' needs; I integrate vocabulary and grammar instruction throughout the day based on students' needs; I explicitly teach vocabulary and word study as part of a systematic school-wide approach and facilitate student inquiry; I continually monitor the effect of word study on students' independent writing; I use our word wall effectively to teach spelling and vocabulary; my students and I continually develop, add to, and delete words from our word wall; I provide clear, ongoing communication with parents about how I teach word study, spelling, and vocabulary, and how families can provide support at home

Word Study

Writing Instruction (School Rubric)

	NOVICE	APPRENTICE	PRACTITIONER	LEADER
Word Study	☐ In most classrooms, teachers rely on a published program and teacher's manual or a designated spelling list for spelling instruction; in most classrooms, teachers give weekly spelling tests with little instruction; in most classrooms, teachers rely on worksheets and memorization to teach vocabulary, grammar, and punctuation	☐ In most classrooms, teachers use a published program and teacher's manual flexibly to determine which spelling skills and strategies to teach; in most classrooms, teachers group students for spelling instruction and give weekly spelling tests; in most classrooms, teachers rely on memorization and activities to teach vocabulary, grammar, and punctuation; most teachers introduce the entire word wall all at once and students occasionally refer to it	☐ In all classrooms, teachers use a variety of resources to teach spelling skills and strategies; teachers begin to develop a schoolwide philosophy and plan for spelling instruction; teachers are beginning to replace weekly spelling tests with individualized and group spelling instruction and assessment; teachers use minilessons, exemplars, word sorts, and student activities to teach vocabulary, grammar, and punctuation; teachers in most classrooms use their word walls effectively to teach spelling and vocabulary; in most classrooms, students are beginning to use the word walls when they are working independently; in most classrooms, teachers develop and add to their word wall throughout the year; all teachers provide information to parents about how word study and spelling are taught	☐ In all classrooms, teachers systematically use a variety of resources to intentionally teach word study, which includes spelling, vocabulary, and grammar based on student needs as part of a schoolwide approach; spelling skills and strategies are taught individually or in small groups; all teachers integrate vocabulary and grammar instruction throughout the day; all teachers explicitly teach word study including vocabulary as an inquiry approach; all teachers continually monitor the effect of word study on students' independent writing; all teachers use their word walls effectively to teach spelling and vocabulary; teachers and students continually develop, add to, and delete words from their word walls; grade level teams collaborate to provide parent communication about word study instruction and home support

Afterword

Carrie and I hope that as you've read this book, you've found yourself nodding and thinking, "I have students like that" and "I do that in my classroom," and that you've felt affirmed for all the great work you're doing. However, it's hard to be an expert in every aspect of teaching writing and to keep on top of all the new professional books and ideas, so we hope you've also picked up some new strategies, minilessons, and ideas to ponder and have added some titles to the Professional Reading Log form in Appendix A. We will continue to add annotations to the database on my website as new books are published and will add new photographs as we visit exemplary classrooms so that this book can become part of a shared conversation.

When I talk to students, they often tell me that writing workshop is their favorite part of the day. When something funny happens at home, they tell their parents, "I can't wait to write about that tomorrow at school." They use carefully chosen words in their poetry and write persuasive letters to make a difference in their world. These students keep an ear tuned to lovely language as they read like writers. In the third book in our series, *The Next-Step Guide to Enhancing Reading Instruction* (forthcoming), Carrie and I will explore how reading workshop and reading instruction can be equally exciting. We would love for you to send us your book recommendations, classroom stories, and photographs as part of our ongoing collaborative exploration of cutting-edge literacy practices in elementary schools around the world.

Appendix A

Professional Reading Log

Name _____

As you read through this book and notice other books you might like to read, record them here. Code whether you want to read the book right away (R), later this year (L), or sometime in the future (F).

BOOK TITLE	AUTHOR	PUBLISHER/ COPYRIGHT DATE	INSTRUCTIONAL CATEGORY	NOTES	WHEN TO READ

Appendix B

Anne Klein's Parent Newsletter About Writing

Dear Parents,

A main focus in the classroom is writing workshop. Students have the opportunity to be real authors by selecting topics, drafting, revising, editing, and publishing their own creations. Students become actively involved in more purposeful writing through this process.

Our classroom workshop routine begins with a whole-class minilesson in which I teach a formal writing skill/strategy. I often give examples of quality writing from student work or published children's literature. During these focused lessons I also introduce different forms of writing (such as narrative, expository, persuasive, technical, or poetic).

The minilesson is followed by an independent work period during which students proceed through the writing process:

❶ **Prewriting**—involves brainstorming a list of topics and considering what to write. This might include talking with a friend, drawing a picture, looking through a list of possible topics, or brainstorming best choices. Possible topics could be discussed at home as well.

❷ **Drafting**—involves the first attempts at writing. Students are just getting their ideas down on paper.

❸ **Revision**—involves checking a piece of writing to see if the wording says what the author wants it to say. The writer focuses on making sense, adding details, cutting unnecessary parts, and so on. The focus here is on meaning.

❹ **Proofreading/Editing**—involves correcting spelling and mechanics. This fine-tuning step is used only for pieces students select to be published. The teachers, parents, or peers may offer help.

❺ **Publishing**—involves presenting the final product in an attractive form (final paper, book, poster, banner, scroll, and so on). This should always show care, effort, and quality.

QUESTIONS YOU COULD ASK YOUR CHILD AS THEY WRITE:

❶ How is it going?

❷ What is sounding really good? Why?

❸ Where are there problems? What could you do about them?

❹ Is there anything that doesn't fit or seems to sound wrong?

❺ What do you think about the piece so far?

❻ What will you do next?

❼ Where might the reader of your writing have questions or want to know more?

❽ What would you like me to respond to with your writing?

PUBLISHING SUGGESTIONS

❶ Discuss the natural writing process. Let them know if something doesn't make sense; talk about verb tense, writing mechanics, using "spell-check," and so on.

❷ Keep the "kid" language. The writing should sound like your child—try not to supply words that you think might sound better (though you can help with a brainstorm list of possible words or use a thesaurus).

❸ Encourage them to do their best. They should use their neatest handwriting and lined paper if not using a computer. Students should also take time and care with illustrations when applicable. Consider a variety of publishing forms.

❹ Enjoy their writing—it is so much fun to read. We want to celebrate where they are in the writing process.

DUE DATES

❶ Some writing will be published at home. Look for due dates on the homework cover sheet and specific assignment sheets. Drafts should be returned with the published final copy and placed back in the writing workshop notebook at school.

❷ Students (and parents) should refer to the scoring guides (rubrics) located in the assessment section of the notebook when turning in published work. These are reviewed and used in class.

Please keep this paper in the writing section of your child's notebook and use as needed throughout the year.

Thanks ☺!

Anne B. Klein

Appendix C

The Writing Process: A Parent Handout from Ben Hart

Why do we write?

We write to relate our thoughts, clarify misunderstandings, ask and answer questions, make a point, disagree, explore ideas, make connections, express feelings, make meaning, develop thinking skills, understand ourselves, and tell our stories. We write to make sense of the human experience.

What does good writing look like?

Good writing explores something that is important to the writer. It reveals the engagement of the writer, whether it's about personal experience or something learned from another source—reading, research, experimentation, calculation. Good writing begins with detail. It is honest; it shows, it doesn't tell. It focuses first on what the writer wants to say. It has voice; it takes risks. Students write well, regardless of the genre or the discipline, when they own and are engaged in the assignment, when they make personal connections to the content. The voice of the writer will take into account purpose and audience.

What does writing in process look like?

In early drafts, writing is thinking on paper. It is messy, tentative, flawed, incomplete, fragmented, disorganized, rambling, inaccurate, generalized, unstructured, clumsy, unpolished, searching, exploring, risking. Some writing needs to go no further. Its purpose is to stimulate thought, to explore ideas and concepts. Journal writing, reflections, self-assessments, and brainstorming are examples of writing to think. Sometimes the writer doesn't want to go further—at least not yet. At other times, students continue through the writing process—redrafting, seeking response, revising, editing. As they do, they gain insights about what they are writing and how they are saying it. They learn that the writing process is recursive and dynamic.

What does writing look like at the end of the process?

When writing is ready to go to final draft or publication it should show evidence of proofreading. At this point, writers need to take responsibility for examining their pieces for possible mechanical difficulties and fixing what they can; after this point, it is appropriate for writers to seek help in editing and proofreading their piece.

What can parents do?

Ask the writers in your family where they are in the process and what they want at this stage. If it is a reflection or a self-assessment, they may need only an audience; if it is a first draft going further, they may need some encouragement, particularly with detail. In this case the appropriate response identifies strengths and focuses on the message. *First-draft writing needs nurturing, not fixing.*

RESPONDING TO FIRST DRAFTS

As difficult as this may be, parents should put their pens away and listen. Commenting on structure or mechanics at this stage discourages writers from taking risks and developing their ideas, and shifts the focus from exploration to error. Issues of correctness belong at the end of the process, before a piece of writing goes public.

RESPONDING TO SUBSEQUENT DRAFTS

Ask them what they want feedback on. At this point, they may be working on being specific—showing, not telling; embedding detail; eliminating clichés and generalizations—and gaining confidence in their voice. The focus should still be on what the writer is saying and how effectively she or he is saying it.

PREPARING FOR PUBLICATION

When writers decide they are ready to submit their final draft to an audience— their peers, another class, their teachers, parents, friends, colleagues, readers of magazines and newspapers, employers—it is their responsibility to ensure that their product is polished. They need to proofread for themselves, then ask someone else to proofread; all writers do that. It is the job of the editor or proofreader to point out errors in mechanics and syntax—spelling, punctuation, tense, word choice, and any phrases that still sound awkward.

At all stages of the process, the writing belongs to the writer. It is up to the writer to make use of a responder's advice; it is not the responder's job to mandate the changes.

Why use the writing process?

Students learn to write by writing. Learning to write well takes time. Good writers learn to use the writing process effectively; they do not learn to follow a mechanical formula. In the same way, responding effectively to writing takes time. It is unfortunately all too easy when looking at a student's piece of writing to focus on errors. Absence of error, however, is not a measure of good writing. Focus on errors at any point, other than at the end of the process, is inappropriate and detrimental to the development of writing that is honest, detailed, committed, engaged, and clear; takes risks; and has voice.

Appendix D

Writing Conference

Name _____

DATE	OBSERVATION	INSTRUCTION & NEXT STEPS

Appendix E

Phonological Awareness Development, Prekindergarten–Grade 1

Developmental stages are approximate. Students may progress through the stages at times different from the indicated grade levels. All tasks are assessed orally rather than through printed text.

	PREKINDERGARTEN	KINDERGARTEN	FIRST GRADE
Separating Words	• Identify the separateness in very familiar words (e.g., *youcancome = you can come*) • Recognize violations of word order • Engage in sentence play	• Identify the separateness in known words (e.g., *out of breath*)	• Identify the separateness in some words in unknown phrases (e.g., *pledge of allegiance*)
Segmenting words	• In a string of sounds or words, listen for and identify the missing sound or word	• Identify syllables in one-, two-, and some three-syllable words	• Identify syllables in words
Rhyming	• Listen and play with rhythm of language • Recognize and enjoy rhymes (e.g., nursery rhymes)	• Play with words (e.g., jump rope jingles) • Recognize pairs of rhyming words and produce rhyming words	• Produce rhyming words
Alliteration (phoneme matching)	• Play with songs, alliteration, and word substitution	• Identify two out of three words that begin with the same sound	• Play with alliteration in more complex words (e.g., *alligator* and *astronaut*) • Play with tongue twisters
Initial consonant segmentation	• In a string of sounds or words, listen for and identify the first, middle, or last sound or word in a string	• Isolate initial consonants in single-syllable familiar words	• Isolate initial consonants
Segment onset and rime		• Segment the onset and rime in simple single-syllable words	
Phoneme segmentation		• Segment the onset and rime in single-syllable words (e.g., *c–a–t*)	• Segment individual sounds of simple words to use for spelling (e.g., *c–a–t*)
Blend phonemes and syllables	• Initial play blending familiar word parts orally (e.g., *butter–fly*)	• Blend onsets and rimes to form words (e.g., *c–at*) • Blend segments of simple meaningful words (e.g., *m–o–m*)	• Blend phonemes of simple one-syllable words (e.g., *mmm–ahhh–mmm = mom*)
Phoneme manipulation		• Begin to substitute phonemes in simple words (e.g., *bat/hat*) • Begin to add phonemes to simple words (e.g., *at/cat*)	• Substitute phonemes in words (e.g., *stamp/clamp* or *map/mad*) • Add phonemes to words (e.g., *lamp/clamp* or *pass/past*) • Delete phonemes from words (e.g., *mail/mate*)

Acknowledgments

f it takes a village to raise a child, then it's taken an international community to craft this book. We want to thank Lois Bridges, Leigh Peake, and Deb Eaton for supporting us initially as we envisioned a series of books about literacy. Kate Montgomery helped us create a vision for this ambitious project and cheered us along the way. We wish that all of you who write could be lucky enough to have Alan Huisman as your editor. He kept our voices and ideas but trimmed and pruned like a bonsai gardener. Lynne Costa did her magic with the appealing layout and gorgeous cover. It's truly a joy to work with the Heinemann team.

Laura Benson (literacy consultant from Denver) and Sandy Figueroa (principal at Peña Blanca Elementary, in Arizona) helped us write annotations for the 300 resources about writing that are posted on my website. We spent a great deal of money every time we saw Jennifer Yriondo (our local professional book rep), but it was well worthwhile. Her expertise about professional resources kept us up to date and eager to learn more.

Our biggest thanks go to our patient families who put up with our overflowing piles of books, constant emailing, and perpetual guilt as we worked on this book. Special thanks to Carrie's husband, Glenn, who helped collect and organize our photographs, and Bonnie's husband, Steve, who patiently stepped in whenever there was a technical crisis. And thank you to Bonnie's two sons, Keith and Bruce, who helped create her web-based database with their brilliant computer and artistic skills.

We would also like to thank the following teachers, principals, coaches, and staff who patiently responded to our requests for the classroom stories and examples, quotations, and photographs that enrich this book immensely. We're constantly amazed by your dedication, commitment to your students and education, and openness to new ideas. You all are amazing teachers and reflective practitioners.

UNITED STATES SCHOOLS AND TEACHERS

Anne Klein, grade 5, Maplewood Cooperative School, Edmonds, WA
Susan Lockhart, grade 5, Maplewood Cooperative School, Edmonds, WA
Megan Sloan, grades 2/3, Cathcart Elementary, Snohomish, WA
Kate Morris, grade 4, Horizon Elementary, Mukilteo, WA
Sherri Ballew, grade 4, Sunnyside Elementary, Marysville, WA
Linda Lee, multiage class, Willard Elementary, Spokane, WA
Doriane Marvel, grade 1, Spicewood Elementary, Austin, TX
Holly Reardon, professional development specialist NAEYC, Washington, D.C.
    (previously at the International School of Beijing)

Jan Mayes, grades K–2 literacy, social studies, and world languages coordinator, Kent, WA

Shannon Stanton, instructional coach coordinator, Kent, WA

Tina Criste, grade 2, Martin Sortun Elementary, Kent, WA

Colleen Oliver, grade 6, Carriage Crest Elementary, Kent, WA

Jolene Granier (retired), grade 6, Colorado

Julie Ledford, Edmonds, WA (soon to be teaching in Dubai, UAE)

Cindy Flegenheimer, grades 4–8, Brighton School, Lynnwood, WA

Barb McCallister, grade 1, Campbell Elementary, Arvada, CO

Happy Bell, grade 2, Austin, TX (previously at Hong Kong International School)

Carol Dulac, grade 3, Sant Bani School, New Hampshire

AMERICAN COMMUNITY SCHOOL OF ABU DHABI, UNITED ARAB EMIRATES

Jen Munnerlyn, literacy coach

Priscilla Wilson, grade 3

AMERICAN EMBASSY SCHOOL, DELHI, INDIA

Bob Hetzel, director

Susan Young, elementary principal

Kathy Zabinski, literacy specialist

Stacey DuPont, literacy specialist (currently a part-time literacy coach at Ras Tanura Elementary in Saudi Arabia)

Gene Quezada, grade 5

Cheryl Perkins, grade 1

Kendra Daly, grade 1

Melissa White, grade 2

AMERICAN SCHOOL IN JAPAN, TOKYO

Ranu Bhattacharyya, grade 4 (previously at the American Embassy School in Delhi and the International School of Beijing)

AMERICAN SCHOOL IN LONDON, ENGLAND

Amy Walter, grade 3

Jennifer Abastillas, grade 1

Julie Ryan, principal

Patrick Lee, grade 4

Sally Disher, grade 4

AMERICAN SCHOOL IN DOHA, QATAR

Tanya Shahen, literacy coach

THE AMERICAN INTERNATIONAL SCHOOL OF MUSCAT, OMAN

Tommy Duncan, grades 5/6
Kenneth Ingram, ESL/ELL coordinator/teacher
Kerry Harder, literacy coach

ANGLO-AMERICAN SCHOOL, MOSCOW, RUSSIA

Alexandra Caso-Gustafson, literacy coach

CAIRO AMERICAN COLLEGE, EGYPT

Theresa Marriott, grade 3

HONG KONG INTERNATIONAL SCHOOL, CHINA

Ben Hart, grades 3/4 (currently assistant principal)
Chris Langdon, grades 3/4 (currently at the American Cooperative School of Tunis)
Kasey Perry, grades 3/4
Keith Stanulis grades 3/4
Colin Weaver, grade 5
Trudy Nelson, grade 1
Eliza Lewis, grade 1/literacy coach
Donna Koehneke, grade 1

INTERNATIONAL SCHOOL OF BEIJING, CHINA

Cindy Curtis, prekindergarten
Fiona Sheridan, literacy coach
Linda Brubaker, grade 1

NESA REGION

Bridget Doogan, curriculum consultant

SAIGON SOUTH INTERNATIONAL SCHOOL, VIETNAM

Susan Hahn, literacy coach

SINGAPORE AMERICAN SCHOOL

Louise Donaghey, primary school literacy coach
David Hoss, primary school principal
Peggy Moineau, grade 2
Melissa Clark, grade 1
Michelle Morton, grade 1
Stephanie Zarikow, grade 5
Jodi Bonnette, intermediate grade literacy coach
Debbie Woodfield, grade 1
Jemma Hooykaas, grade 5
Beth Burnett, grade 5

SHANGHAI AMERICAN SCHOOL, CHINA

Erian Leishman, grade 4

SHEKOU INTERNATIONAL SCHOOL, CHINA

Treena Casey, curriculum director

TAIPEI AMERICAN SCHOOL, TAIWAN

Cathy Hsu, grade 5
Susan Winter, kindergarten

References

Akhavan, Nancy. 2009. *Teaching Writing in a Title I School, K–3*. Portsmouth, NH: Heinemann.

———. 2008. *The Content-Rich Reading and Writing Workshop: A Time-Saving Approach for Making the Most of Your Literacy Block*. New York: Scholastic.

———. 2007. *Accelerated Vocabulary Instruction: Strategies for Closing the Achievement Gap for All Students*. New York: Scholastic.

———. 2004. *How to Align Literacy Instruction, Assessment, and Standards: And Achieve Results You Never Dreamed Possible*. Portsmouth, NH: Heinemann.

Allen, Camille. 2001. *The Multigenre Research Paper: Voice, Passion, and Discovery in Grades 4–6*. Portsmouth, NH: Heinemann.

Allen, Janet. 2007. *Inside Words: Tools for Teaching Academic Vocabulary, Grades 4–12*. Portland, ME: Stenhouse.

———. 1999. *Words, Words, Words: Teaching Vocabulary in Grades 4–12*. Portland, ME: Stenhouse. (E-Book)

Allen, Jennifer. May 2008. "Read Our Walls: Bridging Professional Development and Student Achievement." Holden, ME: Choice Literacy.

Allyn, Pam. 2007. *The Complete 4 for Literacy: How to Teach Reading and Writing Through Daily Lessons, Monthly Units, and Yearlong Calendars*. New York: Scholastic.

Anderson, Carl. 2009. *Strategic Writing Conferences: Smart Conversations That Move Young Writers Forward*. Portsmouth, NH: Heinemann. (with DVDs)

———. 2007. *The Craft of Grammar: Integrated Instruction in Writer's Workshop*. Portsmouth, NH: Heinemann. (DVD)

———. 2005. *Assessing Writers*. Portsmouth, NH: Heinemann.

———. 2000. *How's It Going? A Practical Guide to Conferring with Student Writers*. Portsmouth, NH: Heinemann.

Anderson, Jeff. 2008. *Editing Invitations*. Portland, ME: Stenhouse. (DVD)

———. 2008. *Teaching Apostrophes*. Portland, ME: Stenhouse. (DVD)

———. 2007. *Everyday Editing: Inviting Students to Develop Skill and Craft in Writing Workshop*. Portland, ME: Stenhouse.

———. 2005. *Mechanically Inclined: Building Grammar, Usage, and Style into Writer's Workshop*. Portland, ME: Stenhouse.

Angelillo, Janet. 2008. *Grammar Study: Helping Students Get What Grammar Is and How It Works (Units of Study, Mentor Texts, Curriculum Calendars)*. New York: Scholastic.

———. 2008. *Whole-Class Teaching: Minilessons and More*. Portsmouth, NH: Heinemann.

———. 2005. *Making Revision Matter: Strategies for Guiding Students to Focus, Organize, and Strengthen Their Writing Independently*. New York: Scholastic.

———. 2005. *Writing to the Prompt: When Students Don't Have a Choice*. Portsmouth, NH: Heinemann.

———. 2003. *Writing About Reading: From Book Talk to Literary Essays, Grades 3–8*. Portsmouth, NH: Heinemann.

———. 2002. *A Fresh Approach to Teaching Punctuation*. New York: Scholastic.

Atwell, Nancie. 1998. *In the Middle: New Understandings About Writing, Reading, and Learning*. Portsmouth, NH: Heinemann.

Avery, Carol. 2002. . . . *And with a Light Touch: Learning About Reading, Writing and Teaching with First Graders*. 2d ed. Portsmouth, NH: Heinemann.

Baskwill, Jane. 2009. *Getting Dads on Board: Fostering Literacy Partnerships for Successful Student Learning*. Markham, Ontario: Pembroke.

Bear, Donald, Marcia Invernizzi, Shane Templeton, and Francine Johnston. 2010. *Words Their Way: Letter and Picture Sorts for Emergent Spellers*. 2d ed. Boston: Pearson Education.

———. 2008. *Words Their Way: Word Study for Phonics, Vocabulary, and Spelling Instruction*. 4th ed. Boston: Pearson Education. (with CD-ROM)

Beaver, Joetta, and Mark Clark. 2004. *Developmental Reading Assessment 2: Word Analysis*. Upper Saddle River, NJ: Pearson.

Beck, Isabel, Margaret McKeown, and Linda Kucan. 2008. *Creating Robust Vocabulary: Frequently Asked Questions and Extended Examples*. New York: Guildford Press.

———. 2002. *Bringing Words to Life: Robust Vocabulary Instruction*. New York: Guildford Press.

Bender, Jenny Mechem. 2007. *The Resourceful Writing Teacher: A Handbook of Essential Skills and Strategies*. Portsmouth, NH: Heinemann.

Bennett-Armistead, V. Susan, Nell Duke, and Annie Moses. 2005. *Literacy and the Youngest Learner: Best Practices for Educators of Children from Birth to 5*. New York: Scholastic.

Bernabei, Gretchen, Jayne Hover, and Cynthia Candler. 2009. *Crunchtime: Lessons to Help Students Blow the Roof Off Writing Tests—and Become Better Writers in the Process*. Portsmouth, NH: Heinemann.

Bettleheim, Bruno. 1976. *The Uses of Enchantment: The Meaning and Importance of Fairy Tales*. New York: Knopf.

Bhattacharyya, Ranu. 2010. *The Castle in the Classroom: Story as a Springboard for Early Literacy*. Portsmouth, NH: Heinemann.

Blevins, Wiley. 2006. *Phonics from A–Z: A Practical Guide*. New York: Scholastic.

Block, Cathy Collins, and John Mangieri. 2006. *The Vocabulary-Enriched Classroom: Practices for Improving the Reading Performance of All Students in Grades 3 and Up*. New York: Scholastic.

Bomer, Katherine. 2010. *Hidden Gems: Naming and Teaching from the Brilliance in Every Student's Writing*. Portsmouth, NH: Heinemann.

———. 2005. *Writing a Life: Teaching Memoir to Sharpen Insight, Shape Meaning—and Triumph over Tests*. Portsmouth, NH: Heinemann.

Bomer, Katherine, and Randy Bomer. 2001. *For a Better World: Reading and Writing for Social Action*. Portsmouth, NH: Heinemann.

Booth, David. 2001. *Reading and Writing in the Middle Years*. Portland, ME: Stenhouse.

Brand, Gayle. November 2006. "Planning a Year of K–3 Author Studies." Holden, ME: Choice Literacy.

Brand, Max. 2006. *Conferring with Boys*. Portland, ME: Stenhouse. (DVD)

———. 2005. *A Day of Words: Integrating Word Work in the Intermediate Grades*. Portland, ME: Stenhouse. (VHS or DVD)

———. 2004. *Word Savvy: Integrating Vocabulary, Spelling, and Word Study, Grades 3–6*. Portland, ME: Stenhouse.

Brannon, Lil, Sally Griffin, Karen Haag, Tony Iannone, Cynthia Urganski, and Shanna Woodward. 2008. *Thinking Out Loud on Paper: The Student Daybook as a Tool to Foster Learning*. Portsmouth, NH: Heinemann.

Brozo, William, and Kathleen Puckett. 2009. *Supporting Content Area Literacy with Technology*. Boston: Allyn and Bacon.

Buckner, Aimee. 2009. "New Notebook Essentials." Holden, ME: Choice Literacy.

———. 2006. *Inside Notebooks: Bringing Out Writers, Grades 3–6*. Portland, ME: Stenhouse. (VHS or DVD)

———. September, 2006. "The Five-Minute Solution: Mini-Groups after Mini-Lessons to Maximize Conferring Time." Holden, ME: Choice Literacy.

———. 2005. *Notebook Know-How: Strategies for the Writer's Notebook*. Portland, ME: Stenhouse.

Buis, Kellie. 2007. *Reclaiming Reluctant Writers: How to Encourage Students to Face Their Fears and Master the Essential Traits of Good Writing*. Portland, ME: Stenhouse.

———. 2004. *Making Words Stick*. Portland, ME: Stenhouse.

Caine, Karen. 2008. *Writing to Persuade: Minilessons to Help Students Plan, Draft, and Revise, Grades 3–8*. Portsmouth, NH: Heinemann.

Calkins, Lucy. 2009. *A Quick Guide to Teaching Second Grade Writers with Units of Study*. Portsmouth, NH: Heinemann.

———. 2007. *Seeing Possibilities: An Inside View of Units of Study for Teaching Writing, Grades 3–5*. Portsmouth, NH: Heinemann. (DVD)

———. 2006. *Units of Study for Teaching Writing, Grades 3–5*. Portsmouth, NH: Heinemann.

———. 2005. *Big Lessons from Small Writers*. Portsmouth, NH: Heinemann.

———. 2003. *Units of Study for Primary Writing*. Portsmouth, NH: Heinemann.

———. 1994. *The Art of Teaching Writing*. 2d ed. Portsmouth, NH: Heinemann.

Calkins, Lucy, Amanda Hartman, and Zoë White. 2005. *Conferring with Primary Writers*. Portsmouth, NH: Heinemann. (CD-ROM)

———. 2005. *One to One: The Art of Conferring with Young Writers*. Portsmouth, NH: Heinemann.

Calkins, Lucy, and Leah Mermelstein. 2003. *Launching the Writing Workshop* (from *Units of Study for Primary Writing, Grades K–2*). Portsmouth, NH: Heinemann/*first*hand.

Calkins, Lucy, and Laurie Pessah. 2008. *A Principal's Guide to Leadership in the Teaching of Writing*. Portsmouth, NH: Heinemann. (with DVD)

Calkins, Lucy, and Laurie Pesah. 2003. *Nonfiction Writing: Procedures and Reports* (from *Units of Study for Primary Writing, Grades K–2*). Portsmouth, NH: Heinemann/*first*hand.

Cambourne, Brian. 1993. *The Whole Story: Natural Learning and the Acquisition of Literacy in the Classroom*. New York: Scholastic.

Campbell, Robin. 2004. *Phonics Naturally: Reading and Writing for Real Purposes*. Portsmouth, NH: Heinemann.

Celic, Christina. 2009. *English Language Learners Day by Day, K–6: A Complete Guide to Literacy, Content-Area, and Language Instruction*. Portsmouth, NH: Heinemann.

Chen, Linda, and Eugenia Mora-Flores. 2006. *Balanced Literacy for English Language Learners, K–2*. Portsmouth, NH: Heinemann.

Cloud, Nancy, Fred Genesee, and Else Hamayan. 2009. *Literacy Instruction for English Language Learners: A Teacher's Guide to Research-Based Practices*. Portsmouth, NH: Heinemann.

Cole, Ardith Davis. 2009. *Better Answers: Written Performance That Looks Good and Sounds Smart*. 2d ed. Portland, ME: Stenhouse. (with CD-ROM)

———. 2006. *Right-Answer Writing: An All-in-One Resource to Help Students Craft Better Responses*. Portsmouth, NH: Heinemann. (with CD-ROM)

Corgill, Ann Marie. 2008. *Of Primary Importance: What's Essential in Teaching Young Writers*. Portland, ME: Stenhouse.

Cruz, Colleen. 2008. *A Quick Guide to Reaching Struggling Writers, K–5*. Portsmouth, NH: Heinemann.

———. 2004. *Independent Writing: One Teacher—Thirty-Two Needs, Topics, and Plans*. Portsmouth, NH: Heinemann.

Culham, Ruth. 2005. *6 + 1 Traits of Writing: The Complete Guide for the Primary Grades*. New York: Scholastic.

———. 2003. *6 + 1 Traits of Writing: The Complete Guide Grades 3 and Up: Everything You Need to Teach and Assess Student Writing with This Powerful Model*. New York: Scholastic.

Cummins, Jim, Kristin Brown, and Dennis Sayers. 2007. *Literacy, Technology, and Diversity: Teaching for Success in Changing Times*. Boston: Allyn and Bacon.

Cunningham, Patricia. 2009. *What Really Matters in Vocabulary: Research-Based Practices Across the Curriculum*. Boston: Allyn and Bacon.

———. 2009. *Phonics They Use: Words for Reading and Writing*. 5th ed. Boston: Allyn and Bacon.

Cunningham, Patricia, and Richard Allington. 2007. *Classrooms That Work: They Can All Read and Write*. 4th ed. Boston: Pearson.

Cunningham, Patricia, and James Cunningham. 2010. *What Really Matters in Writing: Research-Based Practices Across the Elementary Curriculum*. Boston: Allyn and Bacon.

Cunningham, Patricia, and Dorothy Hall. 2009. *Making Words Fifth Grade: 50 Hands-On Lessons for Teaching Prefixes, Suffixes, and Roots.* Boston: Allyn and Bacon.

———. 2009. *Making Words First Grade: 100 Hands-On Lessons for Phonemic Awareness, Phonics, and Spelling.* Boston: Allyn and Bacon.

———. 2009. *Making Words Fourth Grade: 50 Hands-On Lessons for Teaching Prefixes, Suffixes, and Roots.* Boston: Allyn and Bacon.

———. 2009. *Making Words Third Grade: 70 Hands-On Lessons for Teaching Prefixes, Suffixes, and Homophones.* Boston: Allyn and Bacon.

———. 2009. *Making Words Second Grade: 100 Hands-On Lessons for Phonemic Awareness, Phonics and Spelling.* Boston: Allyn and Bacon.

Davis, Carol, and Alice Yang. 2005. *Parents and Teachers Working Together.* Portland, ME: Stenhouse.

Davis, Judy, and Sharon Hill. 2003. *The No-Nonsense Guide to Teaching Writing: Strategies, Structures, Solutions.* Portsmouth, NH: Heinemann.

DeMille, Ted. 2008. *Making Believe on Paper: Fiction Writing with Young Children.* Portsmouth, NH: Heinemann.

Dierkling, Connie Campbell, and Sherra Ann Jones. 2003. *Growing Up Writing: Mini-Lessons for Emergent and Beginning Writers.* Gainesville, FL: Maupin House.

Dorfman, Lynne, and Rose Cappelli. 2009. *Nonfiction Mentor Texts: Teaching Informational Writing Through Children's Literature, K–8.* Portland, ME: Stenhouse.

———. 2007. *Mentor Texts: Teaching Writing Through Children's Literature, K–6.* Portland, ME: Stenhouse.

Dorn, Linda. 1999, 2006. *Organizing for Literacy.* Portland, ME: Stenhouse. (VHS or DVD)

Dorn, Linda, Cathy French, and Tammy Jones. 1998. *Apprenticeship in Literacy: Transitions Across Reading and Writing.* Portland, ME: Stenhouse.

Dorn, Linda, and Carla Soffos. 2007. *Collaborative Conferences.* Portland, ME: Stenhouse. (DVD)

———. 2003, 2006. *Developing Independent Learners: A Reading/Writing Workshop Approach.* Portland, ME: Stenhouse. (VHS or DVD)

———. 2001. *Scaffolding Young Writers: A Writer's Workshop Approach.* Portland, ME: Stenhouse.

———. 2001. *Shaping Literate Minds: Developing Self-Regulated Learners.* Portland, ME: Stenhouse.

Dragan, Pat Barrett. 2008. *Kids, Cameras, and the Curriculum.* Portsmouth, NH: Heinemann.

———. 2005. *A How-To Guide for Teaching English Language Learners in the Primary Classroom.* Portsmouth, NH: Heinemann.

———. 2003. *Everything You Need to Know to Teach First Grade.* Portsmouth, NH: Heinemann.

Dudley-Marling, Curt, and Patricia Paugh. 2009. *A Classroom Teacher's Guide to Struggling Writers: How to Provide Differentiated Support and Ongoing Assessment.* Portsmouth, NH: Heinemann.

Dufresne, Michèle. 2002. *Word Solvers: Making Sense of Letters and Sounds.* Portsmouth, NH: Heinemann.

Duke, Nell, and V. Susan Bennett-Armistead. 2003. *Reading and Writing Informational Texts in the Primary Grades.* New York: Scholastic.

Edwards, Patricia. 2009. *Tapping the Potential of Parents: A Strategic Guide to Boosting Student Achievement Through Family Involvement.* New York: Scholastic.

Ehmann, Susan, and Kellyann Gayer. 2009. *I Can Write Like That! A Guide to Mentor Texts and Craft Studies for Writer's Workshop, K–6.* Portsmouth, NH: Heinemann.

Ehrenworth, Mary, and Vicki Vinton. 2005. *The Power of Grammar: Unconventional Approaches to the Conventions of Language.* Portsmouth, NH: Heinemann.

Elliott, Janet. 2008. *Using the Writer's Notebook in Grades 3–8.* Urbana, IL: National Council of Teachers of English.

Ellis, Linda, and Jamie Marsh. 2007. *Getting Started: The Reading-Writing Workshop, Grades 4–8.* Portsmouth, NH: Heinemann.

Ericson, Lita, and Moira Frasher Juliebo. 1998. *Phonological Awareness Handbook for Kindergarten and Primary Teachers.* Newark, DE: International Reading Association.

Evans, Janet. 2005. *Literacy Moves On: Popular Culture, New Technologies, and Critical Literacy in the Elementary Classroom.* Portsmouth, NH: Heinemann.

Fay, Kathleen, and Suzanne Whaley. 2004. *Becoming One Community: Reading and Writing with English Language Learners.* Portland, ME: Stenhouse.

Feigelson, Dan. 2008. *Practical Punctuation: Lessons on Rule Making and Rule Breaking in Elementary Writing.* Portsmouth, NH: Heinemann.

Fershleiser, Rachel, and Larry Smith. 2008. *Not Quite What I Was Planning: Six-Word Memoirs by Writers Famous and Obscure.* New York: Harper.

Fisher, Bobbi. 1998. *Joyful Learning in Kindergarten.* 2d ed. Portsmouth, NH: Heinemann.

Fletcher, Ralph. 2010. *Pyrotechnics on the Page: Language Play That Boosts Writing.* Portland, ME: Stenhouse.

———. 2008. *"Dude, Listen to This!" Engaging Boy Writers.* Portland, ME: Stenhouse. (DVD)

———. 2006. *Boy Writers: Reclaiming Their Voices.* Portland, ME: Stenhouse. (Audiobook)

———. 1996. *Breathing In, Breathing Out: Keeping a Writer's Notebook.* Portsmouth, NH: Heinemann.

———. 1993. *What a Writer Needs.* Portsmouth, NH: Heinemann.

Fletcher, Ralph, and JoAnn Portalupi. 2007. *Craft Lessons: Teaching Writing K–8.* 2d ed. Portland, ME: Stenhouse.

———. 2002, 2006. *When Students Write*. Portland, ME: Stenhouse. (VHS or DVD)

———. 2004, 2006. *In the Beginning: Young Writers Develop Independence*. Portland, ME: Stenhouse. (VHS or DVD)

———. 2005. *Lessons for the Writer's Notebook, Grades 3–6*. Portsmouth, NH: Heinemann.

———. 2001. *Writing Workshop: The Essential Guide*. Portland, ME: Stenhouse.

Flynn, Nick, and Shirley McPhillips. 2000. *A Note Slipped Under the Door: Teaching from the Poems We Love*. Portland ME: Stenhouse.

Foster, Graham, and Toni Marasco. 2007. *Exemplars: Your Best Resource to Improve Student Writing*. Portland, ME: Stenhouse.

Fountas, Irene, and Gay Su Pinnell. 2006. *Word Study Lessons, Grade 3*. Portsmouth, NH: Heinemann. (with CD-ROM)

Fountas, Irene, and Gay Su Pinnell. 2005. *Word Study: Phonics and Spelling Minilessons*. Portsmouth, NH: Heinemann. (with CD-ROM)

Franzese, Rosalie. 2002. *Reading and Writing in Kindergarten: A Practical Guide*. New York: Scholastic.

Fraser, Jane, and Donna Skolnick. 1994. *On Their Way: Celebrating Second Graders as They Read and Write*. Portsmouth, NH: Heinemann.

Freeman, David, and Yvonne Freeman. 2004. *Essential Linguistics: What You Need to Know to Teach Reading, ESL, Spelling, Phonics, and Grammar*. Portsmouth, NH: Heinemann.

Frey, Nancy, and Douglas Fisher. 2009. *Learning Words Inside and Out, Grades 1–6: Vocabulary Instruction That Boosts Achievement in All Subject Areas*. Portsmouth, NH: Heinemann.

Fu, Danling. 2009. *Writing Between Languages: How English Language Learners Make the Transition to Fluency, Grades 4–12*. Portsmouth, NH: Heinemann.

Ganske, Kathy. 2000. *Word Journeys: Assessment-Guided Phonics, Spelling, and Vocabulary Instruction*. New York: Guilford Press.

Garan, Elaine. 2007. *Smart Answers to Tough Questions: What to Say When You're Asked About Fluency, Phonics, Grammar, Vocabulary, SSR, Tests, Support for ELLs, and More*. New York: Scholastic.

Gentry, J. Richard. 2004. *The Science of Spelling*. Portsmouth, NH: Heinemann.

———. 1997. *My Kid Can't Spell! Understanding and Assisting Your Child's Literacy Development*. Portsmouth, NH: Heinemann.

Gentry, J. Richard, and Jean Wallace Gillet. 1993. *Teaching Kids to Spell*. Portsmouth, NH: Heinemann.

Gibbons, Pauline. 2009. *English Learners, Academic Literacy, and Thinking: Learning in the Challenge Zone*. Portsmouth, NH: Heinemann.

Glover, Matt. 2009. *Engaging Young Writers, Preschool—Grade 1*. Portsmouth, NH: Heinemann.

Gotthelf, Abi, and Pam Allyn. 2008. *The Complete Year in Reading and Writing: Grade 3*. New York: Scholastic. (with DVD)

Graves, Donald. 1994. *A Fresh Look at Writing*. Portsmouth, NH: Heinemann.

Graves, Donald, and Penny Kittle. 2005. *Inside Writing: How to Teach the Details of Craft*. Portsmouth, NH: Heinemann. (with DVD and *My Quick Writes*)

Graves, Michael. 2008. *Teaching Individual Words: One Size Does Not Fit All.* Newark, DE: International Reading Association.

———. 2005. *The Vocabulary Book: Learning and Instruction* (Language and Literacy Series). New York: Teachers College Press.

Hahn, Mary Lee. January 2009. "The Joy of Letter Writing: An Integrated Unit for Intermediate Students." Holden, ME: Choice Literacy.

Hale, Elizabeth. 2008. *Crafting Writers, K–6.* Portland, ME: Stenhouse.

Hall, Dorothy, and Patricia Cunningham. 2009. *Making Words: 50 Interactive Lessons That Build Phonemic Awareness, Phonics, and Spelling Skills: Kindergarten.* Boston: Allyn and Bacon.

Hampton, Sally, Sandra Murphy, and Margaret Lowry. 2009. *Using Rubrics to Improve Student Writing.* Rev. ed. Urbana, IL: International Reading Association (one book for each grade level K–5).

Harmon, Janis, Karen Wood, and Wanda Hedrick. 2006. *Instructional Strategies for Teaching Content Vocabulary (Grades 4–12).* Newark, DE: International Reading Association.

Hartman, Amanda, and Lucy Calkins. 2008. *Up Close: Teaching English Language Learners in Reading and Writing Workshops.* Portsmouth, NH: Heinemann. (DVD)

Harwayne, Shelley. 2005. *Novel Perspectives: Writing Minilessons Inspired by the Children in Adult Fiction.* Portsmouth, NH: Heinemann.

———. 2001. *Writing Through Childhood: Rethinking Process and Product.* Portsmouth, NH: Heinemann.

———. 2000. *Lifetime Guarantees: Toward Ambitious Literacy Teaching.* Portsmouth, NH: Heinemann.

Harvey, Stephanie. 1998. *Nonfiction Matters: Reading, Writing, and Research in Grades 3–8.* Portland, ME: Stenhouse.

Heard, Georgia. 2007. *Climb Inside a Poem: Original Poems for Children.* Portsmouth, NH: *first*hand/Heinemann.

———. 2002. *The Revision Toolbox: Teaching Techniques That Work.* Portsmouth, NH: Heinemann.

———. 1999. *Awakening the Heart: Exploring Poetry in Elementary and Middle School.* Portsmouth, NH: Heinemann.

Heard, Georgia, and Lester Laminack. 2008. *Lessons for Climb Inside a Poem.* Portsmouth, NH: Heinemann.

———. 2008. *Reading and Writing Poetry Across the Year, Grades K–2.* Portsmouth, NH: *first*hand/Heinemann.

Heard, Georgia, and Jen McDonough. 2009. *A Place for Wonder: Reading and Writing Nonfiction in the Primary Grades.* Portsmouth, NH: Heinemann.

Helman, Lori, Donald Bear, Marcia Invernizzi. 2008. *Words Their Way with English Learners: Word Study for Phonics, Vocabulary, and Spelling Instruction.* Boston: Pearson Education.

Helman, Lori, Donald Bear, Marcia Invernizzi, Shane Templeton, and Francine Johnston. 2009. *Words Their Way: Letter-Name Alphabetic Sorts for Spanish-Speaking English Learners.* Boston: Pearson Education.

———. 2009. *Words Their Way: Emergent Sorts for Spanish-Speaking English Learners*. Boston: Pearson Education.

Hill, Bonnie Campbell. 2007. *Supporting Your Child's Literacy Learning: A Guide for Parents*. Portsmouth, NH: Heinemann.

———. 2001. *Developmental Continuums: A Framework for Literacy Instruction and Assessment, K–8*. Norwood, MA: Christopher-Gordon.

Hill, Bonnie Campbell, and Carrie Ekey. 2010. *The Next-Step Guide to Enriching Classroom Environments*. Portsmouth, NH: Heinemann.

Hindley, Joanne. 1998, 2006. *Inside Reading and Writing Workshop*. Portland, ME: Stenhouse. (VHS or DVD)

———. 1996. *In the Company of Children*. Portland, ME: Stenhouse.

Holbrook, Sara. 2010. *High Definition: Vocabulary Acquisition Through Collaboration, Composition and Performance*. Portsmouth, NH: Heinemann.

———. 2005. *Practical Poetry: A Nonstandard Approach to Meeting Content-Area Standards*. Portsmouth, NH: Heinemann.

Horn, Martha, and Mary Ellen Giacobbe. 2007. *Talking, Drawing, Writing: Lessons for Our Youngest Writers*. Portland, ME: Stenhouse.

Hoyt, Linda. 2008. *Revisit, Reflect, Retell: Strategies for Improving Reading Comprehension*. Updated ed. Portsmouth, NH: Heinemann. (with CD-ROM and DVD)

———. 2000. *Snapshots: Literacy Minilessons Up Close*. Portsmouth, NH: Heinemann.

Hoyt, Linda, and Teresa Therriault. 2008. *Mastering the Mechanics: Ready-to-Use Lessons for Modeled, Guided, and Independent Editing, Grades K–1*. New York: Scholastic.

———. 2008. *Mastering the Mechanics: Ready-to-Use Lessons for Modeled, Guided, and Independent Editing, Grades 2–3*. New York: Scholastic.

———. 2008. *Mastering the Mechanics: Ready-to-Use Lessons for Modeled, Guided, and Independent Editing, Grades 4–5*. New York: Scholastic.

Hsu, Cathy. October 2009. "Writing Partnerships." *The Reading Teacher* 63 (2): 153–58).

Hydrick, Janie. 1996. *Parent's Guide to Literacy for the 21st Century: PreK Through Grade 5*. Urbana, IL: National Council of Teachers of Reading.

Invernizzi, Marcia, Francine Johnston, Donald Bear, and Shane Templeton. 2009. *Words Their Way: Word Sorts for Within Word Pattern Spellers*. 2d ed. Boston: Pearson Education.

Jacobson, Jennifer. 2010. *No More "I'm Done!": Fostering Independent Writers in the Primary Grades*. Portland, ME: Stenhouse.

Jenkins, Carol Brennan. 1999. *The Allure of the Author: Author Studies in the Elementary Classroom*. Portsmouth, NH: Heinemann.

Jenkins, Carol Brennan, and Deborah White. (Eds.). 2007. *Nonfiction Authors Studies in the Elementary Classroom*. Portsmouth, NH: Heinemann.

Johnston, Francine, Marcia Invernizzi, Donald Bear, and Shane Templeton. 2009. *Words Their Way: Word Sorts for Letter Name–Alphabetic Spellers*. 2d ed. Boston: Pearson Education.

———. 2009. *Words Their Way: Word Sorts for Syllables and Affixes Spellers*. 2d ed. Boston: Pearson Education.

Johnston, Peter. 2004. *Choice Words: How Our Language Affects Children's Learning*. Portland, ME: Stenhouse. (Audiobook)

Johnstone, Bob. 2006. *I Have Computers in My Classroom—Now What?* Portsmouth, NH: Heinemann.

Jorgensen, Karen. 2001. *The Whole Story: Crafting Fiction in the Upper Elementary Grades*. Portsmouth, NH: Heinemann.

Kendall, Juli, and Outey Khuon. 2006. *Writing Sense: Integrated Reading and Writing Lessons for English Language Learners K–8*. Portland, ME: Stenhouse.

Laminack, Lester. 2007. *Cracking Open the Author's Craft: Teaching the Art of Writing*. New York: Scholastic. (with DVD)

Lane, Barry. 2008. *But How Do You Teach Writing? A Simple Guide for All Teachers*. New York: Scholastic.

———. 1992. *After The End: Teaching and Learning Creative Revision*. Portsmouth, NH: Heinemann.

Lane, Barry, and Gretchen Bernabei. 2001. *Why We Must Run with Scissors: Voice Lessons in Persuasive Writing 3–12*. Shoreham, VT: Discover Writing Press.

Lattimer, Heather. 2003. *Thinking Through Genre: Units of Study in Reading and Writing Workshop, Grades 4–12*. Portland, ME: Stenhouse.

Lera, Debbie. 2009. *Writing Above Standard: Engaging Lessons That Take Standards to New Heights and Help Kids Become Skilled, Inspired Writers*. New York: Scholastic.

Lucht, Lauren Berman. 2006. *The Wonder of Word Study: Lessons and Activities to Create Independent Readers, Writers and Spellers*. Portsmouth, NH: Heinemann.

Lyon, Anna, and Paula Moore. 2003. *Sound Systems: Explicit, Systematic Phonics in Early Literacy Contexts*. Portland, ME: Stenhouse.

Margolies, Jaime, and Pam Allyn. 2008. *The Complete Year in Reading and Writing: Grade 1*. New York: Scholastic. (with DVD)

Marten, Cindy. 2003. *Word Crafting: Teaching Spelling Grades K–6*. Portsmouth, NH: Heinemann.

McCarrier, Andrea, Gay Su Pinnell, and Irene Fountas. 2000. *Interactive Writing: How Language and Literacy Come Together, K–2*. Portsmouth, NH: Heinemann.

McMackin, Mary, and Barbara Siegel. 2002. *Knowing How: Researching and Writing Nonfiction 3—8*. Portland, ME: Stenhouse.

McNally, Karen, and Pam Allyn. 2008. *The Complete Year in Reading and Writing: Kindergarten*. New York: Scholastic. (with DVD)

Mermelstein, Leah. 2007. *Don't Forget to Share: The Crucial Last Step in the Writing Workshop*. Portsmouth, NH: Heinemann.

———. 2006. *Reading and Writing Connections in the K–2 Classroom: Find the Clarity and the Blur the Lines*. Boston: Allyn and Bacon.

Miyata, Kaz, and Cathy Miyata. 2006. *The Reading Edge: Using Phonics Strategically to Teach Reading*. Markham, Ontario: Pembroke.

Morgan, Bruce, with Deb Odom. 2004. *Writing Through the Tween Years: Supporting Writers Grades 3–6*. Portland, ME: Stenhouse.

Moustafa, Margaret. 1997. *Beyond Traditional Phonics: Research Discoveries and Reading Instruction*. Portsmouth, NH: Heinemann.

Murray, Donald. 2004. *Write to Learn*. 8th ed. Boston, MA: Wadsworth Publishing.

Newkirk, Thomas. 2009. *Holding On to Good Ideas in a Time of Bad Ones: Six Literacy Principles Worth Fighting For*. Portsmouth, NH: Heinemann.

———. 2002. *Misreading Masculity: Boys, Literacy, and Popular Culture*. Portsmouth, NH: Heinemann.

Oczkus, Lori. 2007. *Guided Writing: Practical Lessons, Powerful Results*. Portsmouth, NH: Heinemann.

Oglan, Gerald, and Averil Elcombe. 2001. *Parent to Parent: Our Children, Their Literacy*. Urbana, IL: National Council of Teachers of English.

Opitz, Michael. 2000. *Rhymes and Reasons: Literature and Language Play for Phonological Awareness*. Portsmouth, NH: Heinemann.

Overmeyer, Mark. 2005. *When Writing Workshop Isn't Working: Answers to Ten Tough Questions Grades 2–5*. Portland, ME: Stenhouse. (E-book)

Owocki, Gretchen. 2007. *Literate Days: Reading and Writing with Preschool and Primary Children*. Portsmouth, NH: Heinemann. (With DVD)

Painter, Kristen. 2006. *Living and Teaching the Writing Workshop*. Portsmouth, NH: Heinemann.

Palmer, Sue, and Ros Bayley. 2005. *Early Literacy Fundamentals: A Balanced Approach to Language, Listening and Literacy Skills—Ages 3 to 6*. Markham, Ontario: Pembroke.

Parker, Emelie, and Tess Pardini. 2006. *"The Words Came Down!" English Learners Read, Write, and Talk Across the Curriculum, K–2*. Portland, ME: Stenhouse.

Parsons, Stephanie. 2007. *Second Grade Writers: Units of Study to Help Children Focus on Audience and Purpose*. Portsmouth, NH: Heinemann.

———. 2005. *First Grade Writers: Units of Study to Help Children Plan, Organize, and Structure Their Ideas*. Portsmouth, NH: Heinemann.

Pastore, Laurie, and Pam Allyn. 2008. *The Complete Year in Reading and Writing: Grade 4*. New York: Scholastic. (with DVD)

———. 2008. *The Complete Year in Reading and Writing: Grade 5*. New York: Scholastic. (with DVD)

Pinnell, Gay Su, and Irene Fountas. 2010. *The Continuum of Literacy Learning: A Guide to Teaching, Grades K–2*, 2nd ed. Portsmouth, NH: Heinemann.

———. 2010. *The Continuum of Literacy Learning: A Guide to Teaching, Grades 3–8*, 2nd ed. Portsmouth, NH: Heinemann.

———. 2010. *The Continuum of Literacy Learning: A Guide to Teaching, Grades K–8*, 2nd ed. Portsmouth, NH: Heinemann.

———. 2006. *Phonics Lessons with CD-ROM Bundle* (One binder per grade level, K–2). Portsmouth, NH: Heinemann.

———. 2006. *Phonics Lessons with CD-ROM and Poetry Bundle* (One binder per grade level, K–2). Portsmouth, NH: Heinemann.

———. 2003. *Sing a Song of Poetry: A Teaching Resource for Phonemic Awareness, Phonics and Fluency* (Grades K, 1, and 2). Portsmouth, NH: Heinemann.

———, eds. 1999. *Voices on Word Matters: Learning About Phonics and Spelling in the Literacy Classroom*. Portsmouth, NH: Heinemann.

———. 1998. *Word Matters: Teaching Phonics and Spelling in the Reading/Writing Classroom*. Portsmouth, NH: Heinemann.

Portalupi, JoAnn, and Ralph Fletcher. 2006. *Talking About Writing*. Portland, ME: Stenhouse. (DVD)

———. 2006. *In the Beginning: Young Writers Develop Independence*. Portland, ME: Stenhouse. (DVD)

———. 2004. *Teaching the Qualities of Writing: Ideas, Design, Language, Presentation*. Portsmouth, NH: Heinemann.

———. 2001. *Nonfiction Craft Lessons: Teaching Informational Writing K–8*. Portland, ME: Stenhouse. (E-book)

Power, Brenda. 1999. *Parent Power: Energizing Home-School Communication*. Portsmouth, NH: Heinemann.

Pransky, Ken. 2008. *Beneath the Surface: The Hidden Realities of Teaching Culturally and Linguistically Diverse Young Learners, K–6*. Portsmouth, NH: Heinemann.

Prescott-Griffin, Mary Lee. 2007. *Writer to Writer: Fluency and Craft in the Multilingual Classroom*. Portsmouth, NH: Heinemann.

Ray, Katie Wood. 2010. *In Pictures and In Words: Teaching the Qualities of Good Writing Through Illustration Study*. Portsmouth, NH: Heinemann.

———. 2008. *Already Ready: Nurturing Writers in Preschool and Kindergarten*. Portsmouth, NH: Heinemann.

———. 2006. *Study Driven: A Framework for Planning Units of Study in the Writing Workshop*. Portsmouth, NH: Heinemann.

———. 2002. *What You Know by Heart: How to Develop Curriculum for Your Writing Workshop*. Portsmouth, NH: Heinemann.

———. 2001. *The Writing Workshop: Working Through the Hard Parts (and They're All Hard Parts)*. Urbana, IL: National Council of Teachers of English.

———. 1999. *Wondrous Words: Writers and Writing in the Elementary Classroom*. Urbana, IL: National Council of Teachers of English.

Ray, Katie Wood, and Lisa Cleaveland. 2005. *The Teaching Behind About the Authors*. Portsmouth, NH: Heinemann. (DVD)

———. 2004. *About the Authors: Writing Workshop with Our Youngest Writers*. Portsmouth, NH: Heinemann.

Reid, Janine, and Betty Schultze. 2005. *What's Next for This Beginning Writer? Minilessons That Take Writing from Scribbles to Script*. Portland, ME: Stenhouse.

Resnick, Lauren, and Sally Hampton. 2009. *Reading and Writing Grade by Grade*. Newark, DE: International Reading Association. (with DVD)

Robb, Laura. 2004. *Nonfiction Writing: From the Inside Out: Writing Lessons Inspired by Conversations with Leading Authors*. New York: Scholastic.

Rog, Lori Jamison. 2007. *Marvelous Minilessons for Teaching Beginning Writing, K–3*. Newark, DL: International Reading Association.

Rog, Lori Jamison, and Paul Kropp. 2004. *The Write Genre: Classroom Activities and Mini-Lessons That Promote Writing with Clarity, Style, and Flashes of Brilliance*. Portland, ME: Stenhouse.

Rogovin, Paula. 1998. *Classroom Interviews: A World of Learning*. Portsmouth, NH: Heinemann.

Rosencrans, Gladys. 1998. *The Spelling Book: Teaching Children How to Spell, Not What to Spell*. Newark, DE: International Reading Association.

Roswell, Jennifer. 2006. *Family Literacy Experiences*. Markham, Ontario: Pembroke.

Routman, Regie. 2009. *Regie Routman in Residence: Transforming Our Teaching Through Reading to Understand*. Portsmouth, NH: Heinemann. (with DVD)

———. 2008. *Regie Routman in Residence: Transforming Our Teaching Through Reading/Writing Connections*. Portsmouth, NH: Heinemann. (with DVD)

———. 2008. *Regie Routman in Residence: Transforming Our Teaching Through Writing for Audience and Purpose*. Portsmouth, NH: Heinemann. (with DVD)

———. 2005. *Writing Essentials: Raising Expectations and Results While Simplifying Teaching*. Portsmouth, NH: Heinemann.

———. 2000. *Conversations: Strategies for Teaching, Learning, and Evaluating*. Portsmouth, NH: Heinemann.

———. 2000. *Kids' Poems: Teaching First Graders to Love Writing Poetry*. New York: Scholastic.

———. 2000. *Kids' Poems: Teaching Kindergartners to Love Writing Poetry*. New York: Scholastic.

———. 2000. *Kids' Poems: Teaching Second Graders to Love Writing Poetry*. New York: Scholastic.

———. 2000. *Kids' Poems: Teaching Third and Fourth Graders to Love Writing Poetry*. New York: Scholastic.

———. 1996. *Literacy at the Crossroads: Crucial Talk About Reading, Writing and Other Teaching Dilemmas*. Portsmouth, NH: Heinemann.

Rowsell, Jennifer. 2006. *Family Literacy Experiences: Creating Reading and Writing Opportunities That Support Classroom Learning*. Markham, Ontario: Pembroke.

Ruzzo, Karen, and Mary Anne Sacco. 2004. *Significant Studies for Second Grade: Reading and Writing Investigations for Children*. Portsmouth, NH: Heinemann.

Samway, Katharine Davies. 2006. *When English Language Learners Write: Connecting Research to Practice, K–8*. Portsmouth, NH: Heinemann.

Scharer, Patricia, and Gay Su Pinnell. 2008. *Guiding K–3 Writers to Independence: The New Essentials*. New York: Scholastic.

Scott, Judith, Bonnie Skobel, and Jan Wells. 2008. *The Word-Conscious Classroom: Building the Vocabulary Readers and Writers Need*. New York: Scholastic.

Servis, Joan. 1999. *Celebrating the Fourth: Ideas and Inspiration for Teachers of Grade Four*. Portsmouth, NH: Heinemann.

Shagoury, Ruth. 2009. *Raising Writers: Understanding and Nurturing Young Children's Writing Development*. Boston: Allyn and Bacon.

Sibberson, Franki. March 2008. "Rethinking a Study of Nonfiction Writing." Holden, ME: Choice Literacy.

———. May 2009. "New Mentor Texts for Word Choice." Holden, ME: Choice Literacy.

Slaughter, Holly. 2009. *Small-Group Writing Conferences: How to Use Your Instructional Time More Efficiently*. Portsmouth, NH: Heinemann.

Sloan, Megan. March, 2010. "Exploring the Art of Betsy Lewin." In *Book Links* 19 (3). Chicago: American Library Association.

———. 2009. *Into Writing: The Primary Teacher's Guide to Writing Workshop*. Portsmouth, NH: Heinemann.

———. 2008. *Teaching Young Writers to Elaborate: Mini-Lessons and Strategies That Help Students Find Topics and Learn to Tell More*. New York: Scholastic.

———. 2005. *Trait-Based Mini-Lessons for Teaching Writing in Grades 2–4*. New York: Scholastic.

Smith, Andrea. August 2009. "Living Words: Integrating Word Study, Technology, and Content Literacy." Holden, ME: Choice Literacy.

Smith, Michael, and Jeffrey Wilhelm. 2007. *Getting It Right: Fresh Approaches to Teaching Grammar, Usage and Correctness*. New York: Scholastic.

Snowball, Diane. 2006. *Focus on Spelling.* Portland, ME: Stenhouse. (VHS or DVD)

Snowball, Diane, and Faye Bolton. 1999. *Spelling K–8: Planning and Teaching*. Portland, ME: Stenhouse.

Spandel, Vicki. 2008. *Creating Writers Through 6-Trait Writing: Assessment and Instruction*. 5th ed. Boston: Pearson. (with CD-ROM)

———. 2008. *Creating Young Writers: Using the Six Traits to Enrich Writing Process in Primary Classrooms*. 2d ed. Boston: Pearson.

———. 2005. *The 9 Rights of Every Writer: A Guide for Teachers*. Portsmouth, NH: Heinemann.

Stead, Tony. 2004. *Time for Nonfiction* Portland, ME: Stenhouse. (VHS or DVD)

———. 2002. *Is That a Fact? Teaching Nonfiction Writing K–3*. Portland, ME: Stenhouse.

Strickland, Dorothy, Kathy Ganski, and Joanne Monroe. 2002. *Supporting Struggling Readers and Writers: Strategies for Classroom Intervention 3–6*. Portsmouth, ME: Stenhouse. (E-book)

Taylor, Sarah Picard. 2008. *A Quick Guide to Teaching Persuasive Writing, K–2*. Portsmouth, NH: Heinemann.

Templeton, Shane, Francine Johnston, Donald Bear, and Marcia Invernizzi. 2009. *Words Their Way: Word Sorts for Derivational Relations Spellers*. 2d ed. Boston: Pearson Education.

Terlecky, Karen. May 2009. "Planning to Teach with Mentor Texts: Two Examples." Holden, ME: Choice Literacy.

Thomason, Tommy, and Carol York. 2000. *Write on Target: Preparing Young Writers to Succeed on State Writing Achievement Tests*. Norwood, MA: Christopher-Gordon.

Thompson, Michael. 2006. *Raising Cain: Protecting the Inner Life of America's Boys*. Public Broadcasting Station (see www.pbs.org).

Topping, Donna Hooker, and Sandra Josephs Hoffman. 2006. *Getting Grammar: 150 New Ways to Teach an Old Subject*. Portsmouth, NH: Heinemann.

Topping, Donna Hooker, and Roberta Ann McManus. 2002. *Real Reading, Real Writing: Content-Area Strategies*. Portsmouth, NH: Heinemann.

Vitale-Reilly, Patty and Pam Allyn. 2008. *The Complete Year in Reading and Writing: Grade 2*. New York: Scholastic. (with DVD)

Vopat, Jim. 2009. *Writing Circles: Kids Revolutionize Workshop*. Portsmouth, NH: Heinemann.

Vygotsky, Lev. 1978. *Mind in Society: The Development of Higher Psychological Processes*. Cambridge, MA: Harvard University Press.

Weber, Chris. 2002. *Publishing with Students*. Portsmouth, NH: Heinemann.

Wells, Jan, and Janine Reid. 2004. *Writing Anchors*. Ontario, Canada: Pembroke.

Wilde, Sandra. 2008. *Spelling Strategies and Patterns: What Kids Need to Know, Grades 3–5*. Portsmouth, NH: Heinemann. (with CD-ROM)

Wilson, Lorraine. 2006. *Writing to Live: How to Teach Writing for Today's World*. Portsmouth, NH: Heinemann.

Children's Books

Avi. 1995. *Poppy*. New York: Orchard Books.

Black, Holly, and Tony DiTerlizzi. 2003–2004. *The Spiderwick Chronicles*. New York: Simon & Schuster. Five volumes.

Brinckloe, Julie. 1986. *Fireflies*. New York: Aladdin.

Broach, Elise. 2008. *Masterpiece*. New York: Holt.

Bunting, Eve. 2000. *The Memory String*. New York: Houghton Mifflin.

———. 1994. *The Sunshine Home*. New York: Clarion.

———. 1995. *Once Upon a Time*. Katonah, NY: Richard C. Owen.

Clearly, Brian. 2001. *Hairy, Scary, Ordinary: What Is an Adjective?* New York: Carolrhoda.

DiCamillo, Kate. 2006. *Miraculous Journey of Edward Tulane*. New York. Candlewick.

———. 2000. *Because of Winn Dixie*. Cambridge, MA: Candlewick.

Fleming, Denise. 1991. *In the Tall, Tall Grass*. New York: Holt.

Fletcher, Ralph. 2007. *Ralph Fletcher: Author at Work*. Katonah, NY: Richard C. Owen.

———. 2005. *Marshfield Dreams: When I Was a Kid*. New York: Holt.

Fox, Mem. 1992. *Memories: An Autobiography*. Evanston, IL: McDougal, Littell.

———. 1985. *Wilfrid Gordon McDonald Partridge*. New York: Kane/Miller Books.

———. 1985. *Possum Magic*. New York: Kane/Miller.

Frasier, Debra. 2000. *Miss Alaineus: A Vocabulary Disaster*. San Diego: Harcourt.

Gifford, Peggy. 2008. *Moxy Maxwell Does Not Love Stuart Little*. New York: Yearling.

Greenfield, Eloise. 1998. *For the Love of the Game: Michael Jordan and Me*. New York: HarperCollins.

Grambling, Lois. 2000. *Can I Have a Tyrannosaurus Rex, Dad? Can I?* Mahwah, NJ: Bridgewater Books.

Henson, Heather. 2008. *That Book Woman*. New York: Simon and Schuster.

Hesse, Karen. 1999. *Come On, Rain!* New York: Scholastic.

Hest, Amy. 2007. *Mr. George Baker*. Boston: Candlewick.

Holbrook, Sara. 2010. *Normally Weird: Will You Be My Friend?* Honesdale, PA: Boyds Mills Press.

———. 2010. *Zombies! Evacuate the School!* Honesdale, PA: Boyds Mills Press.

Johnston, Tony. 1994. *Amber on the Mountain*. New York: Dial.

Keats, Ezra Jack. 1962. *The Snowy Day*. New York: Viking.

L'Engle, Madeleine. 2007. *A Wrinkle in Time*. New York: Macmillan.

Laminack, Lester. 2004. *Saturdays and Teacakes*. New York: Peachtree.

Law, Ingrid. 2008. *Savvy*. New York: Penguin.

Lewis, C. S. 2000. *The Lion, the Witch and the Wardrobe*. New York. HarperCollins.

Lockhart, E. 2008. *The Disreputable History of Frankie Landau-Banks*. New York: Hyperion.

Maclachlan, Patricia. 1994. *All the Places to Love*. New York: HarperCollins.

Martin Jr., Bill. 1992. *Brown Bear, Brown Bear, What Do You See?* New York: Henry Holt.

Meet the Author (Series of Books about Children's Authors and Illustrators). Katonah, NY: Richard C. Owens.

Nielsen, Susin. 2008. *Word Nerd*. Plattsburgh, NY: Tundra Books.

Pulver, Robin. 2004. *Punctuation Takes a Vacation*. New York: Holiday House.

———. 2001. *Nouns and Verbs Have a Field Day*. New York: Holiday House.

Salinger, Michael. 2009. *Well Defined: Vocabulary in Rhyme*. Honesdale, PA: Boyds Mills Press.

Shannon, David. 1998. *No David!* New York: Blue Sky Press.

Spinelli, Eileen. 2008. *The Best Story*. New York: Dial.

Teague, Mark. 2002. *Dear Mrs. Larue: Letters from Obedience School*. New York: Scholastic.

Wiles, Deborah. 2001. *Love, Ruby Lavender*. New York: HarperCollins.

Williams, Vera B. 1984. *A Chair for My Mother*. New York: HarperCollins.

Worth, Valerie. 1996. *All the Small Poems and Fourteen More*. New York: Farrar, Strauss and Giroux.

Yolen, Jane, and Jason Stemple. 2003. *Least Things: Poems About Small Natures*. Honesdale, PA: Boyds Mills Press.

———. 1997. *Color Me a Rhyme: Nature Poems for Young People*. Honesdale, PA: Boyds Mills Press.